THE WEIGHT OF HIDDEN WOUNDS

The Weight of Hidden Wounds

A Female Soldier's Memoir of Trauma, Truth, and Transformation

Danielle Shine

The Weight of Hidden Wounds:

A Female Soldier's Memoir of Trauma, Truth, and Transformation

IRON GRACE PUBLISHING

ISBN 979-8-9955048-1-8 (paperback)

ISBN 979-8-9955048-0-1 (ebook)

Printed in the United States of America

To Mom and Dad, your love and support know no limits.
I love you endlessly.

To Terry, you made me feel safe enough to get help,
and your love makes me stronger.

To Ashten, you are my inspiration to be better every day.

To Carlie and Callen, you helped me along my journey
more than you know.

Contents

Author's Note

Without the professional help of my writing coach and editor, Patricia Wilkinson (write-to-win.com), this would have been a very different story. Trish helped me go deeper than I believed I could and fleshed out scenes so you, the reader, could take this journey from darkness to light with me. I have relied on her knowledge and editing tremendously and will be forever grateful for her help and counsel.

Writing this book has been emotionally challenging and mentally exhausting, but so worth the effort to bring hope to anyone who either struggles with their mental health or has a family member or friend who does. Bringing my experiences to light has allowed me to create a positive space for healing and post-traumatic growth. If you are reading my story because you merely thought it would be interesting, that's fine too. May you be entertained and learn a few things along the way.

My memoir may be difficult for some to read, even triggering. Perhaps reading about my trauma and my journey to healing will inspire you to get help. Maybe it will give you a glimpse of understanding about a loved one's behavior.

You don't have to be a military veteran to have post-traumatic stress disorder. Any traumatic experience can cause it. I have listed several agencies and websites with more information about PTSD in the back of this book.

Don't wait. Regardless of your situation, there *is* help, and it is never too late to step into healing. You are *worth* it!

Chapter 1

RUDE AWAKENING

I flopped onto my bunk in the barracks, my muscles trembling with fatigue after a day of marching and calling cadence and shooting at the range. Even the scratchy wool blanket pulled over my head felt like heaven, and I fell asleep before I finished my prayer of gratitude for getting through another day of boot camp. What seemed like seconds later, my body flushed with desire. My breath hitched, and my stomach constricted to my boyfriend's soft touch, exploring the sensitive skin on my inner thighs. *Yes, more please.* The soft lining of the sleeping bag caressed my arms, and I writhed with anticipation, my body ignited, nerves springing to life though my muscles were wrecked with exhaustion.

Wait. I'm not camping. What the hell?

My eyes flew open to see a woman from my platoon lying next to me in my bunk. Her arm was moving under my wool blanket, and I felt her fingers slide inside my panties. Rage seared through me, and my hand-to-hand combat training kicked in. I threw her onto the concrete floor, jumped on top of her, straddled her stomach, punched her right cheek, her left, threw an uppercut to the jaw, and started over—right, left, uppercut. My knuckles burned, yet I kept going. Had to. Couldn't stop.

Strong hands grabbed my arms and launched me backwards. Another set restrained my shoulders. "Private Combs, what the hell is going on here?"

I gasped to catch my breath. "She attacked me in my bunk, Drill Sergeant."

"Combs, come with me."

"Yes, Drill Sergeant."

I followed him into his office, and he pointed to a chair in front of his desk. "Take a seat, Private." The waning adrenalin left me nauseated and shaky, so I was relieved to comply before I passed out. "Private Combs, I need you to tell me exactly what happened tonight. Then we need to make a decision about what to do next. Start talking."

"Yes, Drill Sergeant. I was asleep and woke up to this chick in my bed, with her hands in places they had no right to be, so I launched her off of me and just started hitting her."

"Anything else you remember? Did you provoke her in any way?"

"No, Drill Sergeant."

"There are two things that can happen. One, we can forget this incident and carry on as usual, or we can report this, and she will be discharged from the U.S. Army. What do you want to do?"

"I want to report it. I don't want her here. How do I know she wouldn't try it again—on me or on someone else?"

"Okay. We'll write up a report and deal with it tomorrow. Go back to the barracks. Get things calmed down and the lights out."

"Yes, Drill Sergeant."

When I walked back into the barracks, I noticed my uninvited visitor had been removed, but everyone was out of their bunks and chattering nervously. "Hey," I yelled. "I can see you're scared, but the drill sergeants have everything under control. Everyone, get back to bed. Lights out in five minutes." I appreciated the distraction to avoid the chaos inside me.

The woman who violated me told the drill sergeant she couldn't bear to be dishonorably discharged and was going to kill herself. In response, the drill sergeant scheduled members of our platoon to take shifts on a 24-hour watch to make sure she remained healthy before she left. The following day, we were informed that she had been kicked out of basic training and sent to the hospital. I never knew what happened after that. I had bigger problems being the Training Leader for the Fourth Platoon in Bravo Company, Second and Forty-Eighth Infantry Battalion at Fort McClellan in Alabama. We had no idea we were the first women to be trained as infantry in the United States of America.

There had to have been a better way to get the money I needed for college. What the hell was I thinking?

Chapter 2

LAUGHINGSTOCK

I tried to shake off my uneasiness of waking up to someone caressing my inner thighs without permission and focus on figuring out how to get my pathetic platoon to work as a team. It seemed the drill sergeant had chosen me to be our Training Leader as a punishment. I recalled the first day of boot camp, tripping off the bus, coming face-to-face with a huge man.

"Welcome to Alabama, ladies," he shouted. "Now grab your gear, privates!" He stood with his arms crossed, feet planted, glaring at me when he said, "What are you looking at? You never seen a black person before?"

I looked around and realized there weren't many white faces, which was a new experience for a girl from Central Oregon in 1987. I'd never felt so confused and scared in my life.

"You dumb? You mute? You're on my time now. Hurry up!"

But my wobbly legs wouldn't budge.

"I said, 'Move it!' We don't got all day, ladies. You're burning daylight. Shake the lead out of your butts and get going!" I felt relieved that he seemed to speak to everyone until he widened his eyes directly at me. "Why are you sweating? You outta shape? Double time, private. Get your gear out of that pile."

When I still stood there, frozen, he said, "What? You gonna cry? I said, 'MOVE!'"

But my feet were stuck to the asphalt as if the soles of my tennis shoes had melted into it. The drill sergeant stepped so close; I smelled stale coffee on his breath. "You're mine now, and you're wasting my time. Drop and give me 20."

My mind raced. *What does that mean—Give me 20?*

"Private, I said drop and give me 20 push-ups, and add 20 more for being stupid."

I wanted to drop, to do what he said, anything to get him to leave me alone, but my brain had shut down.

"When I tell you to do something, private, you respond by saying, 'Yes, Drill Sergeant,'" he screamed, spraying spit at my face. "Do you understand, private?"

I could barely breathe. "Yes, Drill Sergeant."

He moved closer. "What was that, princess? I couldn't hear you. Speak up."

"YES, DRILL SERGEANT!"

"I'm waiting for those push-ups, private, so get down and PUSH!"

I dropped to the ground into the push-up position. My palms burned on the hot pavement, but I got started. *I've got this. No pain, no gain.*

After 10 push-ups, my hands felt like they'd caught fire. After 20, my arms trembled with fatigue, my stomach cramped, and my back knotted. *Crap, I still have 20 to go!* I did my best to ignore the pain and push through the second set. My arms gave out on the final rep, and I landed on my face.

But I did them—all of them.

The drill sergeant loomed above me. "Are you about done, princess? My grandma could do better push-ups than you. You're a disgrace. This is not a vacation. This is the United States Army, private! Now get your pathetic ass up and grab your duffle bag."

"Yes, Drill Sergeant." My entire body ached, but I walked as steadily as I could and stepped amidst the bedlam of all the other privates trying to grab their duffle bags. Arms flailed, people cursed and shoved.

"Come on, ladies," yelled a second man in his brown drill sergeant's hat and camouflage fatigues. "We don't have all day. Follow me to your new home."

In the barracks, a large, gray room with rows of bunk beds, we hurriedly picked a bunk, crammed our stuff in a rickety metal locker, and ran back outside to formation. Both drill sergeants divided us into four squads, ten soldiers in each straight line. After roll call, they designated four privates to be squad leaders. *Good. They didn't call my name, so I dodged that bullet,* I thought until I heard: "Private Combs, you get the honor of being the Training Leader for this platoon."

Crap, that's me! What does that even mean?

The drill sergeant who gave me a hard time as soon as I stepped off the bus shouted: "You're responsible for your soldiers' timeliness, cleanliness, whereabouts, uniform, moods, sleeping, eating, cleaning, even breathing! Do you understand, private? If they fail at anything, and I mean anything, you, Private Combs, will be doing push-ups. Do you copy that, private?"

My eyes bulged and my heart pumped wildly. "Yes, Drill Sergeant!"

Four weeks later, my platoon was the laughingstock of Bravo company. We couldn't even march properly. It seemed every non-athletic soldier had been assigned to me. My group came in dead last for target accuracy, hand grenade competency, and physical training. And I didn't know how to make us better.

On the metal bleachers outside, which doubled as a classroom, all 40 women in my platoon sat waiting for our daily lesson. While most chattered in private conversations, I sat in the front row, racking my brain to figure out how to make our platoon a more cohesive unit. Our drill sergeants walked toward the bleachers, and the chatter ended, every soldier sitting at attention. The drill sergeants stopped in front of us, side-by-side, with their arms crossed and their eyes trained on us.

The sergeant who made me Training Leader announced: "Tomorrow you will be going to the gas chamber."

Seriously? The gas chamber?

He paced in front of the bleachers while he explained nuclear, biological, and chemical (NBC) warfare. For 30 minutes he described how enemies used chemicals to attack soldiers, leaving them incapacitated and unable to fight. When he said, "The chamber exercise will expose you to chemicals so you can identify them if attacked," my hands balled into fists to hide my trembling.

The other sergeant demonstrated how to secure our charcoal-lined suit, boots, and gloves, and how to properly seal our masks. It was hard to concentrate on his directions when I was trying not to freak out. In high school, I'd read about the gas chambers in the concentration camps in Germany. Thinking about spending time in a gas chamber, even with the fancy equipment, seemed crazy. When they told us someone would tap our shoulders, and we would have to take off our masks, I almost tossed the ham and cheese sandwich I ate for lunch.

But I was the Training Leader for my platoon. I had to keep it together.

The next day, while we marched to the chamber and awaited instructions, I gave myself a mental pep talk: *Okay, you can do this. Be tough. Be a good leader. Show your platoon how to do it right. Suck it up and move on. You've got this.*

With nine other soldiers and sweat sliding down my back, I entered a dark structure with a dirt floor and concrete walls. Seconds felt like minutes. *Just let me get it done,* I prayed. Tap, tap. *Shit! Okay, I'll hold my breath and take off my mask.*

"Private, state your name, rank, and serial number," ordered the sergeant.

You've got to be kidding me. They want me to talk?

I tried to screech out the answers. My throat burned with bouts of pain, like being jabbed with hot pokers. The putrid smell clung to my nose hairs. I coughed, sputtered, and choked on thick, gummy saliva. My eyes and nose watered. Darkness engulfed me, and I lost track of the soldiers in front of me. My mind reeled, and I prayed in desperation: *Oh, God, give me strength to get through this torture. Please, God, help me.*

A hand pressed against my back, and I stumbled forward. I coughed up mucus from my fiery throat, and it took me a minute to realize I wasn't in the chamber anymore. I could only see shadows. My eyes felt sunburned, and I wiped them on my sleeve, which stung them more because of the chemical residue on my suit.

The drill sergeant yelled, "Walk it off, ladies. Just breathe. Walk it off."

I couldn't suck in enough oxygen to get my legs to hold my weight, let alone walk. Gasping for air, I leaned over and let the snot, spit, and tears spill out of my nose, mouth, and eyes. My platoon got through the exercise, but recurring nightmares would haunt me for a long time after that experience.

I'd joined the Army to change my dead-end life working at a record store at the local mall. The recruiter had made the idea sound exciting, though so far, nothing was like what he described. He also told me I had to gain 20 pounds to meet the minimum weight requirement, and I only had three months to do it. I got to eat burgers, fries and shakes, burritos and nachos, and loads of pizza. I gained 22 pounds to "be all I could be in the U.S. Army"—which apparently meant testing my reaction to toxic chemicals, not to mention all the horrors that awaited me.

Chapter 3

TRANSFORMED

My body was bruised and beaten, my hands marred and raw, and between my failing platoon and being molested in my sleep, I didn't know how I would survive basic training. I spent every Sunday at church and took solace in the warmth and comfort of the sun passing through the stained-glass windows that cast a rainbow on the floor near the altar. On those mornings, a deep calm overtook me. I prayed for strength and healing, and guidance to support my platoon of whiners, slackers, overachievers, and criers who were loud, quiet, mean, and a couple who were flat-out crazy.

Being in charge of 40 women, between the ages of 18 and 25, none of whom wanted to listen to me, a 19-year-old peer, seemed impossible. Still, no way would I give up. The constant bitching and back-stabbing, which permeated and poisoned our platoon, had to stop. After a particularly pathetic day of training, I'd had enough and decided to take a chance. I prayed silently, gathered my courage, and yelled, "Hey! Toe the line."

My fellow soldiers slowly placed their toes on the line that ran through the barracks. I inhaled deeply and said, "I'm tired and I know you are too. I'm not sure what to do or how to even talk about this, but we need to figure out how we're going to work together. We won't make it through this without each other, and right now, everyone's just out for themselves. We need to lift each other up instead of beating each other down. Can't you feel it? Don't you see the other platoons laughing and making fun of us? What can I do to make things better?" Everyone stared at the floor in silence." No one will be punished for voicing their opinion. I just want to know what I can do as your leader to make us a better unit."

"Be patient," said the woman at the end of the line.

"Listen," said another.

"Support and encourage us instead of yelling all the time."

"Okay, I'm sorry. I've never done anything like this before, and, truthfully, it's hard as hell," I admitted. "I'll do my best to be more patient and supportive, but I can't do it alone. We all have to lean on each other to get through this."

One of our soldiers who had that beautiful, African American gospel voice burst out with Bill Withers's old song: "Lean on me when you're not strong . . ."

"Ah, cheesy, girl!" someone joked.

But a bunch of us, including me, joined her: ." . . and I'll be your friend. I'll help you carry on for it won't be long till I'm gonna need somebody to lean on." Then everyone, even the those who were rolling their eyes, started to sing: "I just might have a problem that you'd understand. We all need somebody to lean on . . ." It was like some ridiculous Hallmark movie, but we didn't care. We finished the song with woops and high fives. The whole platoon seemed lighter.

The next day, we started to march in unison, and we came in third instead of fourth on our daily run. At the range, we increased our accuracy. Morale soared with our success. We began to trust ourselves and one another, and even our drill sergeants. The barracks became upbeat with lots of high-fives and "Shake it off—you'll get 'em next time" encouragements instead of the sour looks and taunting. The remaining weeks of training seemed to fly by.

Victory Forge, a three-day field outing, was our final hurdle before graduation. We marched to the site, pitched our tents, and began to dig our foxholes with the foldable, kid-sized shovels we carried in our rucksacks. Blisters blossomed and burned on both my palms as my buddy and I dug a two-person hole, two M16s long, one M16 wide, and four feet deep.

Climbing into the hole, I tried not to groan with the pain in my mid- and low-back. My buddy and I sat at the bottom, knee to knee, silent and exhausted. In that mental haze, I thought about going home after graduation to tell my family how much I loved and appreciated them. It had never occurred to me to say those things out loud before.

The next day, as I departed my tent and inhaled the crisp morning air in the wilds of Alabama, one of my drill sergeants approached. "Private Combs," he said, "gather six of your best soldiers. Then report to me."

Oh great. What now? "Yes, Drill Sergeant."

I did as he asked and found him in the warehouse the drill sergeants used for an office while out in the field. "Do you ladies want to be part of an elite team of soldiers?" he asked.

"Yes, Drill Sergeant!" the seven of us said in unison.

"Well, pick a name for your team and report to me at zero two hundred hours."

"Yes, Drill Sergeant."

At the appointed time, we returned to the warehouse to receive our orders and reported our team name: The Lady Assassins.

"There will be five male soldiers on guard duty tomorrow," said the drill sergeant. "I want you to sneak up on them, get their names and rank, and then report back to me." He paused. "Any questions?"

"No, Drill Sergeant," we shouted.

We got up at midnight, applied camo paint to our faces and tucked our hair away. We put on our equipment, checked our weapons, and decided we were good to go. Silently, we made our way through the forest and identified our first targets.

On the other side of a swamp, two soldiers sat under a tree. They didn't appear to be guarding anything. We raised our weapons above our heads and silently stepped into the water—deeper and deeper. The smell of dead grass and stagnant water reminded me of wading through the pond back home in Oregon, to catch frogs with my brother.

Easy does it. Slow and steady. Stay focused. My heart pounded so hard, I was sure everyone around me could hear it.

We approached the male soldiers with stealth and speed, surrounding them. With our M16s drawn, we realized they were both asleep. They hadn't seen or heard us coming. "You're dead," I said. They jumped up, startled. They weren't happy about having to give us their names and rank before we moved on.

Feeling more confident, we scoped out our next targets. Two soldiers were positioned outside the warehouse that housed the ammunition, and another soldier patrolled the fence line. Crouching behind plants in the forest, we looked at each other and counted to three. Then we stood and yelled, "You're all dead!"

"Are you kidding me?" the guy at the fence scoffed. "I got shot by a bunch of chicks?"

"You sure did," I said. "Name and rank, soldier."

Mission accomplished. I was pumped on adrenaline, invincible. We returned to the drill sergeant feeling powerful. *Bring it on! I'm ready for whatever you can dish out.*

The week before graduation, one of my drill sergeants approached me as I stood in line at the mess hall and said, "Private Combs, I need you to write a speech."

"A speech?" *What the hell for?*

"It should be about your training and stuff. Then give it to me, and I'll give it to the commander to approve."

The commander? "Yes, Drill Sergeant."

My speech talked about how scared and alone I felt when I first got to Alabama, but through the rigorous training, with the help of my fellow soldiers, I'd become part of a team. I thanked our drill sergeants and everyone who helped us make the transformation from civilians to soldiers. *Hope that's good enough, whatever he wants to do with it*, I thought, handing two type-written pages to the drill sergeant.

He scanned the pages and then looked up. "Private Combs, invite your family to graduation."

"I'm from Oregon, Drill Sergeant. I doubt anyone can come. My mom and dad are working, and I doubt my brother would come."

"I don't need to know your family tree. Just invite your parents. Someone might want to be here for you."

"Yes, Drill Sergeant."

I called and invited my mom and dad. My mom said she'd come, but my dad hated to fly, so he stayed home. I was disappointed my dad wasn't coming, but he worked a swing shift. He'd missed a lot of my sporting events and school functions, so I was used to it. When Mom arrived, the drill sergeants gave me leave to spend a couple of days with her, off-base in a motel room. We laughed and cried as I regaled all my stories about basic training.

I even told her about the woman who tried to violate me in my sleep. I made light of it by pointing out that no one messed with me after they saw me beat the shit out of her. Mom was amazed and impressed that I had been strong through so many intense experiences. I had felt good about myself, but her acknowledgement gave me a huge sense of satisfaction.

At graduation, the commander announced: "This group of women are the first to be trained as infantry soldiers, and nobody can ever take that away from them."

Did I hear that right?

"If anyone ever doubts you, show them your PT uniform with the 2/48th infantry logo on it as proof," he said. "We are proud of your accomplishment and dedication to become the first women to experience this intense training regimen and conquer the challenges we put forth during your nine weeks of basic training."

Whoa. We're the first women ever. I felt tremendous pride for my soldiers as well as myself and honored to be involved in making history.

Seated on the stage with three other trainees, my insides quivered with anticipation. The commander glanced in my direction and said to the audience, "I would like to announce the Outstanding Training Leader of the cycle, Private Danielle Combs." He beckoned me to the podium with a wave of his hand.

I figured I was there to read my speech, not to receive an award. My heart pounded in my ears, and it felt like I floated to the podium. The commander handed me the pages I'd given him weeks before. My hands shook. I'd never spoken in front of hundreds of people, and my voice was wrecked from calling cadence. I managed to screech out the words I'd written, heard snippets of laughter at the appropriate times, and when I finished, everyone stood and gave me a resounding ovation.

"Thank you," I said, humbled, and walked toward my seat.

I was intercepted by my drill sergeant and the commander. The commander went back to the podium and said, "Private Combs is being promoted from Private Enlisted-1 to Private E-2 today. Her leadership and hard work are being rewarded because her platoon is being named the Most Improved Platoon in Bravo Company for this training cycle. Congratulations, Private Combs." My drill sergeant placed my new insignia pin on the lapels of my dress uniform. All the effort, struggle, and lack of sleep had been worth it.

After the ceremony, Mom threw her arms around me, her eyes moist with emotion. "Dani, I'm so proud of you!"

We walked out of the auditorium together to find my whole platoon waiting for me, and they broke into song. "Lean on me . . ." My eyes welled with tears.

Mom looked at me and smiled. "Is this for you?"

"Yeah, it's an inside joke, the thing that brought us together as a team."

I was glad Mom came to see my promotion and hear my speech, and that she got serenaded by my platoon with me. Though disappointed my dad wasn't there, I discovered, years later, my mom gave him a photo of the Lady Assassins that he still keeps in his wallet.

The morning after graduation, I received orders for Advanced Individual Training (AIT). Like when I'd started this journey, I didn't know what awaited me there. By then, it didn't matter. I felt like I belonged in the military, and I thought I could handle anything.

Chapter 4

THE NEXT STEP

On my way to Fort Eustis, Virginia, to Advanced Individual Training (AIT), the summer was stiflingly hot. Worse, the air conditioner on the bus was broken. Sweat pooled in places I didn't want to think about, and my anxiety mounted. I had been assigned to train to become a traffic management coordinator, an 88N—whatever that meant.

There were two bunk beds in each room, and I had three female roommates. We were grateful to have our own bathroom and enjoy a quieter, more private existence. In basic training, the acoustics of the open barracks had intensified every sound, and sharing with a few women, whom I wasn't responsible for, was a huge improvement.

But I kept thinking, *Why is it so damn hot? Do I have to run and do push-ups in this heat and humidity? I hope I don't pass out—talk about embarrassing. That's not the first impression I want to make.*

I tried to tell myself that I would be fine. I'd made it through basic training. This assignment was supposed to train me for a position, a job, not get me in shape to fight.

Thankfully, calisthenics in the blazing heat weren't assigned, and in the next six weeks, I learned how to move troops, equipment, supplies, ammo, tanks, and all kinds of vehicles—anywhere, anytime my superiors ordered. My training was designed to make me proficient at getting supplies to the right places as quickly as possible, especially in the middle of a conflict.

AIT was more lenient than basic training. We got to go bowling and drink beer on base after we finished work for the day. On a couple of weekends, we even traveled off post and hung out at the beach. Those six weeks flew.

After I graduated from Fort Eustis (or Fort Useless as we liked to say), I took a 30-day leave to visit family and friends. The break would also give me time to arrange my affairs and ship things I might need to Germany, where I'd be stationed for two years. In the back of my mind, I wondered if my boyfriend, Gary's decision to join the U.S. Army had influenced my decision to enlist.

Maybe, I thought. *But it doesn't matter. I'm in the Army now—I'm not behind a plow.* I laughed at my weird brain. I told myself and others that I wanted out of my loser, boring life working at the mall. While this was true, my decision to enlist had been more than that. I was going on an adventure, to a future I'd never imagined.

Chapter 5

FORCED

At Rhein-Main Air Force Base in Germany, I was assigned to Kaiserslautern, the Rhine Ordnance barracks, "Little America" to the locals. A female soldier named Ronnie, who was the secretary for the commander in my unit, came to pick me up and orient me. While she gave me a tour, we talked about basic training, hers at Fort Jackson in South Carolina and mine in Alabama. Ronnie was astounded that I'd been trained as infantry.

Her basic training didn't include hand-to-hand combat, extensive weapon training, and their physical conditioning was minimal compared to what we endured at Fort McLellan. When our commander at 2/48th infantry told us that we were the first women trained as infantry, I didn't know what that meant.

Since this was my first permanent duty station, I was amazed at how relaxed everyone seemed in Germany. I'd soon find out what churned beneath the surface. Like in Virginia at AIT, I remained a member of a small minority, both in race and gender, but we all wore army green.

They assigned me to a room in the barracks, which I shared with an African American woman from California named Jaqueline. She also went to basic training at Fort Jackson. There were several sites where women were trained, but most of the female soldiers I'd met had gone to basic in South Carolina.

One night after a few beers, Jacqueline tried to teach me how to dance. "Girl, you need to unlock those hips. Just feel the music."

"How am I supposed to do that? My hips don't work that way, and I can't feel shit."

"You're crazy. I give up. You're too white. You don't have any rhythm."

We both cracked up, and from then on, we became the dynamic duo. She made me laugh when no one else could, and I cherished her friendship.

Gary and I got to see each other, but not as often as we would have liked. He spent the majority of his time in the field, in infantry, which all the specialties in the Army called "ground pounders." I either traveled or coordinated the transport of supplies from the base via train, plane, or convoy.

The first year went by fast. I explored Germany as much as I could. On my time off, I enjoyed visiting the castle in Heidelberg and touring the grounds. I especially loved the view of the Rhine River from the castle. The water reminded me of the Deschutes River back home in Bend, Oregon and filled me with peace.

Sometimes on my own, but more often with friends, we'd stroll through the market square, shop for odds and ends, and finish the day sitting outside on the cobblestone roads, eating a bratwurst and sipping a German Pilsner. Being surrounded by Tudor-style shops and buildings, painted white or pale-yellow, with elegant dark wood accents and window frames, and the occasional gothic church with lurking, ornate gargoyles made me feel like I was in a fairytale. Life was pretty darn good.

I traveled with Ronnie to Bavaria where we visited Munich, and I participated in my first Oktoberfest. My memory's a little hazy, probably from all the beer I consumed. I do remember the frequent bouts of singing, visiting with lots of strangers, and even picking up some conversational German. I embraced the culture, enjoyed the food, and loved the beer.

One weekend, Jaqueline and I visited Turkey. Flying into Adana felt like color had been leached from the world—beige buildings blended with beige sand. On the taxi ride to our hotel, a few structures broke the monotonous color scheme, and there was the occasional green bush.

The marketplace offered a few more hues. We bought brass ornaments, leather jackets and purses, and we spent way too much time combing through the massive Turkish rug selection. Jaqueline bought a rug, and I've never laughed so hard as when I watched her struggle to put the stupid thing on the top rack of the train to get it back to the base. I wasn't much help—I was too busy busting a gut.

When we could both get time off at the same time, Gary and I would meet in Frankfurt at the Bahnhof, the main train station, because it was an easy trip for both of us. We spent the majority of our day in a military hotel room, since it cost less than a civilian hotel. At night we'd go to Sachsenhausen to dance and drink, hopping from club to club. Then we'd stumble back to the base.

Later that year, Gary and I broke up. We seldom got to see each other, yet he'd given me a promise ring, the precursor to an engagement ring. We were too young to get married, and I felt we'd grown apart. Ending that relationship was one of the hardest decisions of my life.

Jaqueline had gone for the weekend, so when she returned, she was surprised to find me drunk. "Girl, what the hell happened to you?"

"Gary and I broke up," I slurred.

"Damn, girl. I'm sorry. What can I do for you?" she asked and sat next to me on my bed.

"Do you have any chocolate?" I whined.

"Nope, but I can get some."

I relied on her to listen and console me. Broken-hearted, I used alcohol to numb my loneliness, yet I had friends all around me. The breakup happened in November. Christmas was fast approaching, which compounded my depression. Holidays in my family were always festive and magical. I had never felt so far from home.

I neglected my chores, which consisted of buffing the hallway until it sparkled, cleaning the bathrooms, and keeping our room up to army standards by being dust free, organized, and polished. I barely made it to work. After my shift, I stayed mostly in our room—in my pajamas eating chocolate and watching tapes of *Days of Our Lives*, compliments of Mom. Watching TV dramas distracted me from my own.

Kris and Leslie begged me to go to a party with them, so I reluctantly got dressed and tagged along. The party turned out to be more fun than I thought, so I resolved to put myself out there more.

The next weekend, I was invited to one of the soldier's off-base apartments for drinks and games. Ritt worked at headquarters, and my commo shop was down the hall. We were friendly, and he seemed fun, so I decided to go. I didn't really know the other people he invited, but I'd promised myself I would make a point of leaving my room, especially on the weekend.

In the corner of Ritt's living room sat a Christmas tree with several burnt-out lights strung on skimpy limbs among haphazard ornaments. The sad-looking tree made me miss the lights on our house back home, the smell of cookies in the oven, caroling with friends on the back of a hay truck, being surrounded by family and loved ones . . .

A loud squeal jarred me back to the present. Several people sat around a table playing a card game called "Spoons." A girl who ended up without a spoon wasn't happy. "Hey, you wanna join?" Ritt asked.

Why not? Maybe I'll make some new friends.

After the game ended, we cranked up the music and danced. We talked and listened to the stereo until one in the morning. The four other people at the party slowly migrated to the bedrooms and passed out. It was just Ritt and me left in the living room. I prided myself in being able to drink the guys under the table, and in my mind, I had achieved my goal.

I got up to go to the bathroom and saw a flash out of the corner of my eye. Ritt had jumped off the couch. He rushed toward me and shoved me into the kitchen. "Hey, where are you going?" he slurred, grabbing my shoulders and pinning me against the wall. His sour breath was hot on my face. Bile burned the back of my throat. His mouth slammed against my lips so hard I tasted blood.

"Hey, back the fuck off!" I yelled and tried to push him away.

He forced his body against me. "You know you want it. You've been eye fucking me all night long."

"No, I don't. Get the hell off me!" I shouted and managed to wriggle my hands between us. But he towered over me, and pushing his chest with all my strength didn't budge him.

My hand-to-hand combat training kicked in, and I swung my fist at his face, a blow that, had it connected, would have knocked out my opponents in Alabama. But he was lightning fast, and he pinned both my arms. Then he picked me up and threw me on the linoleum floor. I kicked and screamed, but he clamped his calloused, filthy hand over my mouth.

How can the others not hear this? Shit, the music is still blaring. What do I do?

Trapped and helpless, my heart pounded. I hyperventilated, and my vision blurred. His free hand ripped open my jeans, and he yanked them down as I bucked and tried to get free. He pressed his full body weight against mine, crushing me into the floor. My brain shut down, and the last thing I remember thinking was: *Someone needs to clean those baseboards.*

I woke up fully dressed on the couch with my head pulsing to varying degrees of pain—almost bearable to excruciating and back again. I was alone, and the room was eerily quiet with the stereo no longer blaring. The scattered lights were still lit on the sad Christmas tree.

Where's Ritt? I feel like shit. Where did everyone go? To bed, that's right. My foggy brain began to put thoughts together. *I was drinking, dancing, and having fun. Then I went to the bathroom. No, wait. I didn't make it. Ritt . . . oh my god. I need to get the fuck out of here.*

I stumbled from the couch to the kitchen counter and used their phone to call for a taxi. As soon as I hung up, I grabbed my jacket and walked into the crisp air, just before dawn. My whole body hurt. Bruises had bloomed all over my arms and legs. My vagina burned and throbbed as I walked.

I can't believe I didn't fight harder. I couldn't even protect myself. What the fuck? I'm a soldier, trained to kill, and I couldn't fight off one dude? I'm worthless. I failed, plain and simple.

Mortified beyond anything I could have imagined, I vowed never to speak about that night. When my friends asked if I had fun at the party, I lied. I avoided Ritt, ducking him in the hallways and avoiding going anywhere I thought he might be.

The more I relived that night, the more I placed blame on myself. It was my fault for getting so wasted. In the future, I would dress more conservatively and be more careful about going places where I didn't know everyone.

Adding to my distress, some of my closest friends left because they had fulfilled their obligation to the military. Jaqueline was preoccupied with her new boyfriend and spent most of her time in his room. I had seven months left in Germany, and I prayed my next post would be closer to Oregon.

My moods became erratic, my patience non-existent. I didn't have the capacity for small talk, and I got increasingly aggressive toward men. No man would ever use me again. My anxiety had festered into anger and threatened to consume me.

I was desperate to talk to Tani, my best friend since second grade, in Springfield, Oregon where my family lived until we moved to Bend. We were opposites. I liked sports and the outdoors; Tani liked to read and preferred to be at home. But there was no one I trusted more. After the move, through middle school, we took turns riding the bus between Eugene and Bend to spend time together.

It was harder to stay close in high school because I traveled for basketball and volleyball, and Tani usually babysat on weekends. Since I joined the Army, we had only written a couple of times. Still, I needed to hear her voice because she was the one person I felt truly knew me and loved me no matter what. My hands trembled holding the receiver and punching the numbers on the phone in the barracks hallway.

"Hello." Tani's voice was as familiar and grounding as I thought it would be.

"Hi, Tani. It's Dani."

"Wow. It's been a while. Where are you?"

"I'm in Germany. I just wanted you to know I miss you, and when I get back to the states, I hope I can come visit you sometime." I held my breath waiting for her response.

"Yeah, I'd like that. How much longer do you have in Germany?"

"Seven more months." I'm not sure why I'd been so nervous. She was the same Tani I knew and loved.

"Do you like it?

"Like what? The Army or Germany?" I laughed.

"Both."

"I miss home, my family, and you. I still have two more years in the Army, so it doesn't matter if I like it or not. I'm committed."

"I'm glad you called, Dani. When you come to visit, you can meet my boyfriend Andy and his son Jake."

My eyes began to well with tears. "That sounds great. I'm looking forward to it. Um . . . I have to go."

"Bye, Dani. Hope to see you soon."

"For sure, bye." When I hung up the phone, I slid down the wall, and all the emotions I'd shoved down came up in wet sobs. Alone on the shiny barracks floor, I sat cross-legged and let the tears drench my shirt.

I should've told her. But she wouldn't want me around anymore because I'm dirty and worthless. I'm a fake, a total joke. I'm trained to kill, yet I got raped by a fellow soldier. I deserved it—I brought it on myself.

I slowed my breathing and pushed myself up off the floor, shoving my memories, self-loathing, and hatred for Ritt back down as I stood up. The hallway was deserted. Images of the attack tried to surface, but I ignored them, telling myself I couldn't change what happened, so I needed to forget about it. My secret was safe. I just needed to focus on something else.

Donna had been living next door in the barracks. Her horrible roommate had an open-door policy for the men that lived below us and often invited them up to play while Donna was in the room. Jaqueline and I felt sorry for her and told her she could live with us. We were crowded, but we got along well, and I had someone to talk to once Jacqueline stopped coming home.

After the incident with Ritt, my need to control my environment, and everyone in it, became an obsession. My clothes had to be ironed and pristine, every object in my room in a specific place, or my stomach soured. Panic would rise in my throat.

I used sex as a weapon, faking intimacy with guys from the club, sleeping with them, and then ghosting them. I couldn't even allow myself to be vulnerable with my roommates. The emotional walls I built prevented anyone from getting too close.

Nightmares of being thrown to the floor and having my clothes ripped off haunted me most nights unless I drank—a lot. If I drank enough to pass out, I could skip the dreams, or at least not remember them. Eating seemed to calm my nervous stomach, so without noticing, I packed on another 20 pounds. Drinking, overeating, and avoiding scary memories consumed my life. I hid behind false bravado, terrified people would get a glimpse behind my mask and discover the scared, powerless girl that was me.

Chapter 6

TEMPORARILY STATESIDE

Once I finished my time in Germany, the army assigned me to a small detachment unit of 14 soldiers at Fort Lewis, and I was the only female. Washington was beautiful—tall evergreens, emerald grass, majestic mountains. I was so glad to be back in the states only a five-hour drive from my family in Oregon.

Our workplace was in a basement we called "the dungeon." We joked about being lower class than the people who worked at headquarters. They had real offices with windows and fresh coffee. We received no natural light or beverages.

In Germany, the communication department had coordinated train and ground transport of supplies and informed bases of when things would arrive. In the states, that job was done by civilians, not soldiers. I began to get anxious when I realized the Army didn't seem to know what to do with our detachment unit.

The first two weeks, I cleaned and organized everything I could get my hands on in the dungeon. I craved control, and taking charge of organization gave me the illusion I had some. While alphabetizing books, Specialist Gomez, a tough and intense Latino, asked if any of us could type, and it was all I could do not to jump up and yell, "Me! Me! I can type!"

"Follow me, Combs."

We trudged up the stairs to the first floor and walked by the guard duty desk. There, a soldier kept track of who came in and went out of the building, until he/she was relieved by the next soldier, 24 hours a day. The desk divided the first floor. To the left was our recreation room with our motto clearly painted on the wall "Rest Assured." To the right was a hallway with several offices on each side.

Specialist Gomez scowled at me over his shoulder. "The first sergeant needs someone to type up some letters and stuff. I'm not really sure, but he'll let you know."

I tried to smile. "Anything is better than what I've been doing, and hey, there are windows up here."

I worked and lived in this building. The moss-covered, gray stone reminded me of some of the castles in Germany. There were three floors above ground and the dungeon below. Behind the guard duty desk was a flight of stairs that led to the living quarters for enlisted soldiers who didn't have families.

Females lived on the second floor, two to a room. We shared a community bathroom and shower at the end of the hall. I was pleasantly surprised by the size of our rooms compared to the ones in Germany. The third floor was the men's quarters, and they had a similar setup—two in each room and shared facilities.

Gomez seemed angry or annoyed. His glare probably had nothing to do with me, but I had the fleeting thought of running up to my room.

"Well, are you coming or what?" he said.

"Uh, yeah." I hadn't realized I'd stopped walking. I followed him down the small hallway into the third door on the left, the first sergeant's office.

"This is Specialist Combs," Gomez said. "She can type so here she is."

The first sergeant was a short, white, high and tight man with an icy stare. "Glad you're here, Specialist. Here's the papers I need typed. Hope you can read my writing."

"I'm sure it'll be fine, First Sergeant." I took the papers he handed to me wondering: *Does everyone on this floor have cold eyes?* I followed him out of the office, down the hall, and into a stark room with a desk, chair, and typewriter. Our footsteps echoed off the bare walls. *At least I have a mission.*

"Do you have any questions for me?"

"No, First Sergeant, I'm good."

He turned and walked out of the room, and I started typing. I did so well with the first assignment that he asked for my help frequently. Once the commander learned I could type, he asked me to create documents for him too. When I wasn't typing, I spent my time with the guys in the basement, reading military handbooks and the soldier's manual, ad nauseam.

In Germany, where I turned 21, there is no drinking age. I looked forward to getting a drink at a bar in the states. One night, Valerie, Diane, and Russ asked if I wanted to go off base with them. My mind reeled. *Should I put myself out there or keep to myself and be safe? But I don't want to sit alone in my room. What the hell? You only live once.*

We went to a bar in Tacoma and played darts, danced, and had a good time together. Valerie was from Michigan. Petite yet feisty, she held nothing back and never backed down. Gritty and determined, she pulled me in from the minute I met her. She was the commander's secretary at the main headquarters, so she worked in a different building, but we spent time together whenever we could.

Diane grew up in Southern California and was blond and tan. She worked in the same building as Valerie as an administrator. I wished I had her confidence. She knew what she wanted and asked for it. Since the attack in Germany, I had become fearful and unsure of myself.

Russ and I belonged to the same detachment unit. He was an Illinois boy with an easy smile and a love for heavy metal music. He always made me laugh. We became great friends and even better dart-throwing partners. At first, I was wary of him, but over time, I realized he was a stand-up guy who could be trusted.

Russ had a friend named Steve who joined us shortly after that first outing, so our crew became Valerie, Diane, Russ, Steve, and myself. Three months later, Steve and I started to date. But he wanted to move faster than I was comfortable, being that I no longer trusted my instincts. To get my family's take on Steve, I coordinated a camping trip with my mom, dad, grandparents, uncle, and brother. I may also have wanted to see if he could handle my loud and somewhat crazy family. We played horseshoes and cards, drank lots of beer, and by the end of the weekend, my family decided Steve was okay. Except for Grandpa. But Grandpa didn't like anybody except for my brother, so I brushed it off. Since Steve passed the first test, it was time for the next one, which was meeting my "second family" in Springfield, Oregon.

Tani and I had rekindled our friendship, and as we'd fantasized as kids, she asked me to be her maid of honor at her wedding. We felt like members of each other's families. I couldn't wait to catch up with them and show Steve around my old stomping grounds in the elementary school years.

I recalled when I was 10 and my dad saying, "You know that little town we go through when we go hunting called Bend? Well, we're moving there, kids."

I'd wanted to puke, thinking about moving away from Tani. But I was a kid, and moving wasn't my decision. To our parents' credit, once my family settled in Bend, Tani and I took turns riding the Greyhound bus to see each other as often as possible. We camped and fished on my side of the mountains, and we spent time at their cabin, between Waldport and Newport on the Oregon Coast, on her side of the Cascades.

Since I moved to Washington, I had made several trips to Eugene to see Tani, and we hung out with her fiancé and stepson. Andy was the one for her. They made a great team. But Andy didn't realize Tani and I came as a package deal, that we were invested in one another emotionally and mentally. Now that she'd have adult responsibilities, I hoped our relationship would remain as important to her as it was to me.

On their wedding day, when Steve and I arrived at the church, I introduced him to my second family. Steve was polite but saw my mom and dad's familiar faces and sat with them. I headed to the prep area to get dressed.

After fussing with our hair and makeup for what seemed like forever, Tani and I started to go to the staging area to walk down the aisle—until I heard, "Dan, do you think we have time for a bathroom break?"

"Are you kidding me? Right now?"

"Not kidding. I'm not sure I can make it."

"Well, we better hurry."

We stood outside the stall and pondered the logistics. She glanced at me nervously. "Um, you're going to have to come in with me."

I laughed. "For my best friend, I guess I can squeeze in there and help you keep your dress off the floor and out of the toilet."

Once in the stall I grabbed a handful of her dress on either side and ducked under to lift it up off the floor.

"It's not touching the floor, is it?"

"No, it's good. Just get busy and pee already."

Sweaty and itchy in my nylons and satin bridesmaid's dress, the only thing I could do was laugh. Then I couldn't stop laughing. Tani started giggling and couldn't focus.

I composed myself and cleared my throat. "No pressure, but you better get it done. Do you want me to hum? I can't turn on the water."

"Things you never thought . . . you'd do on your wedding day," she said between giggles.

"Good thing I don't get embarrassed easily."

We cleaned up and ran to prepare for the walk down the aisle. We shared a look and a laugh as the ceremony began. At the front of the church, I held her bouquet and cried, marveling at how we'd kept our childhood promise to be in one another's weddings. At least I was keeping up my end. I had no plans to marry anytime soon.

At the reception, we danced until late that evening. The disco point and electric slide were crowd favorites. I soaked up the love in the room, grateful to be myself, without fear of being judged or controlled.

But Steve wouldn't join us. He sat in the corner by himself.

I valued every minute with Tani. Getting to know Andy better was fun too. He was perfect for her. As a bonus, Tani loved kids and was excited to be a stepmom to Andy's young son. The thought of kids made me shudder. Though Tani and I were still opposites, I was so happy to have her back in my life.

The next day, Steve and I headed back to Fort Lewis, and he started in on me. "You ignored me at the wedding. You didn't care if I was there or not."

"Well, you could've interacted with everyone instead of sulking."

"I didn't know anyone, and you just left me there."

"I asked you to dance several times. You wouldn't."

"You should've spent more time with me."

"It was my best friend's wedding. Sorry you felt neglected. You're a big boy. You could've talked to people and been friendly."

"I was uncomfortable, and you didn't even care."

"I shouldn't have taken you." With that, I stopped talking. The remainder of the trip was silent as the miles ticked by. *Just get me home. I'm exhausted.*

We continued to date, but I went through the motions, trying to convince myself I was okay. I pretended to be happy but was miserable. After two months, our relationship went from bad to worse.

He became possessive and controlling, and alcohol made it worse. I was afraid to be alone with him, so I'd ask friends to go out with us. When his military commitment had been fulfilled, he decided to remain in the area and rent an apartment in Tacoma, not far from the base. He got a job cleaning carpets during the day, and we'd hang out at night with our friends.

After he got settled into the apartment, I invited Russ, Valerie, and Diane over to his apartment for a housewarming party. The night started great. We played quarters, a drinking game, then poker, and ended the night listening to music and dancing in the living room.

Around midnight, Steve started insulting me as he often did when he got drunk. "You can't dance," he said. "I don't know why you even bother."

"Knock it off. You're being an ass," I said. "Come here. I want to talk to you in private."

He got off the couch and followed me into the bathroom. I closed the door and turned to him. "What's wrong with you? Why can't you just have fun and quit being mean?"

"You haven't even seen me mean yet." The menacing gleam in his eyes scared me. I flung open the door to run, but he grabbed my arm and pulled me back inside. "Where do you think you're going?"

"Back to our friends because you're drunk." My voice was calm, but my heart pounded.

He shoved my shoulder. Hard. I stumbled backwards and fell into the bathtub. My left elbow thwacked the rim of the tub. Pain exploded to the point of dizziness and nausea. "Get away from me!" I screamed and burst into tears.

Russ appeared in the doorway. "What the fuck is going on in here?" he said and pulled Steve into the hallway. Then he came into the bathroom and offered me his hand. "Let's get out of here, Dani."

"O . . . kay," I managed between sobs and was grateful for his help out of the tub.

As Russ escorted me out of the bathroom, Valerie and Diane ran over yelling, "Oh, God. Dani, are you okay?"

"Let's just get out of here," I said.

Diane and Valerie grabbed our jackets, and I headed for the front door. Steve tried to grab me so I couldn't leave, but Russ got between us and said, "Stay away from her. We're leaving. Don't ever try to contact or talk to her."

"We're over," I said through clenched teeth. "I don't ever want to see you again."

The next day, I had an ugly bruise on my elbow, and I went to the military police to place a restraining order on Steve. He was restricted from the base and wasn't allowed to come near me off-base either. Steve kept harassing my friends, but they wouldn't tell him how I was doing or where I was staying.

Valerie had recently moved to an off-base apartment, and I stayed with her. Steve had no idea where she lived, which made me feel safer. A month later, he gave up trying to find me and moved back to his hometown in Maine.

Steve's attack made me crave the comfort of family and friends, but I was embarrassed. Not only had I gotten raped in Germany, I'd been battered by the guy I had brought camping with my family. My grumpy grandpa had been right about Steve.

How do I pick these guys? I wondered. *What's wrong with me?*

The painful memories tormented me. At first, I tried to drown them in alcohol, but even that stopped working. Embarrassed or not, I had to go spend time with Mom and Dad, have lots of laughs, and eat home cooked food in a place where I felt safe. Maybe I would stop to see Tani too, so I could reset and move on.

But my trip home got canceled when our detachment was placed on alert because Saddam Hussein threatened to invade Kuwait. No traveling was allowed. Any time I felt like someone else was making decisions for me, my heart rate increased, my thoughts raced, and I became easily irritated. The more I tried to suppress my anger and fear, the more they spilled out, and with them came a cascade of violent memories. I needed to break the cycle and channel my anxiety into something constructive.

My prayers were answered the next day when we started to prepare our equipment in case we had to go to war. I reminded myself that I needed to be present for my unit. Instead of crying over past events I couldn't change, I threw myself into getting ready for whatever might happen if we had to fight an enemy and defend our country.

Then we heard disturbing news.

The war strategists presumed Saddam would use chemical weapons if we went to war since he didn't hesitate to use them on his own people. The hair rose on the back of my neck. *He's a psychopath. We better get comfortable in our MOPP gear.*

To the extent possible, Mission Oriented Protective Postures or "MOPP gear" protects soldiers during a chemical, biological, radiological, or nuclear strike. We were trained to put on our gas masks first, being that breathing is essential, then help others when possible. The suit was supposed to allow maximum air movement for cooling and to keep biological agents from reaching our skin. The fabric was also lined with charcoal to help neutralize harmful chemical agents.

I shuddered with the memory of burning in every sensitive area in the gas chamber at basic training. I did everything I could to get comfortable and agile in my bulky suit. We learned how to drink, eat, relieve ourselves, and sleep in our MOPP gear.

Are we really going to have to use this thing?

The answer came soon enough. Our detachment was activated on September 16, 1990. We were scheduled to depart from Fort Lewis via McChord Air Force Base at 4:00 a.m. The staff sergeant told us we were headed for Egypt. We knew that wasn't likely. The conflict was in Saudi Arabia where there were already U.S. soldiers. We were a transportation unit. Our job was to provide soldiers with ammunition, equipment, food, and their vehicles.

Our detachment of ten, nine males and myself, decided to have one last blowout party at our favorite Mexican restaurant before we left, and

I paid dearly the next day. When my alarm sounded, I groaned with too much food, drink, and anxiety churning in my gut. I sluggishly got out of bed, took a shower, and fought off the urge to puke. With my rucksack over one shoulder and the strap to my duffle over the other, I headed outside to formation thinking: *Damn. This is really happening. We're being deployed and possibly going to war.*

Chapter 7
DEPLOYED

Well before the sun came up, we drove our vehicles the short distance from the motor pool on Fort Lewis to McChord Air Force Base. Fresh air from the open windows mellowed the pain in my head, and my stomach felt almost normal. We drove our vehicles onto the military cargo plane and parked them in a row in the center of the aircraft. Then we were instructed to pick a seat.

Attached to the walls, lengthwise, our metal seats formed long lines, from the front to the back, on both sides of the plane. Behind the seats, cargo netting ran halfway up the walls in a poor attempt to provide back support. Sadly, airflow control knobs don't exist on military aircrafts, and soon after we took off, the musty netting in the stagnant air brought back my headache. The pain throbbed with my heartbeat, and I grew queasy again. Worse, my metal seat cut off the blood flow from my legs to my feet. Pins and needles forced me to seek a more comfortable location if I was to endure the long flight.

Making my way in the dark, in the narrow space between our vehicles and the line of my fellow soldiers' knees, I stepped on a couple of boots but was too tired to apologize. I found a Commercial Utility Cargo Vehicle (CUCV), otherwise known as a Chevy pick-up truck painted in army-green camouflage, and slipped inside. On previous excursions, it had never occurred to me that the truck was comfortable, but at that moment, the padded, upholstered seat felt like pure luxury, and I fell fast asleep.

We stopped three times for fuel. I slept through the first one but was awake for the stop in Ramstein, Germany and the one at Hellenikon Air Base in Greece. In Greece, we disembarked for a few hours, but we didn't get to see much. I'd always wanted to go to Greece. Greek mythology had been a secret obsession, so I promised myself I would go back as a civilian—maybe on my honeymoon if I ever got married.

When we returned to the cargo plane, everyone was irritable because we were tired, cranky, smelly, and extremely uncomfortable. As we'd suspected, we didn't land in Egypt. We landed in Riyadh, Saudi Arabia.

Why didn't they tell us the truth? I wondered. *Oh, that's right. G.I. stands for "government issue." Soldiers are as expendable as sleeping bags.*

When we left Fort Lewis, it was 40 degrees. When we walked off the plane in the Middle East, a wall of heat smacked into us—a sweltering 95 degrees at 6:00 a.m. *How hot is it going to get when the sun comes up?*

My unit was assigned to the Port of Dammam, which was a four-hour bus ride from Riyadh. Our small transportation detachment from Fort Lewis was attached to the 7th Transportation Group, 24th Transportation Battalion from Fort Eustis, Virginia, where I'd gone to AIT.

The ten of us loaded onto a bus with no air conditioning. Four hours, soaked in sweat, seemed like an eternity. When we arrived at Compound 3, a military campground we called "Tent City," I gagged on the stench of ripe trash mixed with raw sewage. Flies zig-zagged everywhere.

The word "bleak" popped into my head. Rows of army-green general purpose (GP) medium tents stood in contrast with the beige sandscape. The lack of color reminded me of Turkey. I'd been there less than an hour and already missed the evergreens, mountains, and rivers of the Pacific Northwest at a cellular level.

The only water came from the showers and sinks. The bathroom facilities were communal—women and men shared them. The toilets were reminiscent of the old outhouse on my grandparent's rural property in Crooked River Ranch.

Men outnumbered women, 80 to one, so the base commander posted a schedule for the showers. More than once, I'd gotten all ready and psyched up to get a lightning quick wash in the unmonitored bathroom, only to find a guy or two there during the time designated for females. Usually, I would use wet wipes to get relatively clean and skip trying to take a shower, but some days I needed running water over my body.

On the days I was desperate for a shower, I'd keep checking the bathroom until there were no men in sight. Then I'd jump in and frantically wash the funk off as fast as possible. I felt vulnerable and scared and berated myself for being such a sissy. *What's your problem? Suck it up!* I scolded in my head. At the time, I hadn't realized how much the rape and the attack had impacted my daily life. I kept denying and burying my emotions and forcing myself to go on.

The GP-medium I was assigned to housed nine other women. At first, I kept my head down and minded my own business. I went to work, washed my clothes, and tried to sleep in the musty, hot sleeping bag without falling off the narrow cot. On my time off, I wrote letters to my parents and Tani. Making friends seemed out of reach. I wasn't sure I could care for myself, much less anyone else. I was surprised when, about a week after my arrival, an African American female soldier introduced herself.

"Hi, my name's Sharon."

"I'm Dani."

"What unit are you with and where did you come from?"

"My detachment unit was assigned to the 7th Transportation Battalion. We're from Fort Lewis, Washington. What about you?"

"I'm with 7th Trans too, out of Fort Eustis, Virginia."

I couldn't place her accent but found out later she was from Antigua. She had an easy manner, a beautiful smile, and a great laugh. We both complained about our living situation, especially the sketchy showers, and Sharon came up with a solution.

"Maybe we could watch the door for each other if we're off at the same time," she said. "What do you think?"

"That sounds like a great idea. I'd feel so much better knowing someone had my back."

"Me too."

My whole body seemed to relax. I hadn't realized how tense this shower predicament had made me. *Maybe I do have the capacity for a friend,* I thought. *It's nice to have another woman to talk to and hang out with.*

After a month in Tent City, my detachment got reassigned to the Batar Compound. Sharon's detachment was assigned to the same place, so we decided to be roommates. Two to a room and private showers seemed like a step up until a few days later, our sergeant told us to use only bottled water to bathe and brush our teeth. He didn't give a reason, but being good soldiers, we followed orders.

A week later, we found out the Army tested the tap water at the compound and discovered the water table had been contaminated by the sewer—the same water we'd used to brush our teeth and wash our faces and hands those first three days! I was horrified. But I reminded myself it could be worse—I could be out in the desert with the ground pounders, preparing to fight the enemy.

Instead, my job required me to be near a port so I could help manage the supplies from the cargo ships and distribute them where they needed to go. The stevedores, U.S. soldiers trained to load and unload cargo, would drive the vehicles off the ship and line them up in the staging area nearby. Then we'd scan the barcode on each vehicle with handheld lasers. Once all the vehicles were scanned and accounted for, transportation headquarters would notify the company of soldiers they'd been assigned to that the vehicles were ready for pickup. The soldiers would come to the dock, form a convoy, and drive the vehicles to their assigned destination. At my level, I wasn't privy to the details. I did what I was told and didn't ask questions.

If the cargo was ammunition, the boxes were scanned, and then the stevedores would drive the ammo via military police (MP) escort to the "ammo dump," a specific warehouse at the port. The ammo was stored and guarded 24 hours a day by MPs until it left the port in a convoy to the companies out in the desert.

When the cargo was food, the boxes were scanned and taken to a refrigeration trailer or "reefer" to await the scheduled delivery to designated troops within Saudi Arabia. All non-perishable supplies were stored in another warehouse after they were scanned. Once the ship was confirmed to be empty, we'd compare our list with the ship's manifest to make sure everything was accounted for.

Next, we instructed drivers, who didn't speak English, where to deliver the items. Most of the drivers were Sri Lankans earning money to send home to their families. We used maps and crude drawings to communicate where to take the goods that the stevedores had loaded onto semi-trucks. We never knew if the supplies would arrive at their proper destination. Sometimes a load would end up in the wrong place, or it got "lost," never to be found. I wondered if some of the drivers sold our supplies on the black market, but I never knew for sure. My mission was to ship supplies. Finding the source of the losses was above my pay grade.

About two weeks into the daily 30-minute trip from Batar to the Port of Dammam, my buddy Russ and I parked in the container yard and saw a female MP climbing a crane ladder. *What the hell is she looking for?* I thought. *She shouldn't be there.*

When she reached the top of the crane, she jumped into the water, fully dressed in her flak jacket and helmet with her M16 rifle strapped to her back. That gear was heavy. We ran as fast as we could to the water, but she'd already disappeared. A male soldier had jumped in after her, but he couldn't find her.

Nausea passed through me. *What was she doing up there? Was it an accident? Had she meant to do it?*

A Navy SEAL dive team spent hours looking for her body. When they finally pulled her corpse onto a raft, she was ghostly white and bloated. She no longer looked human.

I cried silently, confused and saddened as I prayed for her and her family. I'd never seen a dead body, and her lifeless, flaccid form being lifted out of the water would be etched in my memory forever. Russ and I found out later she was pregnant and depressed. Maybe she couldn't see any other way to deal with her circumstances.

Nightmares impacted my sleep. I'd bolt upright in bed—sweaty, breathless, and fearful. I didn't want to wake Sharon and stress her out, so I tried to calm myself and go back to sleep. I'd told her about the suicide, but I didn't let her know how much it impacted me. Sharon and I were friends, but I was raised to be self-reliant. I didn't want to burden her with my problems.

During the day, I'd get distracted by flashes of that MP being pulled out of the water, but I reminded myself that my job was essential to getting troops what they needed. If I were trying to win a war, I'd take out the supply chain first. Without food, ammo, or transportation, troops were vulnerable to defeat.

I remembered talking about this in Germany with my mom, grandma, and Gary. At first, Gary and I argued about who was more important—infantry, the soldiers fighting the war, or supply people, the ones who got the soldiers what they needed to fight. In the end, we decided everyone involved played a critical role, and there was no safe place in a war zone.

At that point, war still hadn't been declared. We all hoped the politicians could work out their differences before it came to a real-live international conflict. In the meantime, I tried to stave off panic. *Take one day at a time. Just do your job.*

I took pride in working hard at the port, taking my job as a soldier seriously. When something got in the way of my work, I wasn't one to keep quiet about it. My grandpa called me ornery and opinionated. He was right. And I was about to explode over not being allowed to take off my jacket.

Male soldiers could work in their t-shirts, but women had to stay covered. It was incomprehensibly hot—often 120 degrees. Though I used all of the water allotted to me, my lips remained cracked and my skin hot. I also battled constant abdominal pain, cramping, and diarrhea, which dehydrated me even more.

Every soldier was given a case of water bottles each day and encouraged to drink frequently. I had to squander two bottles for personal hygiene due to the contaminated tap water. About a month into scanning vehicles being offloaded from ships' containers, I remember looking around for shade to take a break—then nothing.

"Specialist, wake up! Are you okay?"

I opened my eyes to see two soldiers staring down at me. I slowly sat up and said, "What happened?"

"One minute you were standing; the next you were out," said the tall, muscular soldier.

The skinny soldier reached out his hand and pulled me to my feet. "Come on, there's a medical tent over on pier one. We'll escort you."

They walked with me to the medical tent where a medic placed an intravenous catheter into my arm to replenish my fluids. After I recovered and went back to the compound, Sgt. Gomez told me to go see the commander. When someone was called to see the commander, it usually wasn't good, but I forced myself to put one foot in front of the other and took a few deep breaths to steady myself.

His office was in a small beige building with white windows, about ten feet from the dorm where I slept. Gooseflesh spread over my arms when I entered the building. The air conditioning felt glorious on my hot, sweaty skin. *Must be nice to be in charge. I wish I was in charge.* I knocked on the wall outside his office because it didn't have a door.

"Come in, Specialist Combs."

I walked inside a room that was little more than the length of his desk, stood at attention, and began to raise my arm to salute.

"At ease, Specialist," he said. "I need you to tell me what the hell happened to you today at the port."

I finally had my chance to speak out and hoped I wouldn't be punished. "Sir, I passed out because it was so hot. I can't wear my t-shirt like the males. I was trained that a soldier is the same regardless of sex, so when I'm working at the port, why can't I wear my t-shirt too?"

"Well, you make a good point. The Army has trained you to be a soldier, and it doesn't matter if you're male or female. The problem is the Saudi nationals have a difference of opinion, and we are trying to honor their customs. I'll look into it. You're dismissed."

The next day, I was sitting on the tailgate of the truck, waiting to go to work, when Sgt. Gomez approached me. "I'm not sure what you said to the commander, but he told me you can wear your t-shirt while you're working at the port, but only while you're working. And you're moving to the night shift. Apparently, he doesn't want you to pass out again."

Sgt. Gomez looked me up and down and stopped at my chest. I shifted slightly sideways and tried to distract him. "Thank you, Sergeant. Should I go back to my room and start my shift tonight?"

"Yep, that's what the commander wants."

"Okay, thanks." I jumped off the tailgate and walked back to my room. *Shake it off, Dani. It's not like he hasn't looked at you like an object before. Just steer clear of him.*

I wondered if I had been put on night shift because of heat exhaustion or to keep me from taking off my jacket in daylight, to keep the Saudis happy. But work was work. Sharon and I could go to the port together since we'd be on the same shift. Even at night, we sweat in the oppressive heat and had to guzzle water, but I didn't pass out again.

After 12-hour shifts at the port, I needed something to help me decompress. When I started working nights, I ran in the early mornings, after my shifts, when the air was relatively cool. Almost daily, I ran six miles, loving the feeling of my feet pounding the pavement. I would put on my headphones, plug them into my Walkman, and lose myself in the music. The miles would fly by in my private bubble, which kept me half-way sane. Running my body to exhaustion before going to bed made it easier to sleep during the heat of the day too.

Still, it was hard to keep my spirits up. The occasional care packages and letters from home seemed to come at just the right times to give me the boosts I needed. I felt appreciated and connected to my family, which made all the difference.

Mom sent non-perishable items since mail service was slow. A letter could take up to a month to get delivered. That meant I received a lot of Hickory Farms and Vienna sausages—too many for any one human to consume. Having such a regular supply gave me the opportunity to share my goodies with my unit, and I slowly began to trust my male counterparts.

Playing volleyball with them during downtime, a sport dear to my heart, also helped me to feel more secure. When Russ and I had the same days off, he'd play. Even Sgt. Gomez decided to join in the action, and he treated me like one of the soldiers instead of leering at me.

I guess he's not that bad, I thought. *He's fun when he's not bossing everyone around. Maybe we could be friends.*

I asked Sharon if she wanted to participate, but she said, "Sports aren't really my thing. I'll cheer you on."

"Okay, your loss. It's super fun. You might like it."

"I have two left feet," she said. "I'm just not built for sports."

"Suit yourself." I was bummed she wouldn't even try, but nothing was going to keep me from playing. Volleyball helped to ease the frustration of the constant "hurry up and wait" mentality in the Army.

Between impromptu volleyball games and my regular routine of working, running, and sleeping, with an occasional poker game on the side, I'd settled into a groove. Though an underlying tension tugged at all of us, life seemed to go smoothly.

One night at work, a male soldier came toward me in the staging area where the latest shipment of vehicles had been parked for inventory. The hunched gait reminded me of someone. My breath caught when he got close enough to see his round, pale face. It was Steve. *What is he doing in Saudi? He got out of the Army. He's supposed to be stateside.*

Sharon glanced up at me from a truck she was scanning. "Are you okay? You look like you've seen a ghost."

"You could say that."

Out of the corner of my eye, I noticed Sgt. Gomez headed our way. He knew Steve from Fort Lewis and was aware of the altercation between Steve and me, and the restraining order.

"Hey, Soldier!" Sgt. Gomez yelled at Steve. "You're in the wrong area. You need to get the hell out of here before I call the MPs."

Steve moved toward Sgt. Gomez. "Hey, you know me. I just wanted to see how Dani's doing—you know, check in on her."

"She's fine. Now leave before I make you leave."

Steve forced a laugh. "Dude, no need to get violent. I was recalled for active duty. We're on the same team. I just wanted to say 'Hi' to my old crew."

"No one wants you here, so leave."

"Fine. Is Russ around?"

"He's off right now."

"Maybe I'll go find him and say 'Hi.'"

Sgt. Gomez leaned closer to Steve. "Whatever, dude. Just leave."

Steve turned and walked back to his CUCV and drove away.

"Specialist Combs, you okay?"

"Yes, Sergeant. Thank you."

Sharon moved away from the truck she'd finished scanning and came closer to me. "I know there's a story so spill it."

I told her about my relationship with Steve, the altercation, the MPs, everything. It felt good to get it out. She was quiet and respectful and gave me a hug. "Damn, girl. You've been through some shit. Good thing Sgt. Gomez came by when he did."

"Yeah, I owe him one. I'm glad I have tomorrow off. I need a good long run and some downtime."

The next day after my run, I spotted Russ getting ready to leave for the port and headed over to him. "I had an unexpected and awful surprise last night," I said. "Steve showed up and tried to talk to me."

"Yeah, Steve found me. I told him I wasn't happy to see him, but he kept ignoring me. Let's just say, Sgt. Gomez and I convinced him he needed to leave and gave him a taste of what would happen if he ever came back. Steve was more than eager to get into his truck and go back to his unit in the desert. I don't think you have to worry about being bothered by him ever again."

"Wow. Sorry you had to get involved but thank you for sticking up for me."

"What are friends for?" He smiled and jumped in the CUCV. "Catch ya later."

"Yeah, later."

I was conflicted. Sgt. Gomez could still raise the hair on the back of my neck with the predatorial way he sometimes looked at me. But he'd stood up for me twice. In fact, after what Russ told me, I felt like I owed him. Russ seemed to think he was okay, and Sgt. Gomez had gotten pretty good at volleyball.

Nothing to worry about, enjoy your day off, you idiot!

After that, I settled back into my routine living at the compound and working at the port. Two weeks later, on January 17, 1991, the U.S. Air Force launched the first attack—35 conventional cruise missiles obliterated Iraqi targets—and Desert Storm began. The war would challenge my core values, and the person I thought I was would be confronted and distorted beyond recognition.

Chapter 8

WAR

The night Desert Storm began, I was assigned to guard duty at the battalion headquarters, two miles from the compound. There were four single-story, beige buildings inside a fenced area. One served as headquarters, two were shipping offices, and the fourth was the military police station.

After I checked in at headquarters, I joined three soldiers in front of the only entrance to the facility—a male U.S. soldier and two troops from the Saudi Arabian Armed Forces. The U.S. soldier sauntered over to me. "Hey, I'm Specialist Buck," he said. "I'll be your guard duty buddy tonight."

"Hey, I'm Specialist Combs—nice to meet you."

His bright blue eyes and warm smile were humble and disarming. "Hope tonight goes smoothly. This is my first time on guard duty at battalion."

I smiled in return. "Yeah. Me too."

Our instructions were simple: Check all identification of incoming personnel. Let no one pass through the gate without proper credentials.

My shift started at 11:00 p.m. and would last 12 hours, with a few quick pee breaks. I had thought my trusty M16 rifle under my arm would make me feel safe, but my pulse quickened, and breathing seemed hard as I waited with the others for someone to show up and try to enter.

Inhale - two three, four; exhale - two three, four.

My stomach tightened, though no one had rolled up to the gate. I decided my discomfort came from the Saudi soldiers' disapproving stares from the opposite side of the entrance. Occasionally, they pointed at me and spoke in Arabic. I was sure they were talking about me and tried to ignore them by focusing on keeping the battalion safe.

Specialist Buck stepped closer and said quietly, "Ignore them. They'd be stupid to try something, and if they did, we could take 'em. Look at how sloppy they look in their uniforms. They're small and don't look well trained. They need us more than we need them."

He was right. They weren't standing at attention, and their uniforms looked like they were pulled off the bottom of a dirty clothes pile. "Yeah, they definitely need us more," I said.

We both laughed.

Four hours into my shift, I was relieved for a quick break and decided to take advantage of the phone center to call my mom and dad. The phone rang and Mom answered.

"Hi, Mom."

"Dani, oh my God! How are you?"

"Well, I'm pretty good at the moment. I'm safe—just wanted to let you know I love you."

She began to sob, and my dad came on the line. "Hi, honey, your mom can't talk right now. How're you doing?"

"I'm okay, Dad. I just wanted you guys to know I love and miss you. I have to get back to guard duty, but I'll write a letter soon. I promise."

"Sounds good. We're watching CNN, and they said the war has officially started."

"Wow. You guys know more than I do. I'm just here at battalion keeping out the riff raff at the gate." I forced a laugh.

"Well, I'm proud of you honey. I love you. Keep your head down and be safe."

"I'll try. Love you too. Tell Mom bye."

"Will do."

I hung up the phone and walked quickly through the quiet night back to my post. I took my place in the pool of light in front of the gate, about six feet from Specialist Buck, and every cell in my body seemed to be on high alert. *What the heck?*

Seconds later, the alarm to warn of an incoming missile shrieked. I froze for a moment, then my training kicked in. I donned my mask and MOPP gear. My grip tightened around my M16, and I gasped for air. I hadn't realized how hard it would be to breathe in my gas mask while hyped on adrenalin. *Calm down. Slow down. Just breathe. Okay, this is it. God, please keep me safe.*

The sky remained dark, full of stars—no streaks to indicate an incoming missile. After several excruciating minutes, concentrating on breathing in my mask so I wouldn't pass out, they gave us the "all clear" signal. The air strike didn't reach us. "Thank God," I said under my breath.

"No kidding," said Buck.

As I removed my mask, my whole body shook, inside and out—whether from adrenalin, anxiety, or the damn nerve pills we'd been ordered to take, I didn't know. The nerve pills were to counteract possible nerve agent poisoning. I heard some soldiers refused to take them, though Sharon, Russ, and I had followed orders. A day later, the higher-ups in the chain of command found out not everyone took them. After the initial air strikes from the Iraqis, we were ordered to stand shoulder to shoulder in a long line, between the medical and office buildings at the compound, and take the pills in the presence of the commander.

The commander's assistant would hand us the pill, we'd put it in our mouth, swallow with a gulp of water, and get a mouth inspection to make sure the pill was gone. The procedure felt juvenile. And they wanted to protect us, but the nerve pills had side effects. For example, after taking the pill, I couldn't think or spell—even the word "the." My handwriting looked like kindergarten scrawl, jerky and illegible, and the side effects lasted for three days. I held off on writing home, concerned my childlike penmanship would frighten and worry my family.

Sharon's side effects were worse. Her belly ached, and she couldn't breathe. I told her to drink some water, lie down, and try to relax. She tried to respond, but she could barely talk and garbled that her tongue felt thick and numb.

Walking to my post at the gate, I wondered if the pills had caused these strange reactions, along with the constant butterflies that whipped inside me, or if the wailing siren and anticipation of an incoming missile had caused them. When I returned from my shift, Sharon could speak normally again. The symptoms had only lasted a day. Although scary, the damage didn't seem permanent.

Sleep that night didn't come easy. I tossed and turned and fretted about going to work the next day at the Port of Dammam during wartime. I woke up more tired and anxious than when I went to bed.

In the truck on the way to the port, Sgt. Gomez assigned a guy named Lewis from my unit and me to scan the barcodes of equipment and vehicles as they were offloaded from a ship and reconcile each object with the ship's manifest. Lewis was a tall, African American with a great sense of humor and laid-back attitude—easy to like and work with.

We walked toward the entrance of the ship, and the air raid sirens went off. This time, I didn't hesitate—I threw on my mask and MOPP gear and looked at Lewis. He waved an arm in his MOPP suit for me to follow him, and we ran toward shelter.

Panic tried to take over in fast, ragged breaths. *Just run. Get to safety. Keep breathing.* A truck careened past us and screeched to a halt. Sgt. Gomez and Russ yelled for us to jump on. Relief flooded me as Lewis and I hopped onto the back of the CUCV. My head throbbed, and I fought the urge to puke with the combination of sour latex and surging adrenalin. *Shit. This war is really happening.*

We reached Warehouse 33, the designated "safe zone" and ran inside. Sgt. Gomez, Russ, Lewis, and I sat on the concrete floor and leaned against one of the vehicles offloaded from the ship. We stayed in MOPP 4, our charcoal-lined suits, gloves, boots, and masks, for what seemed forever. Cold sweat trickled down my back, and I concentrated on taking deep breaths to keep from vomiting, which would be both disgusting in my suit and embarrassing.

How safe are we in this tin can of a warehouse? Will I die tonight? I don't want to do this anymore. God, my brain hurts, and I'm so tired.

I glanced outside and noticed a cat. *Is that really a cat, or am I losing it?*

The cat walked by the entrance without stumbling or drooling, so I took that as a good sign. An hour later, the "all clear" alarm sounded. *Thank you, God.*

No one in the warehouse knew what had happened. We did what we were trained to do—we took cover and waited it out. Sgt. Gomez ordered us to get back to our assignments. Everyone returned to work in silence, and the rest of the shift remained quiet. While en route back to the compound, we heard on Armed Forces Radio that an MIM-104 Patriot, a surface-to-air missile, intercepted the SCUD missile the Iraqis had aimed at the city of Dhahran, a mere six miles away!

The next day, our commander decided to put us back on the nerve agent pills. This time, the pills gave me diarrhea, which made my predisposition for dehydration even more tenuous, and any little noise put me on edge. I practically jumped out of my skin with every bang, crack, or yell. Every moment of the day came with unrelenting hypervigilance to anticipate what might happen next.

Two nights after the raid on Dhahran, Sharon and I scanned vehicles at the port and decided to go to the bathroom when the stevedores unloading the ship took a break. The bathrooms at the port were referred to as the "howdy-neighbor johns" because the top half of the entrances were screens instead of solid doors. Anyone who walked by could see you and say, "Howdy, neighbor." The only other bathroom option was a hole in the ground that required good aim, so we chose the lack of privacy.

On our way to the johns, the air smelled of smoke and oil, and the thick haze made nighttime at the port even darker and more difficult to see. Not only were the port workers burning the waste we soldiers created in nearby pits, but Saddam's Iraqi soldiers had also lit several Arabian oil wells on fire. Our noses and throats burned.

The air quality at the port was so bad we covered our faces with handkerchiefs, though we should've had substantial respiratory protection. The thick, black smoke from the oil wells caused most of us to have coughing fits. The layer of dark, tar-like residue that collected on our skin probably coated our lungs as well. I hoped I wouldn't suffer from lung disease later in life.

As I stepped out of my side of the john, I looked up. "Hey, Sharon, I just saw a flare or something streak across the sky," I yelled. "I'm nervous. You better hurry up!"

Within seconds, the air-raid alarm started blaring. Out of reflex, I put on my mask and started to run while looking for somewhere to take cover—ah, the warehouse. It happened so fast; I assumed Sharon was behind me.

I glanced over my shoulder and realized she'd frozen near the johns. I turned around and ran toward her, motioning for her to put on her mask. She fumbled with her mask in slow motion. My blood pumped frantically, and bile soured my tongue.

"We need to take cover," I shouted through my mask, over the alarm. "Look at me. Can you run?"

She didn't respond, so I grabbed her arm and dragged her along with me. We didn't take time to put on the rest of our MOPP gear. My legs burned, but I kept running toward the warehouse. Explosions lit the darkness all around us. Fragments of wood and metal rained on us. Fire engulfed the area. A bomb was coming—I could feel it. We needed to take cover, but it was hard to see through the thick smoke and chaos. *Where's the damn warehouse?*

Confused and panicked, I continued to drag Sharon because she didn't seem to be able to move on her own. I realized we were close to a wall, though I didn't know from which building. I did my best to follow it until we saw a light over a door showing the number 43, our designated warehouse. Relieved, I slammed open the doors. Sharon and I barreled inside and collapsed on the concrete floor. I glanced up to see the stevedores we were working with had made it to safety. Throughout the port there were four such warehouses, and we were lucky enough to be assigned to the ship that was near this particular warehouse.

Within minutes, the "all clear" alarm sounded. I forced myself to stand and extended my hand to Sharon to pull her to her feet. We went back to the staging area next to the ship and continued to scan cargo.

Stuff it down. Move on. Don't let them see how afraid you were. Don't be a pansy.

Sharon remained eerily quiet and zombie-like, going through the motions.

"Hey, roomie!" I said, and she turned toward me with vacant eyes, like she didn't see me. "Are you okay?"

"Uh . . . I'm not sure . . . I don't think so . . . but maybe."

What the hell did that mean? "Well, it's over for now. We just need to stay focused on the job and keep busy."

Two hours later, she seemed to be coming around when she yelled, "Hey, you know what?"

"What?"

She laughed so hard, she could barely spit out her reply. "I've never seen a white girl run so fast!"

We both cracked up. Just as we'd started to relax a little, the air-raid alarm went off again. We masked up and got into a truck this time, instead of seeking shelter on foot. I couldn't see very well through my mask and the smoke, and my peripheral vision was blocked, but I drove anyway. People ran everywhere. I stomped on the accelerator toward the ramp of a ship, determined to get inside. Two stevedores yelled at me to slow down, but I ignored them and launched the truck onto the ramp, screeching to a halt inside the ship.

The ramp closed right after we passed through. I felt safer inside a ship than the flimsy metal warehouse. Sharon and I got out of the truck and tried to find someone, anyone on the ship. What seemed like an hour later, but was probably minutes, we located a ship mate who escorted us up to the dining hall. We'd landed on the Norwegian ship, and lucky for us, they spoke English. They offered us food and drinks and were extremely nice. Being of Norwegian descent, I felt a weird sense of pride.

While we waited for further instructions via our walkie-talkies, or the "all-clear" alarm, we chatted with the crew members and appreciated their company. The time stretched on—because why should the Army's hurry-up-and-wait be any different in war? Three hours later, my walkie-talkie chirped, and we were cleared by Sgt. Cook, another member of my team from Fort Lewis, to return to the dock.

We thanked the Norwegians for their hospitality, went back down to our truck, backed up, turned around inside the ship, and headed down the ramp. I looked at Sharon. "Longest night ever!"

"You got that right! I'm beyond tired."

"Me too. I might actually get some sleep."

"Wouldn't that be nice?"

Once we arrived back at the compound, Sharon glanced over at me as I jumped out of the truck. "Hey, thanks for helping me out tonight," she said.

"No problem. You'd do the same."

"I'm not sure I would—or could."

"Sharon, it's all good. I'm just glad we're safe."

We gathered our gear from the back of the truck and headed for our cots.

The following night, we began with two SCUD missile alerts. The radio announced the first target was Al Jubail, an hour's drive from the port, but the missile crashed into the water. Riyadh was the next target, but our Patriot missile intercepted it. A few hours later, the alarm sounded again. Two more SCUDS were shot down by Patriots, right over our heads!

Saddam seemed to attack earlier each day and more frequently. I protected my frayed nerves by operating on autopilot. The hyper-vigilance war demanded overwhelmed me. In the past, I had been under the illusion that I was in control of my destiny. Life as I'd previously known would soon cease to exist.

Chapter 9

Moral Injury

Random flashes of being pinned to the floor and violated, pushed into a bathtub, and fleeing for my life with explosions and fires all around me invaded my mind, day and night. Sometimes I was unsure if I was awake or dreaming. One night, after two exhausting air raids, I dreamed of an alarm that wouldn't turn off—constant beeping that went on forever, no matter what I did to try to stop it. I sat next to a wall shaking, gasping, and sweating.

Oh no! The alarm is emitting from me—it's going to give away my location! How do I make it stop? They're going to find me. I'm going to die!

I jerked awake. The dream dissipated, and I realized my alarm clock was blaring. I grabbed it and barely stopped myself from hurling it at the wall. Music. I needed music. The dance beat on the radio muffled the bombs and sirens going off in my head while I got dressed, though I was still shaky.

Paranoid and edgy, I kept a keen eye on everyone and everything. Meanwhile, the mind-numbing counting, scanning, and checking off items on a list at the port sapped my energy. Worse, my end-in-time-of-service (ETS) date had come and gone. My job as a transportation specialist had been deemed "mission essential," so the Army extended my commitment by six months. A trained monkey could have done my job at the port. I just wanted to get out of the Army, go home, and go to college.

The war ended as fast as it had started. In May 1991, our new mission was to return equipment and troops to the States. But I should have been one of the soldiers boarding an airplane. The more people I helped to send home, the deeper I sank into depression. My brother was getting married in July, and I didn't know if I'd get out of that hellhole in time to attend.

Phones were scarce, so I called home when I had guard duty. "I've postponed the wedding twice," Wade said. "My fiancé hasn't even met you yet. She's been patient. I can't put off the wedding again. I'm so sorry." When I hung up the phone, the sound of the phone receiver hitting the cradle and my boots clomping along the linoleum floor in the hallway at the battalion echoed in my head—hollow, vacant.

My brother and I had always been close, and I didn't want to miss seeing him get married. *Please, God, let me be released in time. I miss my family. I just want to get home and put this war behind me.*

After guard duty that day, I didn't want to bother Sharon with my dark mood, so I wandered out to a picnic table in the yard by the barracks and sat with my head in my hands. At the table a few feet away, I overheard two soldiers from a different transportation detachment mention they were going to Kuwait City to deliver food and water to civilians—and they needed help. I recognized Specialist Black. I'd seen him around the port, but I didn't know the guy he was talking to. Still, I needed a change and rushed to their table.

"Hey, I'll go with you and help out," I said.

"That'd be great," said Specialist Black. "Be ready tomorrow morning at 6:00."

"We need a few more," said the shorter, more intense guy. "You know anyone else who can come?"

My gut clenched, but I ignored it. "I'll ask my roommate."

"Cool. The more the merrier."

He made me feel uneasy, but I felt leery of anyone I didn't know by then. I took off in search of Sharon. Back at the barracks, I burst into our room.

"Sharon, I have a huge favor to ask. Please come with me to deliver food and water to Kuwaiti citizens. I volunteered, but I only kind of know one of the soldiers. Please say yes."

She sat up on her bed. "Why would I do that? It's our day off. I need some downtime. You do too."

"It'll be downtime. We'll get to see some of the country. You know, see the sights, get some pictures, do something good for the people."

"I don't know."

"It'll be simple—deliver the stuff and get out."

She stared at me for a beat. "Well, I would like to see something other than this damn port."

"Awesome! You're the best. This will be fun, and we can help others in need."

At 6:00 a.m. Sharon and I walked out of the barracks and headed toward the CUCVs. There were seven of us—four males and three females. Again, my stomach clenched, and I glanced at Sharon, the only person in the group I trusted. The bad vibe felt similar to the paranoia I'd often experienced, and I desperately needed a change of scenery. *Chill out. We'll be fine.*

We loaded up three CUCVs with 50 boxes of "meals ready to eat" or MREs—a dozen in each case, 600 per truck, 1800 meals total. We stacked as many cases of water bottles as we could fit in the back of each truck next to the boxes of food. Two soldiers each rode in the other two vehicles. Specialist Black drove the truck Sharon and I rode in, which was cramped since the back of the truck was full, and we both had to sit on the bench seat with the driver. Since I'd talked Sharon into this excursion, I sat in the middle. Doubt and fear quickened my pulse, and my stomach churned.

Calm down. At least you're not with the weirdo in the other truck.

We departed from the barge at 6:30 a.m. Somewhere between

Dammam and Khafji, my sense of foreboding deepened, but I did my best to push it away. Three hours into our five-hour trip, we stopped at Khafji, the town where Saddam Hussein and his Iraqi Army initially took over.

Bullet holes scarred the brick and concrete walls that remained. Other structures were left in unidentifiable heaps from Iraqi bombs. The black, smoke-stained rubble erupted gooseflesh on my arms. An intense chill came over me—a sense of pure evil, a darkness that permeated my soul. *The war's over. I'm safe. We won.*

Sharon and I walked side by side and snapped pictures of the bullet holes on a building. Ten minutes later, the three of us silently got back into the truck and drove toward Kuwait City. After an hour, we entered what looked like hell on earth.

The area was eerily quiet. Hundreds of burned and smashed vehicles, upside-down and sideways, littered both sides of the highway. The soul-wrenching darkness I'd experienced in Khafji intensified. My palms sweat, my throat constricted, and pulling enough air into my lungs to stay on my feet seemed impossible.

Knock it off! Don't be a sissy!

My wolf-like sense of smell picked up the horror before it hit Sharon or Specialist Black. I swallowed bitter bile when I realized the stench came from the decaying flesh amidst the destruction all around us, on the road that would become known as the "Highway of Death."

Who did this? Did our bombers do this?

Black parked the vehicle and jumped out of the truck. I glanced at Sharon. Her face held the same disconnected expression as when we'd run for shelter at the port. My head turned slowly, my gaze unseeing until a pile of burnt clothing and books, on the ground several yards from my window, came into sharp relief.

"Sharon, are you okay?" I asked. "Do you want to get out?"

She shook her head. "Nope. I didn't sign up for this. I'm staying right here."

"Fine. I'm going to check it out. I can't make you come." I slid out of the truck on the driver's side and stomped off, pissed but not sure why.

I peered inside one of the wrecked cars, leaned in to make sense of a badly burnt white object, and froze. The figure was a scorched human being! I swallowed a scream and staggered backwards, realizing all around me were decomposing corpses on the ground and in charred vehicles. The putrid smell seemed to thicken. I felt foreign in my own body but tried to stay present to survey the area for enemies. The five other soldiers came over to see what had caught my eye.

"Is that a corpse with no head?" one of the guys asked.

"Looks like it," the female soldier said. "His head's in the back seat. Jesus. That's gross."

My ears rang and my heart throbbed. I held my breath, and the lack of oxygen started to cloud my vision. *Push it down. Don't think about it. People die. That's what happens in a war.*

If I killed an Iraqi soldier, even though I was following orders, would that make me a murderer?

I walked away from the group and continued making my way through the bodies and vehicles in a daze. *Be aware of all movements. Watch everything and everyone—women, children, men, old, young, and in between. All are threats. They could have a bomb or another weapon. Focus. Don't miss anything or you'll die. Don't let your guard down. Breathe. Don't pass out.*

I heard something that seemed out of place. *Laughter? How the hell could someone be laughing?*

I walked toward the noise and found the three guys from the other trucks. "What's so funny?"

I looked down and felt the blood drain from my face. *They're kicking around a badly burned corpse.*

"That's what you get, you fucking raghead," one of the soldiers yelled.

I stared at the charred, battered remains and couldn't move. They'd crossed a line. This had been someone's husband, brother, father, uncle, or friend, and they treated the body like a piece of trash. In war, evil seemed to lurk everywhere, and if you let your guard down, it would sneak in and fester, take hold of your soul.

"Stop," I screamed when I found my voice. "Leave it alone. Just stop!"

Specialist Black walked over and said, "Quit being such a pussy. Leave if you can't stomach it."

Revolted and ashamed, I turned away, ran to an abandoned truck, and grabbed onto a door handle, needing to feel something solid.

"Hey, look! There's someone's head," someone shouted. "There's an arm—maybe a leg."

Between the putrid smell of rot and death, adrenaline, anger, and disgust, I could no longer hold back the vomit. I heaved and heaved until nothing came out, and still I continued to gag. *Forget about it. Keep breathing. Don't think about the stench, the bodies, the wreckage, the horror.*

I tried to save my sanity, but I could never unsee what I saw that day. Whatever was left of the trusting, carefree, naïve girl had been whittled away over the past few years, replaced by a hardened, hypervigilant, mission-focused, emotionally unavailable person. The happy-go-lucky girl from Bend, Oregon had changed. Death and destruction seemed everywhere I turned, no safe place, no happy ending.

With a heavy heart, sour stomach, and the taste of vomit in my mouth, I meandered on stiff legs between the corpses and rubble, back to the Army truck. When I opened the door, Sharon's eyes went wide. "Jesus, you look awful. Are you okay?"

"No, I don't think so." I got into the truck and slammed the door.

"Do you want to talk about it?"

"I . . . I don't really have the words."

Specialist Black got back in the truck and stared at me. "You okay, princess?"

I didn't answer, so he put the truck in gear, and we headed down the road. Ten minutes later, we approached Iraqi bunkers. I found myself wanting to see if there were any living Iraqi soldiers left in those bunkers, though I hesitated with my hand on the door handle. *This probably isn't a good idea,* I thought, but I opened the door and stepped out anyway. I glanced over my shoulder at Sharon.

She shook her head. "Nope. Not going."

For a fleeting moment, I thought about staying with her. *Just check out the bunkers. No big deal. This is a once-in-a-lifetime experience. Take some pictures.*

I swallowed hard and felt heaviness on my chest. Something stirred inside me that I couldn't identify in my overwhelmed state. Distracted but determined, I marched on. I came upon a mound of sand and noticed an entryway. I cautiously walked down four concrete block stairs to see bunk beds covered with ratty wool blankets, in a room with concrete walls and a dirt floor.

Whoever lived there had run off in such a hurry that some of their belongings were still in the bunker—magazines, newspapers, ammunition, and vials of some kind of liquid. I picked up an Arabic newspaper, put it in the pocket of my camouflage combat uniform, which we called a BDU, and went back outside, relieved to breathe fresh air.

Heading toward another mound of sand in the distance, my boot scraped instead of swishing on the sand. I froze. The hair rose on my neck and arms. My stomach lurched. I had stepped on a landmine.

My heart raced and I became lightheaded. Darkness closed around me. I'd let my guard down and made a fatal error. Time seemed to slow and my raspy breathing grew loud in my ears.

Do I jump off? Step off? Call for help? No, don't call for help. If someone comes running, we may both get blown up.

Images flashed in my head of my body exploding into a million pieces. Every nerve seemed to buzz with anticipation. My stomach ached and churned, and I thought I might lose control of my bowels.

Hold still. Don't move. Don't twitch. Don't cough. I'm 23, and today I'm going to die. I'll never get to go home.

The next mental image was of my family getting a form letter:

Dear Mr. and Mrs. Combs,

We're sorry to inform you that your daughter died in the line of duty. You can be proud that your child served our country well . . ."

I looked down at my combat boots and wondered if this would be the last time my legs would be whole. Shame filled me. *How could you be so stupid?* Then a string of other emotions followed—anger, sadness, confusion, and despair. *How is it possible to feel all these things at once?* Others had faced a similar moment, and it hadn't turned out well.

Lord, please take care of my family. I hope my brother's wedding is awesome. Ease the pain for my parents and watch over my friends. Please make it fast. I don't want my last memory to be one of pain.

As I prayed, warmth filled me. My breathing slowed as did my heart rate. A sense of utter peace and gratitude came over me. It seemed I could literally float off the mine. A pure and holy calm surrounded me. I felt the warmth of an embrace that defied all logic. Stillness, love, and acceptance soothed my soul. I knew the time had come.

Except my mind returned to the present, and I realized I was still alive. Confused, I glanced at my feet and noticed the land mine had somehow moved to my left, or I had stepped to the right, and all my limbs were present and accounted for. I wasn't screaming, there was no blood, no agony, no explosion, no ringing in my ears.

What happened? I stepped on a landmine, waited to be blown to bits, and now I'm standing next to it, completely unharmed. Thank you, God, for saving my life.

After several deep breaths to steady myself, I walked back to the truck and climbed inside. "You're whiter than white," Sharon said. "You okay?"

I stared out the windshield until I could put what happened into words. "I almost died out there."

"What?"

"I stepped on a landmine. I'm not sure what happened, but I must've stepped off of it. I took a picture of the land mine. You can see my footprint." My voice sounded like I was reporting the news.

"Shit, Dani. That's intense."

"I guess, kinda." I forced a laugh.

No one found Iraqi soldiers or any other survivors. When the others returned to the vehicles, we headed to Kuwait, still intent on completing our mission to give food and water to those in need. We drove by the oil wells, burning bright, set on fire by Saddam Hussein's troops. About 30 wells spewed flames that danced in the air—huge plumes of black smoke rose even higher. We stopped on the side of the road to take pictures.

Heat radiated from the oil field like I'd stuck my face in an oven. The soot coated my skin and throat, and it burned my nose. The acrid smell of burnt oil made me feel like I might puke again. It was such an incredible waste of oil. Depressed, I took a picture and went back to the truck.

A half-hour later, we made it to Kuwait City. We could tell the area had been cleaned up a lot. The broken tiles had been replaced on some of the buildings, and the air felt lighter. *Is that hope?*

We pressed on to what looked like an outdoor market and pulled into an empty lot. Kuwaitis gathered around our vehicles, shouting in Arabic. Sharon and I jumped out of the truck, opened the tailgate, and climbed into the back. I grabbed a box of MREs, ripped it open, and handed Sharon some of them.

"Where's Black," I asked. "What does he want us to do?"

Sharon shrugged. "Not sure. I guess just hand out the stuff."

American voices caught my attention above the noisy crowd. I looked up at the truck next to us to find the other five soldiers shouting,

"Two dollars for water, five dollars for MREs."

My jaw dropped. This wasn't a trip to help people in need as I had assumed. The other soldiers came to pocket Iraqi cash, to take advantage of the downtrodden, pawning goods that weren't even theirs to sell.

Sharon and I felt betrayed and angry. We handed out meals, water bottles, and candy as fast as we could to people in filthy clothes, extending dirty hands, begging for water. Joy lit their faces, and they began to chant: "USA. USA. USA. . ."

I wanted to share their excitement, but I couldn't let my guard down. My eyes flitted into the crowd, scanning for someone hiding a bomb or a sniper ready to pick us off. A deep sadness came over me, and I wondered if I'd ever enjoy gift giving again.

Before the others could get their mitts on the provisions Sharon and I had loaded onto the truck, we rushed to put all the food and water we'd brought into the townspeople's hands. When the boxes were empty, I got into the truck and glared at Black, sickened that I had to sit next to him for hours on the trip back to the base.

He glanced at me before he turned the key to start the engine. "What, princess? You got a problem?"

"You asshole!"

"Hey, the Army owes me this for putting up with all their bullshit."

"You lied to me. You said we were going to deliver food and water to the Kuwaitis."

He snorted. "We did deliver food and water."

"You took advantage of these people. I thought we were giving them stuff, not making them pay for it!"

"I never said we were giving it away. I got paid—you didn't. Your choice."

My face heated and my chest tightened. I wanted to punch Black in the face, but I sat rigid in my seat, staring out the windshield at nothing. *What a jerk! Why did I volunteer for this? And poor Sharon.*

I looked at my roommate, silent, her head turned to the side, facing the passenger window. She was one of the few people I trusted in the Army. I felt like a terrible friend for talking her into coming on that horrible trip.

On the drive home, I remained uncharacteristically quiet, fearing the worst. My mind conjured images of getting ambushed, bullets flying everywhere, then getting blown up driving over a mine, and a bomb dropping out of the sky. Sharon and Black didn't talk either and seemed as tense as I felt. Dread hung heavily in the truck. Black put on a tough face—stiff jaw, eyes glaring straight ahead as he drove.

Nothing happened on the return trip, but the experiences of that day would remain in visceral memory forever. I never saw those soldiers again, but their deception intensified the anguish and guilt that the trauma left behind. Still, like any good soldier, I moved on.

We received orders to move to the accommodation barges at the port. Each of the two floating vessels had three levels and housed up to 350 soldiers. The barges were anchored next to one another in the gulf. These would be our final living quarters in Saudi Arabia.

Originally white, years of accumulated rust had turned the barges reddish-brown, and they smelled like mold and wet socks. Sharon's and my units were reassigned to the barge, so we chose to be roomies again. We shared a bathroom with two other women, Tasha and Jenny. The water worked, and we preferred the musty odor over the smell of urine while sharing bathrooms with male soldiers. Our new rooms were within walking distance to our jobs at the port, and on our days off, we sunbathed on the upper deck, a flat area designed for helicopters to land.

The hot lieutenant also moved onto the barge. I felt alive whenever he walked my way or glanced at me. After strolling down the Highway of Death, my senses had gone numb, and I craved the thrill he sparked in me. Our romance began with clandestine meetings at the port and progressed to trysts in his room. His handsome face, dark hair, and smoldering eyes provided enough distraction to give me a break from flashes of burnt bodies and my footprint in the sand on the landmine. The army prohibited relationships between officers and enlisted, which heightened our desire. We talked about everything and loved to run together before work.

A month into our taboo relationship, my mom sent me Gary's address and said I should reach out to him. Missing home, I wrote and told Gary my unit had been in Saudi Arabia since September 1990, and I asked how he'd been. When we started writing, I had no idea we'd decide to meet up when we got back to the states and maybe give our relationship another chance. A possible future with Gary meant I had to break up with the officer. I figured he would tire of me anyway. He had a higher rank and more education. Frankly, I felt I didn't deserve him.

The nights became lonely, so I learned how to box and sparred with other soldiers. When I wasn't pummeling people, I wrote letters, listened to music, and ran by myself around the perimeter of the port. I missed the lieutenant, but I didn't want to feel guilty when Gary and I got together.

Gary gave me comfort. I'd known him since fifth grade. He was safe. We continued to write and make plans, and I couldn't wait to see him. Stationed at Fort Hood in Texas, he promised to come see me when I got discharged from the Army and finally arrived home in Bend.

Two days before I was scheduled to leave Saudi Arabia, I began my official out-processing. I called home to let my family know I'd completed my mission and would be flying to Seattle. Next, I called Gary to tell him it looked like I'd be back in Bend the first week of June and hoped to see him. My heart broke with the thought of leaving Sharon, so as soon as I got off the phone, I tracked her down at the mess hall.

"Well, it's official. I leave in two days. The only thing I'm going to miss about this place is you." I clunked onto the bench opposite her at the table. We hugged each other and cried. I knew in my heart once I left Saudi Arabia, I would never see her again, and I was right.

Chapter 10

COERCED

On May 31, 1991, I walked over to Russ, waiting to board a commercial plane. He hugged me and said, "You okay?"

"Yeah, just bummed about leaving Sharon. I'm going to miss her."

"Me too, but it will be great to be back in the U.S.!"

I clicked my combat boots together. "There's no place like home."

We both laughed.

Russ, Sargeant Gomez, and I walked onto the Boeing 737 headed for the United States. We slept most of the way to Chicago. Everyone on the plane from Chicago to Seattle wanted to buy the "war heroes" a drink. I didn't feel like a hero, but I wouldn't pass up a free beer. Alcohol is prohibited in Saudi Arabia, so we hadn't had a drink since leaving for the Middle East in September. By the time we landed in Seattle, to finish out-processing to leave the U.S. Army, I felt pretty tipsy.

Control yourself. Behave. Mom and Dad are waiting.

As we came out of the breezeway, into the airport, I saw my parents in the crowd and ran into their arms. Warm in their embrace, I started crying like a baby. *I'm home. I'm safe. I'm loved.*

My mom loosened her arms around me and said, "Honey, you're so skinny. I can feel every bone."

"Yeah, I ran six miles a day and didn't eat meat, because I wasn't sure what kind of meat it was. I lost about 30 pounds, but I feel amazing."

"Well, that's good." She pulled me close and tight again. "I'm just so glad you're back home. Safe and sound."

My mom had driven my convertible Volkswagen Cabriolet from Bend while Dad followed in their car to Seattle airport. Shiny black from top to bottom, my car had a new vinyl black roof, fresh paint, and a huge yellow ribbon around it. My breath caught in one of my happiest moments in the past four years. I pictured driving away from Fort Lewis, a proud veteran of the US Army, in a few days, putting the horror behind me, riding away into the sunset in my classy little car.

I ran to my VW and wrapped my arms as far as I could around the top and the windshield. My mom snapped a picture to capture my euphoria over the symbol of my new beginning. Sending money home to have Mom spruce up my ride had been a good decision.

Since I was too tipsy to drive, Mom drove us to a seedy Motel 8 in Tacoma where the stucco was peeling and the vacancy sign flickered. Dad pulled in behind us and checked us in. The rest of the guys had gone back to the barracks.

That evening, while my parents and I waited for our meal at a restaurant, my first real Mexican dinner in nine months, Mom told me Sergeant Gomez had written a letter to them saying he'd keep me safe. I'd never heard of sergeants sending letters to their specialists' parents, but I soon forgot about it while munching on delicious chips and salsa to mariachi music. The next morning, I hugged my parents goodbye and choked back tears, annoyed with myself because I would see them in less than a week.

I headed back to Fort Lewis to pack up the rest of the stuff I'd left in my room at the barracks, before going off to Saudi Arabia. Within the next few days, I was expected to fill out what seemed like reams of paper so I could finally go home. On the second day, while I was filling out forms at the out-processing office, Sergeant Gomez walked in and said, "Hey, Combs, want to get a drink tonight? The rest of the unit will be there."

"Uh, I guess so." Though he'd stood up for me in the Middle East, I still felt awkward around him. But I didn't want to miss getting together with our unit one more time. Soon we'd scatter all over the country and maybe never see each other again.

"Meet up in my room. We'll pre-party, then hit the town."

"Everyone's going to your room?"

"Yep. Nineteen hundred hours."

"Cool, see you then."

At 7:00 p.m. I walked upstairs to his room in the barracks and knocked on the door. The door swung open, and Sergeant Gomez waved me inside. "Right on time. Come on in."

"Where is everyone?"

"They're coming. They must be running late," he said with a slight slur. "Have a drink—beer, wine, vodka? Pick your pleasure."

"Uh . . . beer's fine."

He popped a bottle and handed it to me in the doorway. "To being home," he said and clicked his tumbler to my bottleneck. I hadn't eaten since I figured we'd all order food when we went out, and the beer went straight to my head.

He sat on the end of the military twin-sized bed and waved his hand for me to sit in the chair by his desk—an arm's length from him. *Please hurry up, you guys,* I thought as I obeyed the motion, so used to following his orders.

"Combs, I want you to know I'm proud of you and the way you handled yourself during the war. You're an impressive soldier. I'd say you're one of the best I've been in charge of."

I shifted in my seat, unsure of what I should, or shouldn't, say.

"I took care of you over there. I picked you up during enemy fire and whisked you to safety. I took care of that asshole Steve when he bothered you at the port. I watched your back and kept you safe. I made sure you came home in one piece and even told your parents what a great soldier you are."

"Um . . . I'm not sure what you're saying." The walls started to close in, and I glanced at the door.

He leaned in close. "You owe me."

"Owe you for what?"

"For keeping you safe and taking care of your problems. You don't want me to tell your parents about all the guys you've slept with. I've kept my eye on you, and I've always been there for you, helped you out with the Steven situation in Saudi, and now it's time to pay me back."

"With what?" I slowly stood from the chair.

"Have sex with me, and I won't tell anyone that you're a slut and a lousy soldier." He stood in front of me, blocking the way out.

"You just told me I was a great soldier." *How's it possible that this is happening again? What should I do?*

He grabbed my arm and pulled me toward him. When I tried to yank away, he clamped his hands on both my upper arms and threw me on the bed. I kicked and punched and tried to stand up, but he managed to crawl on top of me. Still, I pushed and pulled at my arms and legs, but he had me pinned to the mattress.

"You'll give it up to everyone else. The stevedore, the lieutenant . . ."

My eyes went wide. *Was he stalking me?*

"Yeah, I know about the lieutenant. If you don't have sex with me, I'll report you to the commander. Then you won't get to go home. They'll charge you and extend your service. But if you have sex with me, I'll keep quiet. No one will know. It's no big deal—just sex. You owe me."

I can't stay in the military. I'm done. I just want to get the hell out of here . . .

My mind left the room, which saved me from being present while I was raped for the second time. The next thing I remembered, I was standing in the communal shower on my floor. Deep, soul-wrenching sobs wracked my body. Scalding water burned my flesh, and I scrubbed my neck, chest, and thighs until they bled. *I should've stopped him. Why am*

I so weak and stupid? How could I let it happen again?

The following day, suffocating from shame, I told no one about Sergeant Gomez. Terrified I'd be kept in the Army and punished for my relationship with the lieutenant, I returned my gear and got my paperwork stamped and submitted. I was officially honorably discharged. I'd completed my mission and served my time. I just wanted to put all the shit behind me and head home.

With my meager possessions loaded into my VW, I said a tearful goodbye to Russ and left Fort Lewis. I bawled, off and on, for three of the six-hour drive home to Bend. I'd suffered untold injuries in the past four years, many that wouldn't come to light for decades.

Chapter 11

ROCKY TRANSITION

I drove into Bend and saw "Welcome Home, Dani and Gary!" on the message board at Cummins Northwest, Inc., the diesel engine company where Dad worked in the parts department. I swallowed hard and a happy tear trickled down my cheek. *I'm home. I'm really home.*

When I turned onto my parents' street, "Welcome Home, Soldier!" was sprawled on butcher paper and taped to the side of the house where I would see it immediately. I became nauseated with anticipation and fear of being exposed as an absolute fraud because I wasn't a tough combat veteran, merely a scared, violated and broken person. As I pulled into the driveway I glanced around nervously and counted approximately 20 people waiting for me. They swarmed my VW, vibrating with excitement. As soon as I got out of the car, they passed me from one to the other, taking turns throwing their arms around me, telling me how glad they were that I'd made it home.

The sign, the people, the hugs, the chattering—I tried to enjoy their affection and return their enthusiasm with smiles and greetings, but I felt trapped, as if in a tunnel. Their voices reverberated in my ears. The air lay thick and hot on my bare arms. Their updates on shopping and opinions of the latest movies seemed foreign and confusing. All I wanted to do was go take a nap on my old bed.

Finally, enough people had gone so that I could gracefully go inside the house—where I found the spare room had been rented to one of the mechanics where Dad worked. My parents offered their couch until I could find another place to live. Relieved to be close to them, my stabilizing influences, I ignored my hurt feelings and focused on figuring out how to get back to what most people thought of as normal.

No book had been written yet on what to expect or how to transition from military to civilian life. My days had been filled with structure and discipline. Not having anywhere to be at a given time made me nervous, and my body reacted with constant diarrhea. My nightmares of burnt bodies and reliving rape started again, so I drank to keep them at bay. And when my stomach fluttered with nervousness, I stuffed it with food, which gave me temporary comfort.

A few of my high school friends decided to have a homecoming party for me. They came to pick me up, declared the location had to be a surprise, and they blindfolded me. At first, I enjoyed the anticipation, but as they walked me out of my parents' house, my heart started to race, sweat bead on my forehead, and my gut clenched.

These are my friends. I'm not in Saudi Arabia anymore. Just relax and have fun.

Two of my friends helped me get into the car. The moment my butt hit the seat, my pulse sped even faster, my palms sweat, and my breath heaved like I was on a full sprint. *Where are they taking me? It's dark. Wait, my friends won't hurt me. I'm safe. I'm in the States. It'll be okay.*

When we arrived at our destination and they took off the blindfold, I could restore my breathing to somewhat normal, but my hands still shook. I didn't recognize the two-story gray house that belonged to the boyfriend of one of my friends. We entered the front door to a room full of people, all seeming to talk at once. The noise grated on my raw nerves, and I wanted to leave. *Wait. I used to love parties. Just drink. Everything will be fine.*

The party migrated to the backyard where I sat in a chair with my back against the wall so I could keep an eye on everyone. I mostly listened as people welcomed me home. Some I didn't know, and they told me what they'd been doing for the past few years. I grew more comfortable as the evening wore on—until the first firework burst into the sky.

A SCUD missile appeared in my vision. I was at the port looking for cover, waiting for the explosion on impact. *These are fireworks probably left over from their fourth of July party—not missiles,* I tried to tell myself, but my body reacted anyway. I bolted from my seat on the grass and ran into the house. A friend found me hunkered in the corner of a dark office with tears streaming down my face.

"Please take me home," I said. She put out her hand and pulled me to my feet. Neither of us spoke on the drive back to my parents' house.

The next week, my stomach flip-flopped with anticipation waiting for Gary to arrive from Texas. When his Toyota 4Runnner pulled to the curb in front of my parents' house, I ran into his arms and finally felt safe. He was the grounding I desperately needed—comfortable, familiar, and had some understanding of my last four years. He had come home to see me and to attend Wade's wedding.

The night before the wedding, Mom and Dad had a barbecue for the family. Gary and I imbibed in too much alcohol, and much of the night was a blur. When Gary and I woke up on the hideaway bed at my parent's house, both our heads felt like they were splitting in two. We stumbled out of bed, threw on our clothes, and raced out of the house, but we didn't arrive in time for family pictures. Mom glared at me with disappointment, but otherwise, the ceremony and dancing at Shevlin Park was a blast.

Wade and Susie had asked me to watch their house and dog while they honeymooned in Mexico. While I cleaned up their house and watched Buffy, their black lab, Gary split his time between me and catching up with his buddies from high school. When he left the following week, my heart was heavy, but I knew that soon he'd be out of the Army, and we'd be together. Cleaning up the dog's messes kept me busy. Buffy loved to shred paper into confetti, including a newspaper she'd found on the lawn. I tried to pick up the pieces and realized it would take forever, so I got out the vacuum and sucked them up instead. The neighbors probably thought I was crazy, but I didn't care.

Back inside the house I thought, *You're destined to be alone. No one will want you. You're damaged goods. Wade and Susie will only be gone a week. Where will you go when they get home from their Mexican cruise?*

Sleeping on my parents' couch had intensified the feeling that I didn't belong anywhere. I needed to find a more stable place to live. But how? I didn't have enough money for the first and last months' rent to get an apartment, and I had no idea what kind of job I wanted or would know how to do.

The dreaded day came when Wade and Susie returned from their honeymoon, tanned and relaxed. I hugged them hello, pet Buffy, and started to throw my few things into a duffle when Susie said, "Where're you going?"

I stared up at her from the couch because I still didn't know.

Wade glanced at Susie. "Yeah, we've been discussing your housing situation. I know it's not much, but you can stay in the little room upstairs."

I looked from Wade to Susie and back again. "Are you kidding me?"

"No, Susie and I want to help you out until you get settled. We have the extra room, so it's no big deal."

"Wade, thank you so much, but you just got married. I don't want to intrude on you guys."

"We all get along, and it'll be nice having you around again. We have a lot of catching up to do."

"Oh my gosh. Thank you so much. I love to clean, and I can help with groceries and stuff."

"We'll make it work. No big deal."

Susie smiled and seemed genuinely pleased. "Go check out your new room."

I walked up the steep, narrow steps and opened the door to a small space, but I didn't have much. A thorough cleaning would get rid of the dust and cobwebs. Wade told me the baseboard heater didn't work, and the heat from the wood stove downstairs wouldn't reach my area. Still, this was a place to stay that wasn't on someone's couch, and I was happy for the opportunity to reconnect with my brother.

We'd lost touch when I was in Germany, so rehashing old times and making new memories together with Susie would make that little room a real home. Wade had always been mellow, and I definitely needed some mellow. Sometimes people wondered how we were related. But we complemented one another, and I was excited to spend more time with my new sister.

Dad told me to go to Cummins Northwest, Inc. to interview for a job. He'd talked to his boss who said they may have a position for me. I needed to earn money, but I'd been in the Army four-and-a-half years and didn't know how to behave as a civilian.

What do I wear? How should I act? What should I say?

I walked into the main office in khakis, a casual button-down blouse, and a sweater because I was freezing. I'd climatized to Saudi Arabia, and Bend's Summer was much cooler. No one sat at the desk to the left of the entrance, so I waited. Then I noticed a tall, red-headed, bearded man in the corner office.

He glanced up at me, stood from a squeaky chair, and lumbered over with an outstretched hand. "Hi, I'm Matt. I'm the branch manager here."

I shook his hand. "Nice to meet you. I'm Dani."

"I feel like I know you already. Your dad talks about you all the time."

"Hopefully he says good things." I laughed, remembering my tough teenage years.

"Ah, yeah. He's so proud of you."

After some basic questions about typing and filing, Matt hired me as the office and warranty manager. I would be responsible for billing and payroll for 15 employees. Sitting at my own desk, I felt like a grownup for the first time. Working a civilian job turned out less alien than I thought it would be, and I settled in quickly to my new nine-to-five routine.

When I wasn't working, Wade, Susie, and I camped often, went fishing, watched movies, and loved being together. Gary and I also saw each other as much as possible and wrote often. He was my rock. In six months, he would be discharged from the Army and could come home from Texas.

I began attending Central Oregon Community College (COCC) in the evenings to earn an Associate of Arts Degree. My goal was to transfer to the University of Oregon, close to Tani and her family. The idea of living near Tani, while pursuing my dream of becoming a physical therapist, or something in the medical field, thrilled me.

At the end of Gary's six months, I flew to Fort Hood Texas to celebrate his honorable discharge from the Army and to drive back to Oregon together. We'd never been on a road trip alone and planned to take our time, visiting New Mexico, Arizona, Utah, Wyoming, Montana, and Idaho before we headed home to Bend. In Arizona, we went to the Grand Canyon, picked a hike designated "simple" in a brochure, and went exploring. Two hours into the hike, only a bottle of water and a bag of grapes between us, I concluded whoever wrote that brochure didn't know what "simple" meant. "Treacherous" would have been more accurate. In fact, we ran into four Army Rangers on the trail.

Gary and I grunted a hello as we crawled up and over huge boulders. We grabbed onto tree branches to keep from falling off the steep, narrow path and had to climb another set of rocks to stay on the trail.

Four hours into our "simple" hike, we made it to a mesa covered in sagebrush and a smattering of cacti. I needed shade, so I crawled under the brush and began to peel off my sock to inspect the blister I'd felt forming on my right heel. Gary dropped his backpack on the ground, pulled something out of it, and came over to me.

"Well, this isn't how I'd planned this, but I'm hoping this will motivate you to get you out of this canyon."

Distracted by my painful blister I said, "What are you talking about?"

"Dan, look at me."

I glanced up and saw a box in his hands. *Oh my God! Is he proposing to me? He wouldn't want me if he knew I'd been raped twice. But I know Gary. I love him, right?*

"Well, what do you say? Will you marry me?"

"Wow. I can't believe this."

"I'm waiting here."

My heart skipped a beat, and my mouth had gone dry, but I managed to screech, "Yes!" I laughed at the unusual proposal that made total sense for us. I'd pictured a nice dinner by candlelight, but Gary wasn't the romantic type—sweat, dirt, sunburn, and blisters seemed more fitting.

He handed me the ring, and I slipped it on my finger. The modest diamond sparkled in the sunlight, simple and beautiful.

"Okay, get your sock back on. We have one hell of a hike out of here."

"I'm going to report this shit to someone—this is not an easy hike!"

He laughed. "Use that aggression to get your ass out of here."

We rationed our water and grapes. My skin radiated heat, and my low back blistered where my pack had rubbed all those hours. Several people gawked as we climbed out of the canyon, badly sunburned, dirty, and smelly. We hobbled over to the truck, and I snatched the brochure off the seat. I had misread the stupid thing. We'd been on the trail marked "most difficult" that was next to a trail marked "simple." But I had a ring that I couldn't stop staring at, so it was all good.

We'd been sleeping in a tent at Kampgrounds of America (KOA) sites, but we splurged and got a motel room with air conditioning and clean towels to celebrate our engagement. For dinner, we had the best taco salads on fry bread. When we arrived home three weeks later, people were excited and wanted to hear the story of how Gary proposed. I was so caught up in the fever, I didn't notice some people were less than enthusiastic at our pending nuptials, and I wouldn't find out until much later.

Oblivious to everyone else, Gary and I remained in our happy bubble while we looked for an apartment. We found a two-bedroom place at Carriage Trade Apartments, and since money was tight, we asked Ron, our buddy from high school and a fellow veteran, to move in with us. Until the move-in date, Gary would stay at his parents' house, and I would stay with Wade and Susie.

Susie was nine months pregnant, so the timing was perfect. The night Hali Danielle was born, Mom, Dad, and I went to the birthing suite at Saint Charles Hospital, and I got to hold my niece for the first time. As I gazed at her scrunched face, warmth flowed through me. Her wrinkly little face looked like an old man, and I chuckled. *I'm going to spoil this child rotten.*

I lived with Wade and Susie for a year. When moving day arrived, I picked up my last box from the floor, and Wade asked, "Hey, did you ever check if the heater worked?"

"No, because you told me it didn't."

"Try it."

I walked over to the baseboard heater, turned it on, and spun around. "Are you kidding me? It worked the whole time?"

"Yep, payback."

He got me. When we were in high school, he had to sleep in a tiny room that wasn't connected to the house. Puberty had hit, and I needed space. We previously shared the bedroom, but between my moods and his taste in music, our fights had gotten heated and frequent.

Mom and Dad cleared out the storage room, next to the detached garage, and converted it into a bedroom. Wade worked late stocking shelves at the Green Mint grocery store down the street, so staying in that small room meant he could come and go without waking up anyone. But the building didn't have heat. He snuggled with his dog, Lowboy, in the winters and was often shivering when he came in for breakfast. Frankly, the icebox I'd lived in upstairs seemed fair. Wade got the last laugh, for sure.

Gary, Ron, and I shared a two-bedroom apartment on the bottom floor of the complex. All three of us had been in the military, so we kept the place clean. There were no dishes in the sink, and everything had a place.

This period I refer to as "the apartment daze." After work at Cummins, I'd buy a 12-pack of beer, invite some friends over, and we'd play poker. Eventually, I'd pass out and then get up to go to work in the morning. If I went to bed sober, the nightmares came flooding back. The Army taught the three of us well, drink your problems away, it'll help to blow off steam. What a bunch of crap. Gary and Ron were pretty angry when they drank and ended up fighting both inside and outside the apartment, sometimes with each other, sometimes with some other pour sot. I internalized my shame and just kept drinking more to black out and keep the demons at bay.

Lack of sleep made it difficult to do my job at Cummins. I struggled to keep 15 men in line with their timecards and attitudes. Telling a customer that they had to pay their bill because the repair wasn't covered under warranty was hard enough without being tired and grumpy. People got loud and explosive when it came to money. I hated that part of my job. Every day left me stressed and looking for a way to numb out.

The pattern had been set. Work. School. Home. Drink. Get Drunk. Pass out. Repeat. It's a wonder the three of us survived being roommates.

Eighteen months later, I graduated from Central Oregon Community College with an Associate of Arts degree. My parents were so proud because I was the first in my family to earn a college degree. I took all the classes to transfer to the University of Oregon and major in Exercise and Movement Science, to eventually become a physical therapist.

When August rolled around, Gary moved into my mom and dad's

spare bedroom, and Ron decided to move to Portland to be closer to his mom and sister. The timing was right because the three of us needed a break from each other. Sad but excited, I packed up my VW and headed to Eugene. I couldn't wait to be closer to Tani and her family.

Chapter 12

CREW DAYS

The University of Oregon campus smelled of fresh-cut grass as I followed the map to the buildings where I would need to go for my first day of school. I had four classes, a full load—Anatomy and Physiology, Chemistry, Women's Studies, and Sports Nutrition. All the other students on a treasure hunt to find their classrooms seemed younger, but I didn't care—well, that's what I told myself.

Tani's parents offered me her old room, so I stayed with them in Springfield, a ten-minute drive from the campus in Eugene. Ken and Dee were like second parents. I helped with cooking and cleaning, and I loved being around them. Living in their familiar house felt like wearing a comfortable old shirt and gave me a sense of security I hadn't felt in a long time.

The first couple months of the school year, I visited Tani on most weekends in Eugene and drove over the Cascade Mountains to visit Mom, Dad, and Gary in Bend, whenever I could squeeze in the time. Tani's and my renewed close friendship and Gary's frequent visits to Eugene helped to fill some of my emptiness. Tani was a precious, rare friend who had withstood the test of time.

At Tani's house, we watched the Oregon Ducks play football, barbecued, and I busted a gut watching her try to keep up with her three kids. Her stepson Jake was 12, her son Nate was four, and she had a one-year-old baby girl named Danielle. I was honored to be her daughter's namesake and felt valued in ways I never had before. Tani's patience and energy in dealing with her children gave me even deeper respect for her. I couldn't see myself ever being a mom.

The first few days of school were chaotic, but I figured out a system—where to park, where to eat, and where to nap—on the couches at the Erb Memorial Student Union between classes. I spoke with a veteran representative in the registrar's office who placed me in the work-study program at U of O. To defray living expenses, I checked out and shelved books at the math and science libraries. The smell of the old books and soothing quiet gave me peace. After work I'd go home, help with dinner and dishes, and then study. The routine kept me grounded, though I'd begun to feel anxious for no apparent reason.

In Women's Studies, a girl kept showing up soaking wet, even on days it hadn't rained. She'd eat three sandwiches and guzzle the same number of water bottles. During the lecture, her eyelids drooped, and her head bobbed like she struggled to stay awake. About two weeks into the semester, when the bell rang, I mustered up the courage to say: "Excuse me, but why are you always wet and hungry when you come to class?"

She laughed. "Yeah, it probably seems a little weird. I'm in crew, which is a club sport, so you pay a fee to row. We need more rowers. Do you want to check it out?"

"I've never rowed before, but I'd be interested. Sure."

"My name's Skye."

"I'm Dani."

"Why don't you meet me at the erg house later today."

"What's an erg?"

"Ergometer, a rowing machine. It's what we train on when we aren't on the water. It's great for working on our stroke rate."

Is she speaking English? What's a stroke rate? "Okay, I'll meet you there. Uh . . . where exactly?"

"Across from Hayward Field."

"Thanks, see you later."

After my last class, I went in search of something called an "erg house" and was relieved to see Skye standing outside a tiny white building that had one door and two small windows. When she opened the door, the music blasted so loud, I thought my eardrums would rupture. I did my best not to wrinkle my nose at the stink of body odor, mold, vomit, and other things I couldn't identify. In a line of rowing machines facing the wall, eight guys drenched in sweat pulled on T-bars, spinning the wheels so fast, wind from the momentum blew on my face as Skye led me farther into the room. After a few minutes of the stench and head-banging music, I stepped outside for some fresh air.

Skye followed me and said, "We're running this afternoon. Do you want to come?"

"Sure." Running was something I knew I could do.

The whole crew team, 15 guys and 15 girls, plus me, showed up to Hayward Field. We began and ended our three-mile run on the field, then started the strengthening portion—four sets of running up and down the stadium stairs, followed by push-ups and sit-ups. Everyone joked and laughed. When I slowed down, Skye cheered me on to keep going and the others joined in. The camaraderie reminded me of being in the Army.

Thirty minutes of pumping iron in the weight room finished the workout. My muscles quivered with exhaustion. I wanted more, I longed to be part of the team and to become a rower. "What's the next step?" I asked Skye. "How do I join?"

"Easy. Just bring your club dues in the morning. Make it out to the University of Oregon Club Sports. Meet us at the bus stop by the bookstore at 4:30 in the morning. We'll row on Dexter Reservoir for about two hours and make it back just in time to make it to our 8:30 Women's Studies class. Remember to bring something to eat because you'll be starving!"

"Okay, see you in the morning."

Skye had given me the greatest gift—a new team and a mission:

rowing. My mind buzzed with excitement. I was all smiles when I went home that night. I walked in the back door and said, "Bet you can't guess what I signed up for today."

Ken was cutting vegetables for dinner, and Dee was reading a book in the TV room. "What?" they asked at the same time.

"You are looking at the newest member of the University of Oregon Women's Crew."

Dee put her book on her lap. "Crew? What does that mean?"

"Crew as in rowing. I've never done it before, but tomorrow is my first day, and practice starts at 4:30 a.m."

Ken laughed. "Geez, that's early. Don't wake us up."

When my alarm blared the next morning, I wondered if I'd made the right decision. I dragged myself out of bed, jumped in my trusty VW, found a parking spot on campus, and headed to the bus stop. Skye and I grunted good mornings and waited for the rest of the team to show up. All present and accounted for, we loaded into the bus.

Getting on the bus, I noticed for the first time that most of my teammates were younger than me, many by five years. As Skye and I made our way down the aisle, where men and women sat randomly, she told me the coach was only 25.

I'm three years older than the coach? Kinda weird.

Skye stopped next to his seat to introduce me, and I automatically extended my hand. "Glad you made it," he said, returning a confident handshake. "Once we get to Dexter, we'll talk about what you get to do."

"Okay. Sounds good, thanks."

The 30-minute ride on the bus was quiet. Most people slept, but I was too excited to close my eyes. I stared out the window, into the darkness, trying to calm the butterflies in my stomach.

When the bus parked in the lot next to the reservoir, the coach ambled back a few rows and loomed above me. "Dani, no time to waste. Come with me. I'll show you the boathouse. The first thing you have to learn is how to get your set right before you row."

"What's a set?"

"It's how the boat floats on the water." He turned and started heading off the bus, talking over his shoulder. "If everyone's in sync and rowing together, the set's smooth. If you aren't in sync, the boat rocks from side to side. You'll get the hang of it and be able to tell."

"Okay, if you say so." I hopped down the steps, out of the bus, and hurried to keep up.

"First, you're going to start in a single scull. Once you've mastered the scull, then we'll place you in a four. The ultimate goal for most rowers is to make the eight (the long boat with eight rowers)."

We entered a shed with rowboats stacked on racks against the walls. Other rowers began to join us and help each other take boats from the walls and walk them to the water. The coach pointed out the single scull, showed me how to carry the small boat to the water, attach the oars, and tighten the clamp to hold the oars in place. Next, he showed me how to get into the scull. He made it look easy.

He stepped out of the scull and held onto it so I could get in. I squatted and placed my foot in the scull. *Can't be that hard. Don't hold your breath. Don't pass out.* I sat with one foot still on the dock. *Okay. Next foot.* As soon as my foot left the dock, I knew I was in trouble. The boat started to rock.

"Straight back. Tighten your core. Now push away from the dock. Grab both of your oars and place them in the water. Try to grab the water to help propel you away from the dock."

I sucked in my gut, sat up straighter, carefully placed the oars into the water, and took a deep breath. *Okay, just grab the water like the coach said.* Though the oars went in together, my right oar went deeper, which threw off my balance. I overcorrected, and the boat toppled me into the cold water.

The coach yelled, "Swim back. Drag your boat with you. Try again.

Just keep trying until you succeed. The first time's never easy."

During the first few practices, I spent more time in the water than in the boat. When I wasn't on the water, I hit the erg house where I learned proper stroke technique. I wanted to get into the four. I had a goal, and nothing could stop me. Through hard work and determination, my times in seat races in the single scull eventually proved that I belonged in the four. The blisters, blood, sweat, and tears paid off.

Being the shortest rower, I was placed in the bow, the first person to cross the finish line. The next step was tackling how to effectively maneuver one long oar instead of two. Everyone sits with their backs to the direction they'll be rowing except the coxswain, usually a small person that sits in the stern of the boat and has a voice that carries. Our coxswain, a tiny spitfire whose sole purpose was to make us go faster, scared the crap out of me.

She yelled at us constantly, encouraging words like: "My grandma could row better than you!" and "What a bunch of whiners! Now dig! There's no crying in rowing!"

Blisters swelled on my red, raw, and bleeding palms. Battle scars. My hands hurt so bad, yet the pain filled the void, and I reveled in the teamwork.

We began training for our first regatta. I'd never been to a regatta, so I had no idea how many teams there would be and what the racecourse would look like. We would be racing 2000 meters—that's all I knew. At every practice we covered way more than the race distance, but our team had only been together for a week in the four. We didn't know each other well, and my three teammates were all 19, fresh out of high school. I had a low tolerance for bullshit and had to constantly remind myself that they were young and hadn't been in the military.

We lined up at the start. My stomach flip-flopped, and my mouth went dry. I leaned forward, muscles flexed, oar in the water, waiting and ready. The gun fired to start the race, and I flinched.

Take cover!...No...wait. I'm rowing. I'm in the States, not Saudi Arabia. Don't go there. Focus. Keep digging into the water. Watch the person in front of you. Mirror her. Just keep rowing. You can do this. It's only 2000 meters!

We placed third out of four teams. At least we weren't last. After the race, we decided to get serious. Every rower had the same goal: row hard, row fast, and push yourself beyond human limits. I also developed a ritual before the gun would go off to start each race. *Breathe in and exhale slowly. You're safe. When you hear the gunshot, row like hell!*

In the next two regattas, we placed second. Following every race, I fought the urge to puke from exhaustion. Sometimes I lost the fight. In time, we got into the groove with a stable set, and we rowed in sync. For me, the exertion never got easier. My legs always burned, and my hands were always raw. Improvement came by increasing our stroke rate, which encouraged us to row harder.

Two months after I started, Coach sauntered over to me as I placed my paddle back on the rack in the boathouse. "Dani, I want you to seat-race for the eight."

I was glad my back was to him because my mouth fell open. "What? Are you sure?"

"Yep. Tomorrow. Be ready."

Whoa. Another racer and I would compete for a seat in the eight-person shell. Each rower had 2000 meters to prove the boat was faster with us in it. The best time would win a spot on the women's eight-person crew, which is a huge honor.

The strongest rowers in the eight were tall and usually at the stern, the back of the boat. They controlled the stroke. They were the powerhouses. They set the pace and rhythm. The bow seat, or front, focused on maintaining the set. One bad pull could throw off the entire team. Consistent strokes were critical in the bow seat.

I knew at once when I'd hit my groove. My brain chatter silenced, and I focused on my task to maintain a good set. My muscles burned from exertion, and friction from the water on the oar opened my scabbed-over blisters. Pain seared through my hands, but I dug deeper and pulled harder in the water. The coxswain yelled for more and we obeyed. One stroke after the other, she called for a "power ten" and we pulled with everything we had. My lungs burned, but we had a balanced set. We glided along the water as one. I gave it my all, then gave more. Time seemed to stand still. The shell slid across the finish line, and I fell forward on my oar, exhausted. When the coach walked up to me afterwards, my stomach lurched in anticipation.

"Congratulations, Dani. You're our new bow seat."

I swallowed over my raspy throat and managed to croak, "Thanks, Coach."

"Thank yourself. You did the work."

After joining the eight, stress mounted with the additional effort required for me to compete on the elite team as well as maintain my self-imposed commitment to keep everyone happy. I continued to call and see Gary as much as possible, visit Tani and her family, and make time for my parents. Three nights a week, I worked at the library and wouldn't get home until eight o'clock. I would shove food in my face, head upstairs to tackle my homework, and sometimes pass out before I got my assignments finished. Yet I kept pushing myself. *I'm not a quitter!*

Chapter 13

Decisions

On a typical weekday, I rowed for two hours in the early morning, went to class, did a midday workout in the erg house, attended two more classes, then ran three miles with the team. When my alarm went off at 4:00 the next morning, it would start over again. I ignored the muscle fatigue and lethargy and soldiered on.

My busy schedule made it difficult to spend time with Gary. He still went to Central Oregon Community College in Bend and had moved into my parents' old garage, which we'd aptly renamed the love shack. Since his schedule was less hectic, he'd come visit me at Tani's on weekends whenever he could.

My hectic life also meant I seldom saw Mom and Dad—or Wade, Susie, and Hali. Susie was pregnant with my second niece, and I felt sad that I couldn't be there to help her. When I lived with my brother, during Susie's first pregnancy, I'd done household chores and cooked some meals. Since I'd transferred to U of O, my connection with family seemed to be waning.

Probably the distance, I told myself and decided things would be different if rowing didn't consume my life. Being active was good, right? In reality, I was closing myself off from people.

At one of our home regattas, Gary, Tani, Andy, Ken, and Dee came to cheer for me. I felt blessed and thanked God for these amazing people. Our team placed second, and my friends and I went for a celebratory dinner of beer and pizza at the restaurant down the hill from Tani and

Andy's house. While the rest of us joked, laughed, and clinked glasses, Gary stared blankly out the window.

"Hey, are you okay?" I asked.

"Yeah. I'm just tired of driving all the time to come see you."

I sighed and put down my beer. "I'm busy with crew right now, but it'll slow down."

"It better."

What does that mean? I tried to enjoy the rest of the weekend with him, but if he resented coming to see me, I preferred to catch up on my homework. A long nap would have been helpful too, that is, if my mind would slow down enough for me to relax.

My second semester at U of O required more hours of reading and lab time for Biomechanics, Chemistry, and Advanced Psychology. Sleep deprivation along with rowing demands began to affect my memory. The information I read in my textbooks stopped registering in my brain. My notes from classes were full of gaps because sometimes I missed what the instructor said. I began recording all my classes and listening to the lectures again to fill in the blanks, which ate into more of my sleep time.

Flashbacks began to haunt me night and day—burnt corpses, bombs, and air raid sirens. Focusing became impossible. The nightmares had subsided when I first moved in with Dee and Ken. As my schedule had gotten more hectic, almost every time I dropped into sleep, I ran through fires, stepped on a landmine, or random people would hold me down to rape me, and I'd jolt awake. When my alarm went off at 4:00, exhausted and depressed, I'd drag myself out of bed.

I shoved my emotions and frustrations aside and kept pushing myself. My eyelids would get too heavy to lift in class, and I'd snap awake when my head dipped. With hot cheeks, I'd survey the room hoping no one noticed my catnap.

Exhaustion weakened my immune system. I caught a cold, but I didn't stop. At practice I plopped into the bow seat. We pushed off the dock and started our warm-up, slow rowing for about five minutes. My arms felt rubbery, my core achy and weak. Still, I pressed on.

When the coxswain yelled for us to pick up the pace, I tried to row faster, but my oar caught the water, ripping it out of my hand. Jumping up to retrieve it, a twinge zapped my lower back, followed by pain shooting down my hamstrings. I sucked a breath, snatched the oar, and plopped back onto my seat. My feet tingled with pins and needles, but I forced myself through the two-hour workout, not wanting anyone to notice I was hurt. When we lifted the boat from the water, I turned away to hide my grimace.

After practice, I went to Biomechanics and couldn't sit still. My lower back throbbed. Every time I inhaled, my breath caught. By the end of the period, I could barely get up from my chair.

I hobbled to the doctor on campus, and she gave me an anti-inflammatory drug. She explained how I would need to "log roll" to sit up in bed—that is, put a pillow between my legs and roll onto my side before pushing myself into a seated position. As I practiced the log roll, she said, "Looks good. Remember to apply ice often, don't lift anything, and don't bend or twist. You can't go back to rowing for four weeks."

What? Did I hear that right? Lying on an ice pack, flat on my back, staring at the ceiling in her office, my eyes burned, and I held my breath.

"I'll be back to check on you in a bit," the doctor said and left the room.

I burst into tears. *You're failing your team!* "Stop it," I chided myself aloud. "I served in the Army to get money for college. My classes have to come first."

On the way home, pain seared down my left leg each time I shifted my VW into gear. Fighting not to wince, so I wouldn't swerve or stall, kept me focused. The ten-minute drive seemed like an hour by the time I rolled to the curb in front of Ken and Dee's house. I turned off the key and cried until I thought I could go inside without dissolving into a puddle of goo when I saw Dee.

I wiped my face with the bottom of my sweatshirt, sucked in some air, and got out of the car. Gritting my teeth through the pain, I limped down the walkway and climbed the three porch stairs to the door. Dee met me inside the entryway and said, "What happened to you?"

"I injured my back rowing." I swallowed hard, and a tear rolled down my cheek. "I'm supposed to ice frequently and take ibuprofen every four to six hours."

"Oh, Dani, I'm so sorry. I know how much you love rowing."

"Yeah, I really did love rowing, and now I need to call my coach and tell him I have to quit before I chicken out."

"The closest phone is in the office. Put your arm around my shoulder, and we'll go together."

Dee helped me limp into the office off the living room. Butterflies filled my stomach when I put the phone to my ear. Even with the medication, I couldn't imagine rowing anytime soon. I didn't want to quit, but I had to make a choice.

"Hello?" I winced at the sound of his voice.

"Uh . . . hey, Coach, it's Dani."

"Hey, Dani, how's your back?"

"Not great, but I'm doing what the doctor told me to do."

That's good. They're doctors for a reason."

"Yep. Well, I'm calling to tell you I can't row anymore. My classes are getting harder, and my grades are suffering." I swallowed the lump in my throat, and Dee gently stroked my arm. "I really love rowing, but my priority has to be school. I hope you understand." Hot, salty tears dripped onto my sweatshirt.

"I'm sorry to hear that. You're a great rower, but you're right. School should be the priority. If you change your mind at any time, you know we'd love to have you back. We sure will miss you."

"I'll miss you guys too. Thanks for being so understanding. Well, I guess I'll go take my next round of pills and do my back stretches."

"Hope your back heals quickly. Bye, Dani."

"Bye, Coach." I hung up, fell into Dee's arms, and sobbed.

"You just need to rest and heal," she said. "Everything will work out. You'll see."

I focused on school and didn't look back. I didn't even say goodbye to Skye. Though I knew Coach could fill my seat right away, I still felt guilty for leaving the boat—and Skye and the team—for letting everyone down. I felt like a failure.

My advisor suggested that I enroll in physics during the summer so I could graduate on time in May. The class would cover an entire year of physics in three months. Brutal! Gary would be in Montana doing seasonal work fighting wildfires, like he'd done the previous two summers. He earned enough money to support himself for the entire school year. We had toyed with the idea of me visiting him, but I decided to remain in Eugene instead of hanging out with Gary for a couple of weeks or going home for barbecues and camping trips. I'd never worked so hard in school as I did that summer and managed to get a B.

While taking the physics class, I missed the birth of my second niece, Lindsey Rose. The birth went well, and mom and baby were doing fine. I planned to visit Bend as soon as I could.

But during my minimal off-time, I decided to enroll at Lane Community College to complete a three-month program to earn a Certified Nursing Assistant (CNA) certificate. That summer, it occurred to me that I needed to do something in the medical field to make sure I still wanted to pursue a career in medicine. Part of the CNA training included an internship at a nursing home. I helped the residents shower, eat, and go to the bathroom.

I discovered I enjoyed helping people. I wasn't grossed out by smells, blood, or any other bodily fluids. And if I needed more money than I earned at the library, CNA positions were easy to find. Besides, when I focused on others, I felt valued and comfortable in ignoring my own needs.

My last two semesters at the University of Oregon flew. In May, my family came over the Cascade Mountains to celebrate my graduation with a Bachelor of Science degree in Exercise and Movement Science. Bonnie Jo, "BJ," and Shelley, two of my cousins who lived near Eugene, threw a graduation party. Streamers and balloons decorated BJ's backyard around the gazebo. My heart felt so full sitting at the picnic table with my parents, Wade, Susie, and my little nieces. Hali would start first grade in the fall, and Lindsey was being passed around so everyone could get some baby time. Tani sat across from me while her kids ran around the yard. BJ and Shelley had made a chocolate cake, and they barbecued burgers on the grill.

Gary walked over and said, "Hey, Dan, can I talk to you for a minute?"

"Uh . . . Sure." I glanced at the others and stepped away from the picnic table, happy that I hadn't felt a twinge in my back or hamstring in a while.

Gary stopped under a tree on the other side of the yard. "Doesn't look like I'll get into the Forestry Resources Technology program because I couldn't complete my math requirement, but P-Burg wants to hire me as a crew boss."

P-Burg is the nickname for Philipsburg, the city in Montana where he worked seasonally as a wildland firefighter. The supervisor and crew boss in P-Burg loved his work ethic and how Gary made new recruits feel like part of the team by bonding with them over beers and barbecues. He trained them well, working beside them in explaining their role in fire suppression. Gary took great care in showing them how to use the equipment, their pulaski, for example, a tool with an ax blade on one end and an adze on the other end to dig trenches. He also prepared them to pass their pack test and get ready to battle fires.

"Wow. I guess that's good news," I said, though I worried about what that meant for us.

"Yeah, so we need to make some different plans."

"Okay." I didn't know what that meant.

"If you want to be with me, you're going to have to move to Montana."

"Well, if we get married as planned, why wouldn't I go with you to Montana?"

"I guess you would." His face looked neutral, neither happy nor sad.

"You do want me to come with you, right?"

"Yeah. I never said I didn't."

That wasn't the warm, loving response I'd hoped for, but Gary wasn't a flowery kind of guy. He tended to be direct and opinionated, but I loved him. We butted heads occasionally, probably because ever since getting out of the Army, I thrived on schedules. I needed a plan and a backup plan at all times. Gary jumped out of airplanes, fought fires, and his risk-taking didn't line up with my need to control my environment.

Still, we were to get married in June, and I hoped we would figure out a balance between my need for order and his for recklessness. I envisioned a traditional wedding at his parents' church, lots of family and friends, a lively reception at the Elks Lodge, and a happily-ever-after for us like in the fairytales. Underneath the anticipation, though, I worried about being so far from home—no quick popovers to Tani's when melancholy threatened to set in, no barbecues or camping with the family, no hanging out with Wade and Susie and my nieces. But if being married to Gary meant sacrificing those things, I would suck it up and follow my man.

Chapter 14

WEDDING WOES

Gary struggled with remembering dates, so he suggested we get married on June 6, D-Day. That way he'd never forget our anniversary. I agreed, though the date was unsettling.

The wedding was to be held at the Episcopal Church, where his mom and dad still attended, and he'd been an altar boy. We anticipated a large crowd since Gary and I both grew up in Bend and had many friends still in the area. A catered reception was to follow the ceremony at the Elks Lodge on the Deschutes River, where my parents were members. Tani graciously agreed to spend her 30th birthday being my matron of honor, and Gary asked Ron to be his best man. Hali would be the flower girl, and Tani's son, Nate, the ring bearer.

The day of the wedding, I woke up with a knot in my gut and a lump in my throat. *What am I so nervous about? I love Gary. We're supposed to be together. Just breathe. Enjoy the day.*

Tani and I had planned to meet at my mom and dad's house, then head over to the church to get ready for the ceremony. When I pulled open the back door, Mom rushed over to me and said, "Dani, you're never going to believe what happened."

"What?" A feeling of dread hung in the air.

"Sammy died this morning."

My cat? But . . . "No, not today."

"I'm so sorry. We found her outside. It looked like she was trying to crawl under the deck."

"Are you kidding me?" *Is this a sign? Should I not marry Gary? I'm freaking the hell out!* I felt shaky and sat in a chair at the kitchen table. "What horrible timing."

Tani arrived moments later, and I told her the news. "Now don't get superstitious," she said. "Sammy was pretty old. It was just her time. Let's get your dress and makeup bag, and head to the church to get ready for your special day."

We fussed over my makeup and hair. I still felt queasy and anxious, but I decided it was pre-wedding jitters. Tani handed me my beautiful bouquet of oriental lilies—large white flowers with purple centers and a heady aroma that filled the room. I leaned in to smell them. The back of my throat began with a tickly sensation that soon turned scratchy and dry. My chest tightened. I gulped to catch my breath and started sneezing.

"Dan, are you okay?" Tani asked. "You look flushed."

"I think I'm having an allergic reaction to my flowers." I sneezed again and shoved them at Tani. "Please, get these away from me!"

Tani took the flowers and put them outside the room on a little table. "We will get them when we head upstairs for the wedding," she said. "Is there anything else I can do for you?"

I stared at her with wide eyes and thought: *Am I doing the right thing? My cat died. I'm allergic to my bouquet. We're getting married on D-day. These signs are kinda like a bad country song . . . But I love him. I'm being paranoid.* "No, I'm fine. Just a little nervous. That's all."

I stepped outside and took several deep breaths. Tani came out and said it was time to go. We walked around the corner of the church and up the stairs where Dad waited for me at the top, tears glistening in his blue eyes. He reached for my hand and said, "Dan, you make a beautiful bride."

"Thanks, Dad. You're very handsome in your tux." I smiled and felt calmer holding his hand as we watched the bridesmaids walk down the aisle. My other hand rested on Hali's shoulder, ready to let her know when to start walking. Nate looked cute in his tux, holding the small white pillow where our rings sat on top, tied with a blue ribbon. When the music changed, I nudged Hali. Nate and my niece walked down the aisle together as she dutifully distributed rose petals. When they approached the altar, the bridal march began.

Dad handed me my bouquet and chuckled. "This is it, no going back now."

"You're right, no going back now." I laughed hollowly, held the flowers as far below my nose as possible, and gazed around the church. All the seats were occupied. People stood in a line against the wall. We'd invited 200 guests, but there seemed to be more.

As I walked with Dad, I distracted myself by finding my family. In the front pew sat Wade, Susie, and baby Lindsey on her lap. Grandma Combs was next to Grandpa and Grandma Best. Uncle Don and Aunt Julie sat at the end of the bench. Near the altar, Gary, Ron, and Nate waited on one side, Tani and Hali on the other.

We stopped in front of the pastor. Dad gave me away with a kiss, and he squeezed my hand before letting go. Gary stepped forward and took my hand. Then our vows were recited, short and sweet. Sweat trickled down my back, and the queasiness returned. I started to feel dizzy with everyone's eyes on us and the heat radiating from the crowd. *It's almost over. Just keep smiling and breathe!*

"You may now kiss your bride," the pastor announced.

Gary leaned toward me, and I met him halfway. His blue eyes seemed to sparkle against the black and white tuxedo. A sense of calm came over me as we kissed, something normal and familiar. We faced our friends and family, and the pastor introduced us as Mr. and Mrs. Lambert.

Weird, no more Combs, I thought.

The pastor invited the guests to attend the reception at the Elks Lodge on Newport Avenue, and he explained the wedding party would follow after a few pictures. Gary and I walked down the aisle hand in hand, husband and wife, until death do us part, in sickness and health, and all that jazz.

While our family and friends departed the church we posed for pictures. My face remained flushed from the allergic reaction and nerves, but I pretended the redness was a sunburn. After the pictures were taken, I placed the evil flowers in Tani's care and told her to keep them as far away from me as possible.

Gary and I loaded up into a limousine and headed toward the Elks Lodge. We kissed and held hands. I couldn't believe we really did it. We were married. The reception at the Elks went on for hours. Great food, lots of friends and family, great cake, everyone danced and had a great time. One of Gary's Army buddies had flown in from North Carolina, so we let him stay with us at Mom and Dad's, and we postponed our consummation until the following night. Since Gary had to leave for Montana right away, we vowed to squeeze in a honeymoon later—which never happened.

Chapter 15

Montana Melancholy

At Shopko in Missoula, I bought a four-person kitchen table and a rocking chair. Then I went to an appliance store, picked out a washer and dryer, scheduled delivery, and headed to La-Z-Boy. I chose an L-shaped sectional and purchased a recliner for Gary. After all, he was the only one bringing in money at that time. Besides, the fire season had started, so he was earning "hazard pay." On the drive home from my shopping spree, I decided to stop at the University of Montana and check out their Physical Therapy (PT) program. I needed to devise a plan for my future.

It turned out, due to the limited availability of slots, I would have to retake physics and earn an A to be a competitive candidate. Even then, there was no guarantee that I would be admitted to the PT program. Getting a B in physics over the summer had been rough, and I couldn't imagine torturing myself again with another full year of school with no breaks. Leaving the building feeling defeated, I decided physical therapy might not be the right path for me.

Being a certified nursing assistant, CNA, I applied to work at Saint Patrick Hospital in Missoula, Montana. I was hired to work on the oncology floor, caring for patients battling cancer. The work was not only physically challenging but emotionally draining. After eight hours of hustling to clean, feed, and walk patients, I'd drive the 20 minutes home to Clinton and fall into bed, exhausted. But I had a hard time getting the rest I needed to face another day.

On the evenings Gary worked, I felt alone and vulnerable. When I finally drifted off to sleep, any noise would startle me awake. Darkness would overtake my subconscious and fuel nightmares of fighting off rapists with no faces. Even on the rare nights when I didn't wake up, the next morning my body dragged with fatigue, and a haunted feeling filled my mind. I couldn't shake it, so I stuffed it down and turned to alcohol to help me sleep.

Connecting with patients and their families became both my strength and my weakness. Though I loved caring for those in their final days and comforting their loved ones, when I left work, I carried a heaviness that left me feeling fragile and broken. I drank more alcohol and never talked to anyone about my brewing turmoil, which had become my toxic pattern.

After a year on the oncology floor, I needed a change. There was an opening in the Emergency Room for a ward secretary/CNA, so I applied for the position. Two weeks later, I was transferred to the ER.

I seldom saw Gary, who often fought fires or did prescribed burns with the forest service. Staying busy by tending my gardens, mowing the lawn, watching movies, and exercising helped me to keep some of my harsh memories at bay. But spending so much time alone increasingly strained my ability to avoid the darkness expanding within me.

I decided to enroll in the nursing program at the University of Montana. A registered nurse earned more money than a CNA, and I wouldn't have to retake physics. Once school started, the juggling began. When I wasn't working in the ER, I was at nursing school. Hours were spent memorizing medical terminology and reading textbooks until my eyes blurred and my head pounded.

Any "spare" time was spent keeping up with housework and yard work, which was also a full-time job. When Gary managed to come home, he had high expectations for cleanliness. He didn't like the sight of hair, so I cleaned my hairbrush daily. The refrigerator needed to be organized, as did the pantry and cupboards. I was allowed to have five houseplants and ten pairs of shoes. I didn't analyze these oddities. I adapted to his expectations, no questions asked.

Gary stayed in P-Burg a lot though. The drive to Philipsburg was about 45 minutes, so I tried to be patient, realizing that he was tired after a long day, so he preferred to stay in the bunkhouse. But I knew Gary often took the guys out for beers after work. Then he would opt to stay in P-burg rather than driving home. I couldn't help but feel a little jealous and sad that he'd chosen to drink with the boys over coming home to me.

Mid-semester I had a nervous breakdown, though I didn't know what was happening at the time. I knew something was wrong when I began to pace the hallway in my house. I couldn't sleep, concentrate, or eat. The mere thought of food made me nauseous. I tried to keep my symptoms hidden, but after two weeks, I'd lost 15 pounds and felt perpetually agitated. Thoughts of pills and guns made me fear I might hurt myself.

The only person I could turn to was Jani, my friend who worked with me in the ER. She suggested I come stay with her for a few days until I could see a doctor. We played dominoes and watched movies, trying to keep my mind occupied with pleasant thoughts, but the darkness remained just under the surface.

One night when Gary was home, while I was cleaning up after dinner, he loomed over me at the sink with his eyes narrowed. "Whatever this is, get over it," he said. "You're fine."

My eyes burned with tears as I continued to scrub a pot. "I don't think I am. Jani told me I should talk to a doctor and possibly a counselor."

"Why? You've never needed to before. Just focus on something else."

I dropped the pot in the sink, and my body started to shake. "Don't you think I've *tried*? Besides, how would you know what I should do? You're never home!"

"Yeah, you're right. I have to work. I have an important job training the recruits. They need me."

"But *I* need you . . . Can't you come home?" I asked quietly.

"I can't right now. You know that. We're in the middle of burn season."

"Okay," I said, but I thought: *Doesn't he even care that something is seriously wrong with me?*

I continued to struggle at work, but only Jani knew—or so I thought. Our ER pastor came up to me one day and said, "Are you all right, Dani? I'm worried about you."

This small gesture of concern sent me into full-blown sobbing that I couldn't stop. The charge nurse walked over and put her hand on my shoulder. "Dani, maybe you and the pastor could go to the break room," she said.

Henry, the chaplain, and I did as she suggested and sat on the couch. "What's going on?" he asked. "Is there anything you want to talk about?"

"I don't know what's happening to me. I'm sad. I'm lonely. I cry all the time. I can't sleep. Eating makes me sick. I'm a mess."

"Everything you just described makes me wonder if you're suffering from depression. Does anyone in your family have depression?"

"Not . . . that I . . . know of," I managed to choke out between sobs. "We don't really talk about that stuff."

"I'm concerned for you and think you need to talk to a psychiatrist. Also, you might want to make an appointment with a counselor. I can get you their names and phone numbers if you'd like."

"That's exactly what Jani said. I made an appointment, but they couldn't see me until next week."

He stood. "Let me see what I can do. You're a strong person. Everything will work out. You'll see." And with that he left the room.

Psychiatrist? Am I crazy? Are they going to haul me away to some padded cell? This can't be happening.

Two days later, I had an appointment with a psychiatrist, compliments of Henry. Sitting in my 4Runner, in the lot outside of the doctor's office, my heart pounded frantically. *What if she asks about things I don't want to talk about? I have secrets . . . I'll answer her questions, but I won't say too much.*

The psychiatrist diagnosed that I had been suffering from a major depression episode. I knew what that meant from my studies, but I'd been too close to see it. My symptoms were typical: lack of interest in anything, loss of appetite, panic attacks, inability to sleep, and poor memory. She prescribed an antidepressant and recommended counseling. I called my parents and told them the news.

"No, honey, you've always been happy and optimistic," Mom said. "You can't be depressed. Just think about all the good things. Go to church more, get active, pull yourself up by your bootstraps."

If it were only that easy. "Mom, this is different. And I'm scared because Gary is going to Mississippi to do prescribed burns for three months. I'll be all alone."

"Dani, it'll all be okay. Just try to relax and maybe get some sleep. We love you. You know that, right?"

"Yes, I do. I love you guys, too. I just miss you guys so much. Sorry to unload this on you, Mom, but I don't know who else to call."

"You know you can call us anytime, day or night. Hang in there. We love you."

"Okay, Mom. I will. Love you too." Hanging up the phone, I felt more alone than ever before.

Ashamed and humiliated, I wanted to hide in my house, but I made myself go to school and work. While Gary packed to go to Mississippi, I carefully approached him and asked if we could sit in the living room for a minute. He stared at me for a few seconds before he nodded and followed me out of our bedroom. I sat on the couch, and he plopped onto his recliner. I dreaded telling him about the diagnosis, but it seemed the right thing to do.

"I'm proud of you for going to the doctor. That probably wasn't easy," he said. "I'm glad you're getting help now, Dan."

Wow. He was supportive. "Can't you get someone to take your place in Mississippi?"

He shook his head. "The crew is counting on me. I have to go."

Determined to not fall apart, I spent hours outside, reconnecting with nature. My mind grew calm. Life slowed down, and I could breathe. The only other time I'd felt this way was in rowing. In that quiet, reflective, peaceful place in my brain, where time seemed to stand still, my spirit seemed lighter. Worries seemed to fade away.

I thanked God for the peace I felt, though temporary. I relied heavily on Him during this battle with depression. But even with all the prayer, painting, medication, and counseling, just to manage getting through each day, people still commented that I didn't seem like myself. If they only knew how I hid in plain sight. *There is more to this than depression,* I thought, not realizing I'd barely tapped into the damage inside me.

Chapter 16

HARBINGERS OF DOOM

I didn't feel an intense desire to become a parent. Mostly, I worried that all the chemical crap we ingested in the Persian Gulf War might harm a baby. Still, I wanted to see what Gary had to say about having a family, so I planned a conversation. He'd just gotten off after fighting a fire. I cooked a nice dinner, and after the dishes were washed, I sat next to him on the couch.

"I have a weird question for you," I said.

"What kind of weird question?"

"Well, I don't really know how to ask, so I'm just going to do it. How do you feel about trying to have a baby?"

He stared at me for what seemed like a long time. "Are you pregnant? I thought you were on the pill."

"I'm still on the pill, but we aren't getting any younger. If we want to try to have kids, we should do it. I've been on the pill so long now that it might take some time to get it out of my system." I stared at him, waiting. He just sat there. "So, what do you think?"

"Well, I guess we could try."

He didn't seem enthusiastic, but I took that as a "Yes" and stopped taking my birth control pills the following day. *God, it's in your hands now*, I thought, and life continued as usual—I worked at the hospital, and Gary worked in Philipsburg. Four months had gone by when I started to feel sick at work.

"Are you okay? You look pale," one of my coworkers said. "Do you need to go home?"

"No, I'm okay," I lied and went about my work.

On one of my trips to the lab, a tech stopped me and said, "I have a hunch. You should get your blood drawn."

"Why? And don't we need an order or something?"

"No, I'm just going to run a simple pregnancy test."

"Oh, I don't think I'm pregnant. It's probably something I ate."

"Well, let's just check." She drew my blood and said she'd call me with the results.

Back on the floor, I continued my rounds and anxiously waited. When the lab assistant finally called, she said, "You're pregnant. Only a couple of weeks by the looks of it, but pregnant, nonetheless. Congratulations!"

I'm pregnant? What the hell am I going to do with a baby?

Ten weeks into my pregnancy, I went for a walk, and two crows followed me. They flew around me, squawking for the entire two miles. In the car, on my way to work, their noisy caws echoed in my head. The sound was so vivid, it made me shiver. During a break, my Native American friend joined me at my table in the lounge. I opened my mouth, but nothing came out. *Just tell her,* I scolded myself, and I spit out what had happened.

"The crow must be your spirit guide," she said.

"Wait. What?"

"Crows are known to be the keeper of the souls. They're highly intelligent and can be tricksters."

"Well, that's creepy. How can I make them go away?"

"There isn't any way to do that. Maybe they're just checking in on you."

"Yeah, maybe." Chills spread across my back.

The next morning, I took my daily walk on the trail behind our property, at the base of the Sapphire Mountains. The cool air felt good on my pregnancy-warm skin. Seemingly out of nowhere, though they'd probably been perched in the Douglas fir nearby, the crows dive-bombed me, squawking and screaming. I covered my head with one arm, held my belly with the other, and ran all the way back to my house.

I woke up that night with the worst cramps of my life. When I went to the bathroom, I noticed bright red blood in the toilet. *No, this can't be happening!* I thought. *Not my baby. The crows, the damn crows! You can't have my baby's soul. No way.*

I called my nurse midwife, and she told me she would order an ultrasound. Gary happened to be home, so he drove me to the hospital. The ultrasound tech barely greeted us before she inserted the probe vaginally. I strained to hear a heartbeat, but there was silence. My heart began to speed up, and I thought, *Why can't I hear anything?*

"Wait here," the tech said abruptly and left the room.

Gary and I gazed at each other. Neither one of us spoke. Soon the door opened. The doctor entered and walked to my bedside. "The pregnancy isn't viable," he said.

My head spun.

"Viable? What does that mean?" Gary asked.

My baby's dead.

The doctor looked at Gary. "The fetus is not alive. There's no heartbeat. We need to discuss your options. You can have a D and C, or dilation and curettage, or you can wait and see if your body will abort on its own."

That's it? What did I do wrong?

"These things sometimes happen. I'm sorry. I'll give you some time to decide how you want to proceed. I'll be back in a few minutes." The sound of the door closing seemed so final.

"Dan, what do you want to do?" Gary asked, his face pale and drawn.

"I guess I'll have the D and C," I said, barely above a whisper. *This must be God's way of telling me I shouldn't be a parent. I never want to feel this horrible again.*

The procedure was extremely painful, physically and emotionally. I felt like a failure. The grief nearly overwhelmed me. In the next few weeks, I cried and cried, praying for God to mend my broken heart. Henry, the ER chaplain, suggested I write a letter to my unborn child, then bury the letter somewhere that would be meaningful to me, to get some closure. Writing that letter brought many more tears that blurred my vision and smudged the ink in places.

I bought two small metal angels. Each held a heart that read "Peace." I kept an angel as a memorial for my child and dug a hole near the lavender in my garden to bury the other angel with my precious goodbye. Once these tokens were securely covered with fertile potting soil, so I could grow flowers in that spot the following spring, I sat back on my feet and said this prayer:

God, please take care of my precious baby, and please take some of this pain away. Just help me. I'm afraid. I'm lost. I don't know who I am anymore.

Chapter 17

NEW BEGINNINGS

A few months after I lost my baby, I began feeling nauseous and gassy, symptoms I recognized. Gary and I were shocked that I'd gotten pregnant again so fast. While he continued to work and sleep in P-Burg, I struggled with morning sickness that lasted all day. The puking got so bad that I carried Ziploc baggies with me, to keep from making a mess wherever I went. My midwife kept telling me that being sick was a good thing. It meant the baby was growing and viable, and everything was normal.

Staying out of that dark place in my head was the hardest part. Every time fear and doubt crept into my thoughts, I prayed, "Please, God, let this baby live," more times than I could count. But six weeks early, after a long and grueling labor, the midwife placed our five-pound, ten-ounce baby into my arms. We named her Ashten Riley Lambert.

As I gazed at her, a lump formed in my throat. She was perfect with her soft skin, beautiful, scrunched face, and full head of dark hair. As I held her tiny hand in mine, I was overcome with love for my miraculous, precious little peanut. Sadly, I didn't get to hold her for long. She had to go to the Neonatal Intensive Care Unit to receive intravenous fluids and oxygen for two weeks, until she could breathe on her own and stay awake long enough to breastfeed.

When I got to bring her home a few weeks later, I summoned my inner soldier to deal with the onslaught of baby bottles, diapers, rashes, crying, daycare, panic, frustration, and absolute exhaustion. Being a first-time parent, I didn't know what was considered "normal" baby behavior.

Ashten had a habit of crying from 5:00 p.m. to midnight. Her pediatrician called her a "sensitive child."

Okay . . . sensitive. What does that mean?

In the meantime, Gary stayed in P-Burg for longer and longer shifts, supposedly working. Much later, I discovered he had been in someone else's arms. Devastated and determined to give my child a better life, I packed up my house, got divorced, and Ashten and I moved back to Bend, Oregon. We lived with my mom and dad until I could figure out what to do with my life.

I drank to avoid my pain, my memories, myself. When I wasn't drinking, I was eating chips, cupcakes, cookies, and chocolate. The full feeling gave me comfort in my loneliness. Through the haze, I managed to transfer my Montana nursing license to Oregon and began working at St. Charles Hospital in radiology. Soon after, I migrated to endoscopy in the Medical Diagnostics Unit (MDU).

After Gary's betrayal, I was a bit of a man-hater and generally pissy, but my coworkers in the MDU welcomed me anyway. They were fun and light-hearted. For the first time in a long while, life seemed to get better.

Working four ten-hour shifts at the hospital every week, and living at my parents' house, with my 18-month-old daughter, now mobile and into everything, tested my mettle. I longed for the days I could put Ashten in her seat, walk away, and come back to find her still there. The toddler phase added a dimension of exhaustion previously unknown to me.

Ashten waking up screaming almost nightly contributed to my weariness. The pediatrician called them night terrors. Yes, my daughter seemed terrified, and her mom and grandparents got pretty rattled too. She hadn't yet grown out of being a "sensitive" child.

I secured a loan from the Veteran's Administration (VA) to purchase a small lot in a subdivision on the east side of Bend and had a house built. Four months later, we moved into our two-bedroom craftsman on a cul-de-sac. Traffic was minimal, and the field behind our property gave the illusion of more space. To secure the perimeter, I hired a contractor to build a fence around the property. Military habits were hard to break.

Tony, one of my friends, mentioned he knew a guy who lived near my house. While Susie, my sister-in-law, and I carried boxes from my truck to the porch, the guy showed up and said, "Hi, I'm Terry. I live just down the street. Welcome to the neighborhood. My house is always open, and there's always beer in the fridge. Help yourself." He had an easy smile, warm brown eyes, salt-and-pepper chestnut hair, and lots of muscles under his tee-shirt.

"Thanks, I might just take you up on that." *Like I would ever randomly walk into some guy's house and snag a beer.*

Susie hefted her box onto the kitchen counter with a smirk. "You're into him. You think he's cute."

"Please. Not even. I don't have time for a relationship." Without another thought, I got busy settling into our new home.

The next couple of months, between work and being a single mom, I had little time for self-care. In my weariness, I felt like I wasn't a good mom or a good nurse, or even a good person. My mind swirled with reasons that Gary's betrayal and the divorce were my fault. I hadn't done enough to be a good wife. I brought the situation upon myself. Weirdly, these beliefs gave me the illusion of control, yet I yearned for some semblance of stability.

Chapter 18

CUTE NEIGHBOR

Spring arrived in the high desert. The cherry trees were in full bloom. Daffodils and tulips lit up flower beds all over town. I made a trip to East Side Gardens, where I bought three lavender plants and two-day lilies. It was time to brighten the little patch of dirt between my driveway and the sidewalk.

While I planted, Ashten played in the grass nearby. I stood to admire my work when my phone vibrated in my pocket. Scooping up my daughter, we headed into the backyard and closed the gate so she could be contained for a bit.

"Hello?"

"Hey, Dani, it's Tricia."

"Wow. Blast from the past. How are you?" Tricia and I were high school friends who occasionally reconnected.

"I'm good, and I heard you were back in town. Would you like to come over for a barbecue with Mike and me this weekend?"

"Sure. I'll ask Mom if she can watch Ashten."

"Great. I'll see you Saturday at 5:00."

That Saturday, I met her husband, Mike. The three of us ate steak and vegetables around their firepit and laughed until our faces hurt. Several beers in, and taking the night off from parenting, we had more fun than I had in a long time.

"Are you seeing anyone?" Tricia asked.

"Not really. I'm busy working and mothering. Except, I did meet a cute guy in my neighborhood."

"Does this cute guy have a name?"

"His name is Terry Shine."

Her husband started laughing in the kitchen and shouted through the window screen: "No way. Terry's an old friend of mine. We went to high school together. Great guy. We should invite him over. Do you want me to call him?"

My cheeks felt hot. "No, I'm not ready for anything like that, but thanks. He just seemed nice, that's all."

Several minutes later, the doorbell rang. Mike had called Terry and told him some girl was talking about him, and he should come over. Gotta love small towns!

Terry's warm smile met the three of us out on the deck. Slightly embarrassed, I accepted another beer from Terry's outstretched hand. The fire danced across our faces as we talked about our jobs and our families. At some point, Tricia and Mike slipped away, and we hadn't noticed. Terry made me feel comfortable and relaxed. *How refreshing, a man who wants to have a conversation, even seems to enjoy it.*

After that barbecue, I never looked back. He was handsome, funny, considerate, and kind, and he truly enjoyed life. And I was surprised, but pleased, that he wanted to be around me as much as possible. We went on dinner dates, watched movies, and went for walks. And Ashten loved him too.

Terry played with her and made her laugh. I kept thinking: *He can't be this nice. Something has to be wrong with him!*

His daughter Carlie would be graduating from high school that year. His son Callen was a sophomore. His kids were fun and kind, and they welcomed Ashten and me immediately. Carlie was a cute, bubbly blond with a beautiful smile who didn't see anyone as a stranger. Callen seemed more reserved than his sister, but he would come over for dinner and hang out with his dad, Ashten, and me. I was so thankful that Terry's kids seemed comfortable with us.

Terry played soccer. Ashten and I went to watch his games whenever we could. He also rode dirt bikes. His family—three sisters, mom and dad, who had been married forever, like my parents—made Ashten and me feel like we belonged with them.

My dad and Terry sparred with jokes that got everyone laughing. My mom appreciated his manners and ability to put everyone at ease. Terry and I became inseparable, which was quite the opposite of what I'd been used to in my former relationship. I couldn't imagine not being with Terry. I absolutely loved him and was thrilled that he loved both Ashten and me.

Finally, it seemed I'd caught a break—at least on the outside. Inside, my mind and body were gearing up for an attack. Soon my life would be upended—again.

Chapter 19

NOT THAT SIMPLE

Terry and I got married outside in a friend's woodsy back yard, surrounded by friends and family. Six months later, we went on our dream honeymoon to Greece, Crete, and London, fulfilling the promise I'd made to myself when I was headed to Saudi Arabia. We returned home starry-eyed for each other, but our newlywed bliss was soon overshadowed by Ashten's struggles in school.

Almost from the first day of second grade, she would get in the car when I would pick her up from school and say, "Mom, I feel different from everyone else. Is something wrong with me?"

Though I did my best to point out her strengths, like her ability to memorize a song after hearing it only once, her artistry for short stories and abstract drawings, and her adeptness at solving puzzles, we were concerned about how distracted she had become during the past year. She would begin to put her clothes away and forget what she was doing on her way to her dresser. I'd walk into her bedroom to see the folded pants in a stack on the floor next to her, and she'd be drawing a picture.

At conference time, her teacher mentioned Ashten's reading level was behind where it should be at that point in second grade. When we had her vision checked, the optometrist recommended giving her frequent breaks during reading. Terry and I took turns helping with homework, which was a constant battle. We tried reasoning, pleading, motivating, even bribery. She would drag her feet to the table and sit slumped in her chair. When we could get her to focus on her assignment, she would get frustrated easily and press so hard on her pencil against the paper that the tip would break. Then she would grab her book, hit herself on the head with it, jump up from the table, and run away screaming. Terry and I dealt with our frustration by yelling at each other. Again, I felt like a failure, both as a wife and a mother.

Something had to change. I decided my frequent drinking wasn't helping, so I quit, cold turkey. I replaced the alcohol with more cookies and candy. The temporary sugar rush eased my nervousness and gave me a false sense of comfort. I rationalized that overeating was better than numbing out with alcohol. My daughter needed me to be present and sober if I was going to figure out how to help her.

God, please guide me in the right direction.

One of my coworkers recommended that I take Ashten to see Dr. Debbie Coehlo at Juniper Pediatrics in Bend. Dr. Coehlo did several assessments with Ashten and informed me that my daughter had attention deficit hyperactivity disorder (ADHD), the inattentive type—*plus* anxiety and depression. We decided to try natural interventions before considering medication, so Dr. Coehlo prescribed supplements to increase amino acid production. We hoped this would aid in improving Ashten's memory and concentration.

Dr. Coehlo also suggested that I read *Driven to Distraction: Recognizing and Coping with Attention Deficit Disorder from Childhood through Adulthood*, by Hallowell, E. MD and Ratey, J, MD. I figured Ashten must have inherited the disorder since I had the same ADHD symptoms: lack of focus, poor time management, impulsiveness, fits of rage, forgetfulness, lack of motivation, restlessness, anxiety, and fatigue.

For a year, Ashten and I tried exercise, dietary changes, medication, and behavioral therapy to manage her symptoms. Playing soccer seemed to help alleviate some of her nervous energy. However, while Ashten was getting into shape, I noticed my pants were getting tighter.

I can deal with my weight problem later. It's just food. Everyone needs food.

At least I'm not drinking anymore.

None of the things we tried seemed to make a noticeable difference in how well she could focus at school. We were both frustrated, and my need to be in control left me feeling defeated and desperate. I picked up *Driven to Distraction* again to see if I could find another idea to try. One of the first suggestions was to seek the help of a therapist who specializes in ADHD, so I scheduled an appointment.

For the first session I decided to go by myself, so my nervousness wouldn't scare Ashten. My hands shook as I opened the door to the counselor's office. The waiting room was dimly lit and disturbingly quiet, except for the white noise machine on a table outside of the counselor's door. My heart began to race.

What the hell? Does this counselor think darkness and near silence make people like Ashten and me feel calm? I felt like running to my car, speeding from the parking lot, and screeching onto the street.

A door opened, and a woman dressed in a business suit and glasses entered the waiting area. "Hi, my name is Sally," she said. "You must be Danielle. What brings you here to see me?"

I released the breath I'd been holding. "Well, I believe my daughter and I have ADHD. I want to know if you have coping strategies that can help us."

"Before we get into that, I want to ask you about your history with school and go from there. Tell me a little bit about yourself."

I followed her into a room, where we sat in comfortable chairs, and thought, *Easy enough, okay. Take a deep breath. She just wants to know about your childhood.*

"I was born in Springfield, Oregon and went to school at Brattain Elementary." Memories came flooding back: my grandparents' farm, our house, and spending time with Tani. "I loved school and everything about it. Actually, in second grade, the principal and my teacher suggested to my parents that I should move to third grade and join the TAG (talented and gifted) program. But my parents decided to keep me in second grade with my peers. I had friends and played well with others, and I loved my teachers."

"Let me get this straight. School was easy for you, and you never struggled with homework or making friends?"

"No, I had lots of friends, and homework was easy, pretty much through high school."

"Okay, what did you do after you graduated from high school?"

"I wanted to go to college, and my parents couldn't afford to help with tuition, so I joined the Army. The military offered me the GI Bill, which would reimburse me for my school expenses."

"What did you do in the Army?" The question was simple, but it sure didn't feel like it.

"Well..." Nausea washed over me. I shook inside and out. My throat went desert dry. My chest tightened.

"Danielle, are you okay?"

Tears spilled down my face. I tasted salt in my mouth as I tried to choke out an apology, but I couldn't speak. We sat in awkward silence as I took a few deep breaths.

"Maybe we should go back to before the military. Let's talk about your family," she said.

I exhaled loudly and found my voice. "My family's my rock. They've always been there for me no matter what. They've supported me completely. I'm so blessed to have them. We've always been close, but lately I feel distant, like I'm pulling away from them. I don't know why. I guess life just gets busy."

Sally gazed at me thoughtfully for several moments. "Where did you live after you graduated from high school?"

"I went to Basic Training in Alabama and went to Virginia for Advanced Individual Training. Then I was stationed in Germany for two years, then was reassigned stateside to Fort Lewis, Washington. The last nine months of my service I was in Saudi Arabia." I stopped abruptly, unable to breathe. *I need to get out of here.*

"Okay, Danielle, I want you to think about something that makes you happy."

Happy. Ashten. She makes me happy. My family makes me happy. Flowers, water, hummingbirds.

"Now take a couple of deep breaths," said the counselor's soothing voice. "Focus on your breathing."

Two minutes later, Sally said something that rocked me to my core: "Danielle, I don't think you have ADHD; I think you have PTSD."

Wait, what? PTSD? No way. She's crazy. She doesn't know me. She's wrong!

"I don't think so," I said. "I dealt with all of that stuff. I'm fine."

She leaned forward. "Do you know what PTSD is?"

"Well, yeah. Some vets get it. They have flashbacks and nightmares or something like that."

She stood up, grabbed a brochure from a small stack on the bookshelf next to the door, and walked it over. "Here's some information about PTSD. I suggest you read this. I'd like to see you back in two days. I need to research a couple of things, and this will give you time to process what we talked about today."

"Okay."

"And if you have any questions or concerns before your next appointment, please call me."

"Thanks." I walked to the door feeling like I was floating and detached.

When I opened my car door, it occurred to me that I didn't remember walking to the parking lot. I sat heavily behind the steering wheel. My body trembled, and my face was wet with tears. I shook my head, trying to make sense of what Sally told me. Wiping my cheeks with my sleeve, I started my car and vowed to prove her wrong.

Chapter 20

POST-TRAUMATIC STRESS DISORDER (PTSD)

I went straight to my parents' house, entered through the back door, and marched into the living room. "I was just seen by a counselor who thinks I have PTSD," I told them. Dad looked up from his recliner and clicked the remote to turn off the TV.

Mom put her knitting on the couch beside her. "Well, honey, you never talk about what happened over there, other than the couple of funny stories you've told us." Dad nodded in agreement.

My mind reeled. *What? Wait. I think about it constantly. It haunts me.*

On the outside, I attempted to laugh and wave it aside. "I dealt with all of that, and it was so long ago."

"But maybe there's something to this," Mom said and glanced at Dad. "Just think about it. That's all we ask."

I shrugged and said, "What were you guys watching?"

Dad turned the TV back on to the sitcom they'd been watching. I stared at the screen and left my parents' house an hour later without remembering anything about the episode.

When Ashten got home from school, she grabbed a snack and ran upstairs to watch a show on her iPad. I was thankful for the alone time and sat at the bar in the kitchen, drumming my fingers on the counter. As soon as Terry walked into the house, I pounced.

"The counselor I saw today for ADHD thinks I have PTSD. What do you think?"

"Hi, honey. How was your day?" he said and waited for me to respond. When I didn't answer, he said, "Okay, we're jumping in. Well, I don't know. You told me you were in the Army, but you don't talk about your time in the military."

"Are you sure? I feel like I talk about it all the time."

"Nope. You don't."

I got up and walked upstairs to check on Ashten thinking: *Unbelievable. I do talk about it. I know I do . . . Don't I?*

Two days later, I paced in Sally's waiting room until she opened the door, greeted me, and waved me inside. "Did you get a chance to review the material I gave you?" she asked as I sat in the chair opposite hers.

Again, my heart raced, and my mouth went dry. "Kind of. I'm confused and maybe a little in shock."

"Those are completely normal reactions to something like this. I spoke to a colleague of mine who recommended I give you the information for the Bend Veterans Center and the number to speak with a Veterans' Service Officer."

"Should I call them now?"

"The sooner, the better. I want you to know that I'm not trained to help combat veterans. My specialty is helping people with ADHD. This is unfamiliar territory for me. Are you okay with contacting them, or would you like me to?"

"No . . . I can do it. Thank you." Again, I felt like I was floating somehow, like the words drifted around me without sinking in.

"If you can't get an appointment right away, you can come talk to me until you can see someone."

"Okay, thank you." I stood and walked out of her office. As I closed the door, everything I'd buried wanted to come to the surface. Instead, I pushed the memories down deeper and told myself: *I'm fine. There's no way I could have PTSD.*

For the next year, I convinced myself that if I had PTSD, I wouldn't be able to function. I was a wife and mom. I was a professional. Yet the next five years would redefine my entire being.

Chapter 21

THE VAULT

In the months following that last meeting with Sally, my angry outbursts, crying jags, heart palpitations, and flashbacks grew worse. On a particularly bad day, after Karla, a coworker and friend, spilled coffee on our schedule, I picked up the paper and glared at her. "Are you kidding me?" I said. "You shouldn't be drinking near the schedule. Now I'll have to print a new form and start all over." I stomped to the computer to print a new copy. "I don't have time for this crap!"

"Sorry," she said. "I didn't think it was a big deal. Just wipe it off and move on."

"That's just it. I can't move on until it's right! You obviously don't get it and don't care, but I do!"

She looked at the floor and walked past me, down the hallway.

Do I have to do everything myself? Nobody can do anything right. It's not that hard, people.

Ten minutes later, my boss and Karla met me in the nurses station. "Dani, can you come into my office?" my boss asked.

The three of us headed in silence to the open doorway, opposite the counter. Inside her office, my boss said, "Dani, Karla and I've been talking, and we think it might be time for you to get some help. Your temper is getting out of control. We're worried about you."

My eyes went wide, and my voice came out louder than I intended. "Is this about the stupid schedule? She was being careless."

My boss's gray eyes softened. "No, it goes deeper than that."

"Oh." My throat tightened, and I looked at my feet. "I didn't realize you felt that way. I guess I can schedule an appointment with a Veterans' Service Officer and see what they can do."

"I think that's a good idea."

When the day arrived for me to meet with a Veterans' Service Officer (VSO), I sat in my car, staring at the red brick building, chiding myself. *Other veterans deserve to talk to the VSO more than you. You're not that bad.*

I might have peeled out of the parking lot and driven home if I didn't hate to be late, much less blow off a commitment. My door felt heavier than usual to open. I climbed out of my car in slow motion and checked in at the front desk in a daze. Choosing a chair against the wall, where I could see the whole room, I waited for what seemed like a long time. Eventually, a woman with long dark hair and a bright smile appeared from the hallway.

"Danielle?"

I stood on shaky legs. "That's me."

"Come with me," the woman said and headed toward the back of the building. Once we were seated in her office, she asked, "Why are you here today, Danielle?"

Tears welled. I cleared my throat and tried to speak, but no words came out.

"Take some time. I know this can be difficult." She slid a box of tissues across the desk, and I grabbed one.

"Thank you." I mopped up my tears and blew my nose. "I'm sorry. I've never talked about this stuff, but I can't seem to control my emotions. I was told a year ago by a counselor that I have PTSD. She recommended I go see a VSO, so here I am. Better late than never, I guess." I attempted to laugh.

The VSO folded her hands on her lap and sighed. "I'm sorry. This must be really hard for you. Let's just start with the basics and go from there. I'm going to ask you some general questions related to your time in service. I'll enter the information in my computer and file a claim for compensation from the government due to your PTSD."

"I didn't know you could do that. What kind of claim?"

"The claim, if approved, allows you to get reimbursed for any damages which happened to you while you were serving your country. I work for the veterans, not the government. Let's see if we can get you some financial help." She raised her fingers to her keyboard and started asking questions.

An hour later, my head pounded from the relentless flow of tears as I described my experiences during the war in the Persian Gulf. I didn't even mention the rapes. I'd buried those experiences even deeper than the combat horrors.

After I finished telling her about the bombs, the highway, the bodies, and the landmine, she instructed me to gather any possible evidence to support my history. She suggested I look through my pictures, notes, letters from family members, and anything else that would connect my condition and symptoms to my time in the service.

"I'm sending all of this to the Veterans' Affair Compensation and Pension branch for them to review," she said. "After they review the information, they'll call and schedule you for a comp and pen exam at the VA Clinic in Hillsboro, outside of Portland. In the meantime, I want to suggest you reach out to the Vet Center here in Bend. They're awesome at helping combat veterans with PTSD."

I grabbed another tissue and wiped my sweaty hands. "Okay, thank you for your help. I'll go home and see what I can dig up."

Before I left the parking lot, I called and made an appointment with a therapist named Dee at the Vet Center and drove home on a mission to find proof of my traumatic experiences. When I got home, I walked out the back door and headed for our metal storage containers. Terry was an excavator by trade, and our house was on a hill, so he dug a space to fit two huge storage containers and also used them as the foundation for the carport he built next to the house.

I marched across the lawn, down the dirt path that led to the bottom of the hill and stumbled on the thick layer of pea gravel at the entrance to the containers. I caught my fall with my palms against the metal doors, and in that instant, my mind flashed with the image of my foot over the landmine. Then I saw the body parts along the highway and a human head flying through the air. My breath caught. I stared at the container doors until I could move again.

Just locate the dang pictures. Stay focused.

Hefting open the heavy metal door reminded me of the many containers I had unloaded at the Port of Dammam. But this container held my darkest secrets, the ones I kept trying to shove away and forget. I used the sunlight that seeped into the container to find what I wanted.

Cobwebs caught in my hair, and I coughed to clear the dust from my throat as I opened every box, not sure where I'd hidden my past. Within 15 minutes, the photo album stared up at me, daring me to open it. Lifting the cover, I squelched the wave of nausea and detached my mind from the pictures, like any good soldier.

Just gather the evidence, close the box, and lock the vault in your memory again. Should be easy enough. That lie I told myself would soon collapse, along with my sanity.

Chapter 22

THE VET CENTER

My symptoms escalated. Terry and Ashten avoided me, afraid of getting snapped at, and nursing had become something I loathed instead of loved. Before every shift, as I walked through the door at the hospital, my stomach roiled, and I'd think: *You don't belong here. You're an imposter. You can't even help yourself. You shouldn't be trying to help others.*

Then I'd shuffle to the nearest garbage can to expel the Cheerios and banana I had for breakfast. Still, my relaxed-fit scrubs continued to get more snug. Since giving up alcohol as my preferred coping mechanism two years earlier, I had stuffed any and all memories down with food. I simply replaced one addiction for another. My expanded waistline frustrated me and launched me into a downward spiral of self-loathing.

On the Tuesday that I met Dee for the first time, I waited in a plush leather chair at the Vet Center trembling. Sweat rolled down my back, and my heart pounded in my ears. A lady with gray hair, wearing a navy-blue business suit, finally called my name and told me to follow her. Once seated in her orderly office, she asked, "So, what brings you in today, Danielle?"

"I go by Dani."

"Okay, Dani."

"Well, I was told over a year ago I have PTSD by a therapist who specializes in ADHD, and my VSO recommended this clinic."

She nodded and wrote something on the yellow pad in her lap. "Great. You've been seeing a VSO. Have you filed a Compensation and

Pension Claim yet?"

"Yes, she said my case is strong for compensation for trauma related to my time in the service." Though I tried to squelch them, tears welled up and spilled out.

Dee grabbed a tissue from the box on the table to my right and handed it to me. "Dani, before we start talking about your military history, can you tell me about your family and where you grew up?"

"Sure." I sucked up as much air as possible and exhaled. "I grew up in Springfield, Oregon. I have an older brother, Wade. We used to be close, but he works a lot now. When I was nine, my dad got a job in Bend, and we moved to what he called 'God's country'."

"Are you close to your family?"

"Well, I used to be. Sometimes I feel distant from them. I'm not really sure why. I work a ton at the hospital. I like to stay busy. I have a nine-year-old daughter, Ashten, who was diagnosed with ADHD, anxiety, and depression two years ago, so I'm focused on her. Her biological dad is in Montana. He's also a veteran that probably has PTSD. He copes with alcohol and work." *Hmm. That sounds familiar.*

"How's your relationship with your ex-husband?"

"Strained. I found him in bed with another woman, so I packed up my entire house and moved back to Bend to be near my family."

"Does he see your daughter?"

"Once a year around Christmas; he's busy working most of the time."

She scribbled something on her pad. "Tell me about your current living situation."

"Well, I'm remarried to an amazing man. His kids, my step-kids, Carlie and Callen, are great. We get along really well. Ashten enjoys having siblings, even though they're much older."

"Are you working right now?"

My stomach filled with butterflies that I tried to ignore. "Yep. I'm a registered nurse. I work in the Medical Diagnostic Unit at the hospital where we perform endoscopies, colonoscopies, and bronchoscopies for cancer screenings, difficulty swallowing, and lung problems."

"How are things at work?"

My lips trembled, and my eyes got teary again. "Not great, but okay."

"What's going on at work?"

"I was one of the charge nurses, but it was pretty stressful. I was angry all the time and had trouble remembering things. After I lost control and yelled at one of the gastroenterologists in the procedure room, I stepped down. Now I work in admission and recovery, but I'm terrified I'll forget something that could potentially hurt, or even kill, a patient."

"Sounds like a challenging job."

"Yes, it is. I put a lot of pressure on myself, and I hate to make mistakes." Tears slipped down my face, and I wiped them away with my fingers.

"What's coming up for you, Dani?"

"I feel like a failure. I can't do it anymore. It's just too stressful. I get physically ill when I enter the hospital now. I'm angry all the time, and I have no idea what's going to come flying out of my mouth. I'm a nervous wreck!"

"Exploring your options might be a good thing. Your body is trying to tell you something. Maybe find a less stressful job."

"I never looked at it that way before. Maybe something less stressful will help me not be so angry all the time. I'm just confused and tired—exhausted actually."

"Let me ask you this: What are your goals for counseling?"

"Well, I'd like to not be so angry all the time, and I guess I want to learn more about PTSD. I don't really know much about it."

"I recommend that you look at the government website. There are some videos and articles with information regarding PTSD. Check it out and then we can discuss any questions you might have at our next visit. Let's plan on seeing each other once a week. Does that sound okay to you?"

"Sure, that sounds like a plan." I thanked her, said goodbye, and could barely keep from bursting into choking sobs on my way to my car.

As soon as I pulled my door closed in the parking lot, I hunched over the steering wheel and bawled. My head throbbed. When I could finally sit up, I inhaled slowly and backed out of the parking space thinking: *One step at a time.*

When I got home, I opened my laptop at the kitchen table, fingers balanced on the keyboard. I stared at the screen for several moments before slowly typing PTSD in a search engine. On the va.gov website, the definition read: "PTSD is a mental health problem that some people develop after experiencing or witnessing a life-threatening event, like combat, a natural disaster, a car accident, or sexual assault. It's normal to have upsetting memories, feel on edge, or have trouble sleeping after this type of event. If symptoms last more than a few months, it may be PTSD. The good news is that there are effective treatments."

I clicked on the tab labeled "Understand PTSD." One of the first things mentioned was using avoidance as a common coping technique; that is, sidestepping anything that reminds the person of traumatic events. The site also pointed out that if avoidance became the main way someone coped with past trauma, it could interfere with the healing process.

I felt like the webpage described me, and I slammed my laptop shut. Ignoring my queasy stomach, I made dinner on autopilot. Terry, Ashten, and I carried on a basic conversation while we ate. My head pounded with the beat of my heart, and my mind was still numb when I put Ashten to bed. Every fiber in my body felt used up.

Chapter 23

Desensitization Attempt

Balancing work, home, and therapy left me depleted, praying for strength and energy. After a battle to get my butt out of bed and showered one morning, my manager in the MDU called me into her office. "Dani, I'm not sure what's going on with you, but your coworkers are concerned about your temper and volatile mood swings," she said. "I think you need to take a break, maybe work part time for a while and focus on self-care." She stared at me waiting for me to reply.

"I know, I'm struggling. One minute I think I'm fine, then I'm crying, shaking, or yelling at someone. I have no idea which Dani is going to show up at work, or home for that matter— happy Dani or pissed off Dani." I sighed through tears, utterly sick of crying all the time.

Maybe I need to take some time and get my mind straight. It's just temporary.

It had been 25 years since I was discharged from the U.S. Army, and I finally decided to decrease my hours at the hospital to focus on self-care, to deal with the root of my symptoms. During the first few sessions with Dee, we discussed distressful memories and the beliefs I'd created about myself as a result. My answers prompted her to suggest that I try EMDR (eye-movement desensitization reprocessing) therapy, which was supposed to use my eye movements to reduce my visceral reactions to my memories.

Dee explained we would use a horizontal bar with LED lights mounted on a stand. The device would be turned on, and the lights would repeatedly move side to side while I thought about a disturbing memory or discussed whatever came to my mind. The goal was to bring forth my traumatic memories so the EMDR could help my brain process and store them with all my other memories, instead of in my subconscious mind. This process was supposed to decrease my symptoms from PTSD.

Being a nurse, EMDR sounded interesting. Dad always said, "God hates a coward," so with that mantra in mind, I decided to try it. Before we started, Dee had me picture a container where I could put my memories, and she asked me to identify a safe place where I could visualize myself when I got emotionally charged. These two measures would help me get calm if I started to panic.

"Have you decided on a container yet?" she asked.

"Yes, a metal vault, like a big container that I can open or close when I want."

"Okay, that sounds great. Now can you tell me about your safe, calm place?"

"Sure. Belknap Hot Springs." Memories of camping trips and hikes with my family flooded my mind. I recalled the faint scent of rhododendrons and freshly cut grass. I envisioned huge pink, yellow, and red flowers blooming on the bushes and heard the creek babbling in the background. "There was a hidden garden in Belknap," I told Dee. "After a hike one day, my brother Wade, his wife Susie, my best friend Tani, her husband Andy, and Terry and Ashten and I laid on the grass together in the garden and looked up at the blue sky. I felt so peaceful."

Dee's warm smile almost made me feel like she was on the grass with us. "Sounds like a perfect happy place. Now can you identify a false belief about yourself that you've connected to your trauma?

"Um . . . I felt helpless and trapped when I was there, like I'd failed a test or something."

"Okay, let's use your feeling of helplessness and substitute it with a positive belief, or truth." She relaxed in her chair and folded her hands. "Did you feel like you did the best you could while you were over there?"

"Yeah. Things happened so fast. But I felt like I did my best."

"Why don't we use the positive belief that you did the best you could at the time?"

"Uh . . . okay." *This sounds like hocus pocus.*

"Dani, watch the light bar and just let your mind take you where it wants."

I watched the green light race back and forth and reminded myself to breathe. A memory of my grandpa's face, pinched and gloating, came into view. My body erupted with heat. Tears ran down my face, and I held back a sob.

In my mind, I was five years old, in our camper. I felt angry, scared, and frustrated. Grandpa told my mom and dad that I shouldn't be let outside until I said, "Good morning" to him. Grandpa didn't like me. I could never do anything right in his eyes. I felt like everything I said made him angry, so I did my best not to say anything to him at all.

Wade played cards with me in the camper to pass the time. Finally, around dinnertime, I meekly said, "Good morning." Mom gave me something to eat and then Wade and I went outside to play.

In the present, I thought: *What a miserable way to live—always pissed off at the world.*

Grandpa never understood how powerful and hurtful his words could be. "Do as you're told," he would say. "Respect your elders. Speak only when spoken to." He wanted me to treat him with respect, but given how he treated me, telling me I was worthless and good for nothing, I didn't understand what he meant. He made me feel unwanted and unloved as a child.

Then Uncle Don came to mind. When Wade and I would stay at his house, he would do what Wade wanted, but if I suggested a game or a show to watch, he'd laugh and tell me my ideas were dumb. These two influential men in my life didn't treat my mom or aunts or female cousins well either. They didn't value women.

I'm not one of your horses. You can't break me! I shouted in my head at my grandpa and my uncle with the EMDR lights still flashing. *You think I'm weak because I'm female, but I will remain true to myself and speak my mind. And you don't have to like me.*

My new truth became: I have survived difficult circumstances, and I'm a strong person. With support from my friends and family, I've overcome tremendous obstacles and challenges. I have done the best I could.

Though my new beliefs were positive, when I left the Vet Center, my limbs felt heavy, and my stomach was queasy. As soon as I got home, I went to bed and pulled the covers over my head. Naps allowed my weary brain to recharge and make it through the rest of the day.

At my second EMDR session, Dee asked, "Can you identify another false belief connected to your trauma?"

"I can't trust anyone," tumbled out of my mouth.

"Okay, so what is the truth you want to replace it with."

"It's okay to let people in and trust them." Hearing those words out loud made me wince. I wondered if this was even possible for me.

She placed her hand over the button on the metal stand. "Now follow the lights and focus on what comes up for you."

Continually talking as the lights flashed felt safe, but she encouraged me to sit quietly, to "just see and feel." I was transported back to basic training in Alabama. First, I remembered the girl who crawled into my bunk and ran her hands up my thighs. Heat flashed through my body, and I clenched my fists.

My memory shifted to the drill sergeant picking me to be the platoon guide. *He chose me so I'd fail*, I thought. *I'll prove him wrong*.

Next, I saw myself at the range shooting at the pop-up targets. I became aware that, once again, I had remained strong and true to myself. I felt proud of my service.

An image of a fragile baby, nestled inside several layers of protective containers, appeared in my mind. *How can the baby grow without any light, food, or water?* I thought. *Is that baby me? I need to let her out so she can be loved and appreciated. She needs food so she can live.*

Dee's voice entered my consciousness, muffled as if baby-me couldn't hear her well inside the protective containers. "Okay, Dani. Think about your positive belief and repeat it."

My breath caught. I started to cry. I felt vulnerable, like I got caught wearing someone else's underwear.

"Okay . . . okay," Dee said softly. "Put those memories back inside your vault and think about your happy place."

Blue skies. Sweet smells of rhododendrons and trees, the warmth of my husband's hand. The softness of my daughter's hair as we lay on the grass . . .

My breathing slowed and my muscles relaxed by inches.

"Good job today, Dani. How do you feel?" She looked at me intently, pen poised on her yellow notepad.

"Tired but okay."

The next three sessions with Dee had to be rescheduled. While I waited for the latest new appointment, I received a letter from the Vet Center saying that Dee had to leave due to personal circumstances. Though the center promised to assign a new counselor to help me, once again, I felt abandoned and alone.

Maybe it's not the right time for me to do this stuff anyway. I need to focus on Terry and Ashten and work.

I pulled out my cell phone and called the one person I knew could cheer me up. "Hi, Tani. I'm struggling with therapy. The lady I was seeing left for personal reasons, and they put me with some random guy. Maybe I should just stop doing this. I don't even know if it's working or not."

"Wow, okay." She chuckled. "First of all, hi. Second, I think you shouldn't rush into any decisions. Therapy might be helpful. You've always been the strong one in our relationship. I know you can do whatever you set your mind to."

I swallowed hard. "I don't feel very strong right now."

"Well, *I* believe in you."

If she can believe in me, I guess I can too. "Thanks, Tani. I love you."

"Love you too. Hang in there."

The following week, I walked through the Vet Center doors to meet my new male counselor. The minute I sat in his office, I felt uncomfortable. My restless legs wouldn't stop bouncing, and I couldn't focus on what he asked me. I felt floaty and detached, like I was observing someone else.

I scheduled one more appointment with him, to see if that had just been a rough day for me. During the second appointment, I couldn't make myself stop tensing up every time he asked me a question. Something wasn't right, so I asked for another female counselor.

Talking to a woman felt safer, less triggering, though my new counselor couldn't get me to take off the mask I hid behind—at work, at home, and even in her office. When I made up my face and styled my hair in the mornings, I transformed myself into a person who looked in control on the outside. On the inside, every cell seemed ready to explode and contaminate anyone who came close. My pleasant appearance and friendly behavior belied how closed off I felt from everyone. I lived in mission mode, on high alert, stealthy and careful.

My inward struggle raged. Since I'd given up alcohol, the socially acceptable candy and cake and chips I ate kept increasing. I fooled myself into thinking junk food helped me avoid my fear, anger, frustration, shame, and anything else that overwhelmed me. My growing girth also served as a physical barrier to keep people out, to protect the scared little girl inside me. But in those days, things were seldom what they seemed.

Chapter 24

COMPENSATION AND PENSION

My family members kept me relatively sane in the four months it took the VA to assign a new female counselor to replace Dee. During our first session, I knew I'd found my person. Amy had done the same job in transportation in the military that I did, and I was comfortable talking with her.

Amy used Cognitive Behavioral Therapy (CBT) to help me understand my behaviors, motivations, and problematic thinking patterns. Once we identified a problem area, she would teach me ways to soothe my emotions and increase my self-awareness. Instead of avoiding my fears, she encouraged me to face them so I could let them go. Using these tools, I began to feel less stressed and build self-confidence.

A month into counseling with Amy, the VA sent a letter requesting that I take a compensation and pension (C and P) exam to evaluate my PTSD. Standing next to the mailbox in the front yard, I stared at the paper, panic rising, barely understanding the printed words. *What kind of questions will they ask me? What if I fail the exam and can't get any more help?* I let my arm drop with the letter against my thigh and took several deep breaths. *Amy will explain this to me at my next appointment.*

A sense of calm followed. Looking back, I realize that was a milestone for growth. Still, the minute my butt hit the seat in Amy's office I asked, "What does a compensation and pension exam consist of? I got a C and P letter from the VA. They scheduled an appointment for me."

She folded her hands in her lap. "Well, I'm not going to lie to you.

It'll be mentally exhausting. The exam determines if the trauma you've experienced is related to your time in the military. They have a rating scale from 0 to 100 percent. The government will send you a check each month, depending on the percentage determined from that scale. Don't hide anything. Just let them see how your trauma is impacting your life."

Bile burned in my throat. "I feel sick just thinking about it."

"That's pretty normal. Just be honest and answer their questions to the best of your ability."

"I'll try."

"I know the idea of answering uncomfortable questions doesn't seem ideal, but you'll be fine."

I had to request time off from working at the hospital since the VA scheduled appointments without taking my work hours into consideration. Driving over the mountain pass in the winter alone scared me. I worried that I might drive myself over a cliff to avoid reliving my traumatic memories.

And since I had to take time off from work for the C and P exam, it made sense to extend my request through the following week, to finally get my left knee replaced. More than one doctor had told me that no amount of physical therapy would stop my knee from hurting. I needed a new one. Between the constant ache during the day, and the pain keeping me awake at night, I hoped fixing my knee problem would restore a bit of my good nature and patience. But first I needed to ask for help, which didn't come easily for me.

My legs and hands trembled as I walked into the living room, where Terry was watching a football game. "Honey, the VA has scheduled an exam for me in Hillsboro," I said. "Do you think you could drive me?"

He looked up from the TV. "What day? I might have to shuffle some things around."

I told him the day and time. "If you could take me, I'd really appreciate it. I'm kinda nervous about it."

"Sure. I'll make it happen." He got up and gave me a hug. "It'll be okay."

"And I'd like to schedule my knee-replacement surgery the week after. Could you take me to the hospital and pick me up?"

He chuckled, and his smile calmed my jitters. "You think I'd make you walk home after surgery? Just let me know when so I can plan for it."

That evening, I sat at the kitchen island with my computer, looking up hotels in Hillsboro. I wasn't sure if I'd be up for the three-and-a-half-hour drive home to Bend after being quizzed on my trauma. *Will I be bad enough to get money from the government? Will they think I'm lying? How long will the exam take?* Staring at my laptop, I said aloud, "Breathe, Dani. Take one step at a time."

The following week, Terry and I sat in the truck outside the red brick building in Hillsboro. My mouth watered. Acid churned and burned in my gut. Terry tenderly clasped my hand in his and said, "Geez, your hands are sweaty. Are you okay?"

"Not really. I feel sick."

"Honey, just do the best you can. It'll be okay. I'm right here."

I was seated in an office 20 minutes later. Books were haphazardly stacked on shelves and strewn across a wide wooden desk. In the chair on the other side of the desk sat an old man with caterpillar eyebrows, wearing a sweater vest. He looked like a stereotypical psychiatrist with his pen poised on a long, white form attached to a clipboard. I felt judged before he opened his mouth. Without even greeting me, he asked, "What branch of service were you in and how long did you serve?"

"I was in the Army for four-and-a-half years."

"Did you serve during war time?"

The dam broke. Tears streamed down my face, and I sobbed loudly. My core temperature rose, and my face flushed. "Yes." I grabbed a tissue from the box on his desk and prayed for strength.

In answering his questions, I told him about the nightly bombings, the burning oil wells, the burnt corpses trapped in their vehicles on the Highway of Death, and stepping on the landmine. An hour into the exam, my brain felt beat up. The walls seemed to close in, and I wanted to run, but I remained seated and finished answering his questions.

"Are you receiving psychiatric care through the VA?"

"Yes, I see Dr. Black at the clinic in Bend."

"You might want to discuss different medication options or a higher dose. Your symptoms could be controlled better. And you seem depressed."

I wouldn't be this stressed if I didn't have to be here proving to you how messed up I am. What a horrible system. The trauma from this exam is piling onto the trauma I've been dealing with.

He leaned back in his chair and laced his fingers on top of his desk. "I'm giving you a rating of 70 percent for PTSD. Your symptoms are pretty severe. But I don't want you to let this define who you are. Keep going to counseling and getting help."

He stood up and led me back to the waiting area. I plopped into the seat next to Terry and dabbed at my tears with the ratty tissue I still had in my hand.

"How are you?"

I sighed. "Exhausted."

"Let's go to the hotel and soak in the hot tub. Then you can take a nap. . . unless you're hungry and you want to get something to eat."

"I'm beat. I just want to rest."

He grabbed my hand. "How do you think you did?"

"Well, he rated me at 70 percent on his scale for PTSD and told me to follow up with my psychiatrist to get more medication, so I guess I did okay."

"Whoa. Let's get you into that hot tub, girl."

Relaying my experiences in the war, without even mentioning the rapes and abuse by fellow soldiers, sapped my energy for several days. I kept thinking about the 70 percent rating that validated me in one way and discouraged me in another. The evaluator told me not to let my PTSD define me, but I struggled with the realization that my service in the military had left permanent scars.

At my next counseling session, Amy and I discussed the C and P exam at length. We both agreed that I did the best I could, and overall, the evaluation had gone well. I still hadn't been able to admit I'd been sexually assaulted, even to Amy, because I still blamed myself.

"Dani, I wanted you to be the first to know, after talking to you about the lack of services for women in Central Oregon, we've decided to offer a women's group at the Vet Center."

"Nice. When does it start?"

"I still have to get a few things together, but it should be up and running in a couple of months."

"That should be perfect timing. I'm getting my knee replaced and should be able to walk without pain by then. Hey, did I ever tell you I tried to start a nonprofit called Women of Combat?"

"No, you never mentioned that. What happened?"

"Well, women veterans are hard to find. I scheduled a meet-and-greet at the public library. I advertised the event in the newspaper and on Facebook, but only one woman showed up. We exchanged phone numbers and email addresses, but after several unreturned phone calls and emails, I figured she wasn't interested. I gave out information and invited people at local events, but nothing I did brought in women veterans. So, I decided to call it quits and focus on my family and job. Anyway, enough about that. I'm glad there's going to be something offered here for women."

"Hopefully we can make it work. I'll keep you posted about the group. Thanks for suggesting it."

As I rose from the chair, the hair at the back of my neck prickled with the thought of opening up to a bunch of strangers in a women's group.

By the time I got into my car, I was bawling, hunched over the steering wheel. I was terrified that I wouldn't get better—I'd remain scared, angry, and emotionally out of control forever. I worried that everyone would know I was a fake—someone who only acted organized and composed but was a broiling mess on the inside.

Chapter 25

WOMEN VETERANS' GROUP

I pulled open the door to the Central Oregon Vet Center, three months after my C and P exam. My knee surgery had gone well, outside of a few hiccups with the pain medications, mainly nausea and vomiting. But physical therapy made it possible for me to walk through the Vet Center doors without a limp. The guy behind the desk looked up and said, "Hi, what can I do for you?"

I opened my mouth, but nothing came out. I swallowed, hoping to moisten my tongue. It didn't help. I cleared my throat and choked out, "I'm here for the women's group."

The guy nodded toward the hallway. "It's the first door on the left."

"Thanks." I forced my concrete legs to move in that direction and wiped my palms on my jeans. *Just breathe.* I reminded myself. *Stay focused.*

For ten minutes, I sat in a circle of empty plastic chairs, inhaling ragged breaths, with sweat dripping down my back, under my tee shirt. I was about to push off the chair to leave, feeling both disappointed and relieved, when Amy entered the room and closed the door.

"Well, it looks like it's just the two of us," she said. "We can wait a couple more minutes and see. How was your knee surgery?"

"Great." I didn't feel like elaborating.

We managed small talk for another five minutes until Amy leaned back in her chair and said, "I guess no one else is going to show. So, tell me, what do you want out of the group?

"Um, maybe a couple more people." We both laughed. "I'm not exactly sure. I've never attended a group meeting like this before."

"What did you want for your nonprofit, Women of Combat?"

"I guess I wanted a safe space for women veterans to talk and bond and know they aren't alone."

"Sounds like a great basis for a group—a community of women veterans in a safe space, to discuss and learn about PTSD, symptom management and support. I invited several other women, so maybe next week more will attend. Not everyone lives in Bend, so travel might be an issue."

I shrugged and stood. "Well, I hope they can make it. See you next week."

The following week, the guy behind the desk said I could grab a water bottle out of the fridge, and then I headed to the same room. Four women were sitting in plastic chairs in a circle, with two empty seats between them. I chose one of the empty chairs, feeling both nervous and relieved that I wouldn't be alone this time. Amy came in, shut the doors, and sat in the empty chair across from me.

Amy introduced herself and said, "Let's go around the circle. Please share your branch of service, what you did in the military, and something about yourself."

We all stared at Amy. The other women's faces looked how I felt—careful, unsure of whether we'd made the right choice in coming.

Amy leaned toward me. "Dani, why don't you start?"

My heart pounded. I exhaled and forced myself to speak. "Okay. My name's Dani. I was in the Army during the Persian Gulf War. I'm a nurse at the hospital, I'm married, have a daughter, and two step-kids."

The introductions revealed that between us we had served in Vietnam, the Persian Gulf, and Iraq. Amy asked us to share what we wanted out of the group. Support and connection seemed to be the common theme, so Amy's first assignment was for us to contact one of the other women in the group before our next session. She passed around copies of the list of our phone numbers.

"Call the person directly below your name on the list. If your name is last, call the name at the top. Any questions?" Amy paused. No one responded. "Okay, have a great week, and we'll see you next Thursday."

Afraid to seem overeager, I waited until Wednesday night to look at the list. I plugged in the number for the person below my name and held my breath.

"Hello."

"Hi, this is Dani from the group. I'm just calling to check in. How're you doing?" I swallowed and choked and coughed into the phone. "Sorry about that." I laughed.

"I'm doing okay, how about you?"

"I'm okay too. I was nervous about calling, but I had to do it before tomorrow, right?" I chuckled nervously.

"Me too. I called my person this afternoon. It felt weird."

"I agree but at least we completed our task."

"Yes, we did."

I racked my brain for more to say but came up empty. "Well, I need to start dinner. I just wanted to reach out and check in."

"Thanks. I'll see you tomorrow."

"Sounds good. See you then."

Over the next few weeks, our check-ins became less awkward. We decided to start a group chat and communicated frequently via texts. For the first time since I'd finished my service in the military, I felt understood. These women knew exactly what it felt like to be undervalued and to have their actions misinterpreted. Our ability to truly hear one another and offer acceptance was liberating.

I was astonished to learn my fellow women veterans had all been harassed, made to feel less than their male counterparts, and were disregarded and judged. Just. Like. Me. No matter which branch of service, we all felt like interlopers in the Good Ol' Boy Club. We were all mocked and discredited daily.

We talked about feeling invisible to our fellow male soldiers. When I joined the military, I had expected to be part of a team serving my country. It didn't occur to me that I would be treated differently than any other soldier. I figured that I had their backs so they would have mine—on and off duty. The others in the group shared similar stories.

I admitted to the group how I never discussed that I was in the military with my coworkers. Only my family and close friends knew. I was terrified that people would ask questions they expected me to answer, things I didn't want to talk about. Instead of having pride in my service, I felt ashamed. Again, most of the women in the group expressed similar experiences.

Amy pointed out that every soldier had their own story and not everyone was privileged to know it. This resonated deeply within me. Of course, I tended to avoid sharing my story altogether, keeping it locked up, hidden in the vault.

The group was scheduled to meet for two hours and 15 minutes. Shortly before the end of one of the meetings, Amy passed out a paper to us with a knight in armor, surrounded by the words: helplessness, nightmares, guilt, intrusive memories, poor judgment, depression, flashbacks, hopelessness, apathy, mistrust, communication problems, isolation, irritability, anger and rage, lack of feelings, avoidance, anxiety, poor self-esteem and self-image.

"I want you guys to look at this handout and share with the group next week anything that comes up from reading it," Amy said. "Have a great week!"

Overwhelmed, I folded the page, shoved it in my pocket, and headed for my car. When I got home, I sat on the couch. I unfolded the paper, and stared at it. I couldn't breathe. *How can I have every one of these symptoms?* I crumpled the paper, walked into the office, and stuffed the wad in the back of my desk drawer. Maybe I'll look at this another day. I couldn't process those words at that moment.

At work, management sent me back to the procedure room because they wanted the new hires to learn admission and recovery. I hoped the move would ease my general agitation since every cough or squeak of someone's shoes on the floor seemed to interrupt and derail my thoughts. Setting up for a procedure was second nature, so I looked forward to switching positions for a while. But when my coworker changed my specimen collection table, my face flushed, and I whipped around to confront her.

"Did you mess with my setup? I had it the way I wanted it, just back off," I snapped. "I've done this a million times, and I don't need your help!"

My coworker sucked in a breath and then stared at the floor. "Sorry, I thought I was helping."

"Well, don't think so much." I stomped out of the room still railing in my head. *Why can't people just leave me alone? I'm fine. I don't need anyone's help . . . Just take a deep breath and go get the patient. You know how to do this.*

I wheeled the patient into the procedure room, asked the standard questions, checked the vitals and the airway, and sedated the patient. The doctor requested cautery so he could use a snare to burn off a polyp in the patient's colon. I got up from my stool, placed the grounding pad on the patient's flank, and plugged in the cautery equipment, like I'd done a million times . . . but the beep sounded far away.

I glanced at the linoleum floor and saw sand. The familiar stench of death filled my nostrils. I gazed at a burned carcass in the driver seat of a vehicle, the victim's charred arms extended, still attached to the steering wheel. Distant voices spoke to me, but I couldn't make out what they were saying. My mind floated, dream-like, as I tried to find my way back to the present. Somehow, I managed to get back over to my stool and my patient. My fingers were perched on the computer keyboard.

"Dani, are you okay?" the doctor asked. "Do you need some help?

You seem like you're a million miles away."

Wait. I'm at work. What's going on? Where did I go? Is my patient okay? Oh my God. What just happened?

"Sorry, I must've spaced out for a second. I'm okay though, thanks," I lied.

Sweat had soaked through my shirt. I was embarrassed to get off the stool, afraid to reveal the big wet patches on my light blue scrubs. Once the procedure ended, I unhooked my patient, tied my scrub jacket around my waist, and rolled the gurney into the recovery area. I gave the recovery nurse a brief report, walked to the charge nurse's desk, and asked for a break.

Sucking in as much air as I could, I walked ten steps to the back door and onto the garden patio. On a concrete bench between bushes, I sat, put my head in my hands, and began to cry. Sobs wracked my body, and my muscles quivered from tensing.

My friend Karla, the charge nurse that day, walked outside to check on me. "Dani, are you okay?"

"I don't know what's wrong with me," I wailed. "I think I'm going crazy. I saw sand instead of tile on the floor in the procedure room. When I smelled burned flesh, suddenly I was staring into torched cars. I don't understand what happened."

"Maybe you should go home early, rest, maybe call your counselor. You need to take care of yourself. Work will always be here." Karla smiled and gave me a hug. "Call me if you need anything, okay?"

"Thanks, I will." I walked into the nurses' changing room, sat on the bench, and visualized myself at Belknap with my family—my safe space. When I felt grounded enough to drive, I headed home.

My vault had been ripped wide open. It seemed my thoughts and actions were no longer under my control. I felt like a puppet, manipulated by the force of my subconscious mind, clawing its way to the surface, intent on tearing apart my relationships, my job, and my sanity.

Chapter 26

TRIGGERED

The following week, during the women's group at the Vet Center, we discussed what the word "trigger" means. Amy explained how thoughts, feelings, sounds, colors, smells—really anything—can be a trigger.

Could I have been triggered in the procedure room? I shoved the thought aside because my tongue seemed to take off on its own. "I'm not sure if I've been triggered, but after my knee surgery, I felt helpless and out of control, so I inserted some control by halving my pain meds. It was like I deserved the pain somehow. But I couldn't take the agony and decided to go back to the amount the doctor prescribed." By the time I finished babbling, sweat had glued my legs to my chair, and I felt trapped. I glanced up at the group and then toward the door.

"Is there a reason you didn't ask your doctor to help you get through that feeling of helplessness?" Amy asked.

"Yes, I'm a professional. I feel like I should be able to handle anything medical on my own. Up until recently, I've been able to manage whatever I needed to. I just get stuff done. It takes longer to ask for help than to do things myself."

"Could it be that when you tried to take back control by changing the amount of pain medication, and it didn't work, it added to your frustration?"

I slouched in my chair and tossed up my hands. "Well, yeah. I was frustrated and mad that I couldn't handle the pain. I'm tougher than that. It's just pain. No big deal."

"I think your body was telling you it was a very big deal. You had major surgery—they replaced an entire joint. What would you expect from one of your patients?"

I sighed. She had a point. "I would expect my patient to follow the doctor's orders . . . But I've been hurt when I was vulnerable and let people in. I can't trust anyone but myself."

Amy's head tilted in apparent confusion. "What are you thinking about?"

I sat up slowly, and tears began to flow. "I just realized maybe I was triggered by that feeling of helplessness after my surgery."

Amy straightened in her chair and smiled. "Good. Let it out. That's a huge connection to make. You've identified one of your triggers."

"I guess I'm hard on myself. I have high expectations, and I don't know how to show myself compassion. I feel like I don't deserve it."

"Do your patients deserve compassion?"

"Of course."

"As do you. Just like you deserve relief from your pain."

Sitting in my car after the session, my mind reeled. *What other triggers do I have? How can I identify them or know when they're coming? I'm broken. I'll never get better.* I punched the steering wheel and stared up through the sunroof. *Please help me, God. I don't want to live like this anymore.*

Chapter 27

COGNITIVE PROCESSING THERAPY

Ten months into the Women's Group, Amy asked if we'd be interested in trying Cognitive Processing Therapy or CPT. "People with PTSD think differently about themselves, their environment, safety, control, esteem, trust, and intimacy," she said. "Their thought patterns can cause an increase in feelings of anger, anxiety, and guilt." Our counselor continued to explain that through the process of CPT, she would ask us to identify "stuck points" or thoughts we have about ourselves or situations that may not be true. During the following 12 weeks, we challenged our beliefs, and the way we process and store information in our brains.

I had been raised to believe there was good and bad in the world, but for the most part, people were good, and the world, overall, was a just place. These beliefs were completely shattered by the horrors I'd witnessed and experienced. And I only felt safe at home.

I loathed crowds and would get physically sick with diarrhea or nausea, or both, if I had to go someplace where there would be people I didn't know. Just going to the grocery store made my heart race, my gut tighten, and my adrenaline spike. The thought of going anywhere left me feeling depleted and unmotivated to do anything.

At our first group session of CPT, Amy gave the four of us simple homework: Fill out an ABC worksheet. A stood for an *activating event*. B was the *belief* or "stuck point" that resulted from that event. C represented the *consequences*, or feelings, that came up for us. But for the moment, we only had to do steps A and B.

During our second session, the five of us sat in our plastic chairs, and Amy asked if anyone wanted to share their ABC worksheet. I blurted, "Sure. I don't know if I did it right, but here it goes. For A, I have my parents asked us out for breakfast, and B, I only feel safe at home, so I didn't want to go."

"Good. This brings up a great topic: Emotions," Amy said. "I'm going to give you a handout called the 'Wheel of Emotions.'"

The mention of emotions made my stomach clench. She handed each of us a copy around the circle. I stared at the paper thinking: *I'm supposed to have all these emotions? This reminds me of that stupid knight in armor picture.*

I'd spent the past 24 years avoiding any and all emotions. Soldiers were trained to push down emotions because if you reacted to them, you could get killed or get someone else killed. Glancing again at the handout, I thought, *no way in hell do I have all these emotions. Not possible.*

At the center of the circle were the words: joyful, peaceful, powerful, mad, scared, and sad. More complex emotions stemmed outward. I tried to recall a time when I felt joyful. Ashten's beautiful infant face popped into my head, and a warm, pleasant glow spread through me.

Okay, I know what joy feels like. And I can imitate and fake the emotion, but I haven't allowed myself the luxury of joy for a long time.

Sad, scared, and mad, on the other hand, were all too familiar. *I wake up every day with a mixture of those three swirling about in my mind. Someone like me doesn't deserve happiness and peace because, somehow, I brought this PTSD thing on myself.* The well-worn path of negative self-talk felt familiar, and therefore, reassuring. *Feelings are for the weak. I don't need or want them.*

"Dani, what do you think about this Wheel of Emotions?" Amy asked.

"I don't have all of these. I don't even know what some of them are."

Amy nodded slowly as if making a decision. "My homework for all of you is to identify a time in your life when you've felt these six basic emo—"

"I remember experiencing joy when my daughter was born," I interrupted. "I felt such a warm, loving feeling toward her. But I can't remember any other time I've felt joyful."

"That's a good start. You've identified at least one time. Now try to come up with some other examples for the other emotions. This week, when you're filling out your ABC worksheet, see if you can name a couple of emotions from this wheel in the consequences section."

Not only do we have to identify stuck points, but now we have to tag on emotions? I glanced around the small conference room, and all four of us had the same weary look of fear and confusion on our faces. Several minutes after the session ended, no one had moved except Amy, who had left the room. Our eyes had glazed over, staring at nothing.

"I don't know about you guys," I said into the silence, "but I have no idea what to make of this wheel."

"Burn it," said another veteran, which made all of us laugh.

The next day, while standing in front of the stove, waiting for my oatmeal to boil, I pulled out the wheel. *Powerful. Have I ever felt powerful? I guess being a charge nurse made me feel powerful and in control.*

Then I looked at the word "Peaceful." A trip to Montana with my high school friend, Susie, entered my mind—floating on the water at Flathead Lake, the water lapping gently around us. I remembered how the tension had drained from my body, how my thoughts lazily bobbed and swayed into silence. *Okay, I've felt peaceful.*

"Scared" was easy. During the war I lived in fear, not knowing if I'd survive from day to day.

Thinking about the war brought back a good example of "anger." The memory of finding out I had to stay longer in the Middle East, because I was "mission essential," ignited a white-hot blaze that raced through my body and clenched my fists, as though I were reliving it.

"Sadness" came next. I found myself feeling the weight on my chest, longing to be with my family and friends. The weight grew heavier with the despair I felt at possibly missing my brother's wedding in July.

So, I have examples for joy, peaceful, scared, angry, and sad. That's good enough for now. I stirred the oatmeal in the saucepan, poured it into my bowl, added some brown sugar and milk, and sat at the island with my ABC worksheet.

I recalled the incident watching fellow soldiers kicking a dead body. It occurred to me that my resulting belief was: I can't trust anyone, not even the people I thought were on my team. Anger fired in my chest again, then came the heaviness of sorrow. I wrote about the event in the A section on the worksheet.

The B section asked: Are my thoughts realistic or helpful?

Definitely not helpful. I wrote: Just because those guys weren't trustworthy doesn't mean no one can be trusted.

The last section asked what I could tell myself instead, so I wrote: *I trust my parents and my husband. Not everyone deserves trust, but some people do.*

Every week, I learned more about my problematic thinking patterns and tried to accept how *my* perspectives were the problem. For so long, I blamed everyone else's behavior for my frustrations. Those well-worn neural pathways in my brain were like deep ruts in the mud. I felt as if I were being thrown from side to side in my attempts to move forward.

The fourth week into CPT, Amy handed out another damn worksheet. Our circle of veterans collectively winced. The paper listed common destructive patterns for victims of PTSD, such as: jumping to conclusions, exaggerating or minimizing, ignoring important parts of situations, oversimplifying, overgeneralizing, mind reading, catastrophic reasoning, and all-or-nothing attitudes, to name a few. Staring at the handout, once again, I recognized every single of them.

My default seemed to be "all-or-nothing." This meant I viewed the world as black or white, right or wrong. I'd lost friends as a result and was moving toward losing my job as well. The most glaring example was how I viewed all men as untrustworthy (except my dad, husband, and brother) and remained ever skeptical of their intentions.

At the end of the session, Amy gave us another ABC worksheet. More homework. This one asked us to state a belief. Then it took us through several steps that would show us the belief wasn't true. The next day, when Ashten was in school and Terry was at work, I sat on the couch with my furry babies, Storm and Atlas, for support, and settled into work.

I chose the belief or "stuck point" that if I hadn't volunteered to go distribute food and water for the survivors in Kuwait, my best friend in the military and I wouldn't have been traumatized that day.

Filling in the blanks on the page, I wrote that I believed this 100 percent. When asked how strongly I felt each emotion, I rated anger at 80 percent; overwhelmed at 100 percent; guilt at 80 percent, and sadness at 80 percent. The next step challenged my belief with evidence for and against.

My evidence was simple.

For: The drive and stops on the Highway of Death happened. I signed up for it and convinced Sharon to join me.

Against: There was no way I could have known what would happen on that excursion, being that it was a war zone. I had thought we were going to do something good, to help people.

The next question on the worksheet asked: Is this belief a habit or fact? I wrote the first thing that came to mind: Habit.

Next question: Is this belief based on facts or feelings? I chose feelings.

My heart rate inexplicably accelerated, and my face flushed. *What does this stupid worksheet have to do with anything? How is this supposed to help me?* Suddenly my head pounded. I shoved the paper back into my notebook, left the living room, and stomped upstairs with the dogs trailing behind me.

Several hours later, I settled on the couch again and opened my notebook. The next column on the worksheet focused on problematic patterns. That section helped me realize I'd jumped to the conclusion that once we were on the road, somehow, I could have prevented the events. The truth: I was a specialist, low on the military chain of command. I wasn't in a position to give orders or change the outcome.

The final column was for a new alternative thought. I wrote: I did the best I could at the time. On the space for how strongly I believed this new thought, I wrote: 100 percent.

My old stuck point didn't seem to make sense anymore. My feelings of guilt, anger, and sadness seemed to lift, though I still felt overwhelmed. The process took a lot of energy, though, and I had to take a nap.

Over the next couple of weeks, we filled out more worksheets and discussed them with the group. I started to view things differently. Sometimes I was able to identify the problematic thinking pattern as it happened, and I could stop it. Progress was slow, but I reminded myself that this crap had been ingrained in my mind over decades.

We challenged our beliefs regarding safety and trust, in ourselves and others. I had believed I was in control of myself, and that I should be able to keep myself from harm. Most of us seemed to feel that way. We discovered this was an illusion. We'd been given training and tools to protect ourselves, but sometimes those tools weren't enough. Bad things could happen to good people. I guess I understood these concepts, but I couldn't seem to apply them.

This illusion that I should have been able to protect myself caused me not to trust my own instincts. I was habitually hyper critical of myself and my actions. My standards for myself, at home and at work, were unobtainable, yet I tried desperately to meet them. When I failed, self-doubt and criticism sent me on another round of the vicious cycle that was destroying me.

If I can't even trust myself, how can I trust others? That question reverberated in my mind and consumed me with frustration and sadness. I tried to soothe myself with chocolate and soda, but with that temporary comfort came a big dose of guilt, knowing that stuff would further expand my waistline. Worse, I often took out my frustration on co-workers and family members. Since I'd been off work, recovering from surgery, Terry and Ashten took the brunt of my impatience and snarky comments. Hurting the people I loved led to eating away my distress and guilt. I couldn't see a way out of the cycle, so I sank progressively further into depression.

During the last two weeks of the CPT program, we focused on being kind to ourselves and learning about intimacy. Just the word "intimacy" made my jaw clench. I was under the misconception that intimacy meant sex. I found out that intimacy means so much more.

Intimacy not only pertains to your relationship with another person, but your relationship with yourself. The handout read: "The belief that one can take care of one's own emotional needs, an important part of healthy living, is the ability to soothe and calm oneself. Part of self-intimacy is the ability to be alone without feeling lonely or empty."

My breath caught as I reread the last sentence. I hated being alone, ruminating over past mistakes that left me disgusted and unsettled. Silence triggered overwhelming anxiety and nervousness, which left me feeling unsafe, unworthy, and unloved. I craved the emptiness that allowed me to go numb, to take a break from hating myself.

After 12 weeks of CPT, I still felt crappy. I viewed things differently but still freaked out at the thought of going to work, going to the grocery store . . . basically doing anything.

Great. I failed again. What is wrong with me? Why doesn't anything work?

At the last session, Amy asked the group if CPT had been helpful. I looked right at her and lied. "Yeah, super helpful. I got a lot out of it."

Well, it wasn't a total lie. I learned a lot more about myself and my thinking patterns. Still, my feet felt dangerously close to the edge of a mental abyss. I feared if I teetered off the edge, I wouldn't make it back—ever. The inner chaos would consume me.

Wouldn't it be easier for everyone if I were just gone? Damn . . . that's a faulty thinking pattern. Don't do anything stupid. You have a daughter who needs you.

Chapter 28

INDIVIDUAL UNEMPLOYABILITY (IU)

As I waited for the VA to schedule another compensation and pension (C and P) exam, I tried to adjust to early retirement. I decided my memory and anger issues were interfering with my nursing judgment and professionalism, so I made the difficult decision to medically retire. While my mind understood that I didn't have to go to work, my darn body couldn't seem to catch up, and my eyes would pop open at 5:00 a.m. Occasionally I could go back to sleep, but most of the time I'd lie in bed, and my thoughts would flit from one thing to the next. When I could no longer tolerate my swirling mind, I dragged myself out of bed, showered, and got ready for my long day alone, while Ashten was at school and Terry went to work.

Three days into my new life, I couldn't take the boredom anymore, so I decided to become a super mom. My first action in my new role would be to designate myself Ashten's taxi to and from school. I rationalized that she hated the bus, and riding together would give us more time to bond. I convinced myself that my middle school child needed me more than I needed to process my crap. Being fluent in avoidance made the idea seamless.

My new routine consisted of making breakfast for Ashten, getting her ready for school, then dropping her off. Sometimes the furry babies and I would take a walk to pass the time until I picked her up after school. The days crept by as I waited to hear from the VA about scheduling another exam to assess my individual unemployability (IU). Which meant I could be deemed no longer able to work at the job for which I was trained. The VA might compensate me because my PTSD was severe enough that I could no longer work in my profession.

Six weeks later, I got the call that I would have another C&P exam in Vancouver, Washington the following week. True to form, Terry graciously agreed to take off another day from work and drive me over the mountain pass. On a Wednesday, Terry and I loaded into the truck and headed to a psychiatrist's office. The VA had hired an outside provider to assess the IU claim. I had no idea why. I just did as I was told like a good little soldier.

We barely arrived in time, so we got out of the truck and power walked across the parking lot toward the entrance. Terry grabbed the glass door for me. The lobby was eerily silent, but my heartbeat was deafening. I almost didn't hear the receptionist say, "Can I help you?"

"Yes, I'm here for an 11:00 appointment. My name is Danielle Shine."

She typed something on her keyboard. "Oh, yes. Please have a seat, and I'll let the doctor know you're here."

"Thanks."

Terry and I lumbered over to the chairs and plopped into them. My thoughts raced with questions and self-doubt. My eyes burned with tears again. I ordered myself to get a grip on my emotions and picked up a magazine. Still, my vision blurred, and I couldn't see the pictures on the pages. I replaced the magazine on the small end table and reached for Terry's hand. He wrapped his warm hand around mine, and my body began to relax.

A woman dressed in black slacks and a cream blouse came through the door next to the receptionist's desk. "Miss Shine?" she called.

I stood up. "Yes."

"Please, follow me."

Once in her office, she directed me to a chair across from her desk. "Please, take a seat."

I sat in the padded wooden chair and started picking at my fingernails. I looked around her office to distract myself, and keep from imploding, but I couldn't make sense of what I saw.

"Can you please state your full name for me?"

"Danielle Danine Shine."

She looked at the paper on her desk in front of her. "You're here today for an exam for Individual Unemployability. Is that correct?"

"Yes."

"I've reviewed your chart and see you're currently rated at 70 percent for PTSD, is that correct?"

"Yes."

"You recently had to leave work due to your disability. Can you tell me about what you did and why you had to leave?" She poised her pen on the paper.

Tears that had been welling began to escape. My mouth opened and closed. Nothing came out. I couldn't speak around the giant ball in my throat.

"Take your time, Danielle."

I closed my eyes, took a deep breath, and tried again. "I was a registered nurse for 16 years. I worked as an endoscopic nurse, sedating patients for procedures, and I was a charge nurse one day a week. But I had to change my job because I'd get triggered by the cautery in the room. Then I went to the VA and worked as a nurse care manager. I had to quit that job because talking to disgruntled veterans triggered anxiety attacks. I returned to my old unit, the MDU, but then I injured my shoulder moving a 600-pound man in the ICU and had to have surgery on my rotator cuff. Recently, I had my knee replaced because it was bone-on-bone from walking on the concrete floors. The hospital assigned me to light duty, handling paperwork, but I couldn't stay focused and would forget to note critical things that could be life threatening for patients. I'd get physically sick when I even thought of work because I worried I'd hurt someone, so I felt like I had no choice but to leave." My face flushed with embarrassment when I realized how fast I'd been talking.

"What did you mean by 'you would get sick'?"

"Every time I entered the hospital, I'd puke. I always felt shaky and sweaty, and sometimes I'd snap at people, say inappropriate or sarcastic things, and I couldn't seem to control it, even though I tried really hard."

"So, sometimes you feel angry." She wrote something on the page.

"Yeah, but I don't know when the anger is coming. Someone says or does something, and it's like my mouth goes off on its own. It's unpredictable and scary because it seems to come out of nowhere. It got bad enough that some of my coworkers, and even some of the physicians, avoided talking to me, afraid I'd go off on them for no reason." I started to cry again. "People have always thought of me as a nice, fun-loving person. It's been awful."

After two excruciating hours of answering her questions, she folded her hands on top of her desk and leaned toward me. "Danielle, do you have an appointment with a local psychiatrist in the near future?"

"No." I looked at my lap and tore little pieces from my tissue.

"I'd recommend that you make one. I think you'd benefit from an increase in your medication."

That's the second time a psychiatrist has said that to me. Am I really that messed up? "Uh . . . okay, I'll call and make an appointment when I get home."

"I've gathered enough information from this interview, so I will escort you back to the waiting area." She stood and moved toward the door.

"Thanks." I walked with her to the waiting area and glanced around nervously, looking for Terry.

He looked up from reading his book in the corner of the room. "How're you doing?" His eyes seemed to say he already knew how I felt—rung out, exhausted.

“I’m really tired. I think I’ll take a nap on the drive home.”

“Okay. Do you think it went well?”

“Well, she told me I needed more medication, so apparently she noticed I was a complete mess.”

He stood and put an arm around me. “I guess that’s good.”

“Yeah, I guess so.”

He took my hand, and we walked out to the truck. As soon as we hit the road to Bend, I fell asleep. Terry had to shake me a little to wake me when we pulled into our driveway.

A week later, at the next women veterans’ group meeting, I discussed the Cand P exam and how bone weary I felt after the interrogation. After the meeting, as I got up to leave, one of the women came up to me and asked, “Have you applied for Social Security benefits?”

“No, I didn’t know I could. I’m not old enough.”

“You probably qualify because of your disability. Look it up on their website. You’ll have to fill out some forms, but it’s worth a shot.”

“Thanks, I will.”

Once I got home and situated on my comfy couch, with my laptop and my furry babies, I went to the Social Security website. They had a form I could fill out online to apply for disability benefits, so I said a prayer and sent it off. I looked at figuring out a way to keep my family from financial hardship as my new job. I’d done everything I could. Waiting for the VA’s decision and the response from Social Security was torture.

Sitting alone on my couch, in my eerily quiet house, I thought: *You don’t deserve to be happy, and you definitely don’t deserve this money. Your entire family would be better off if you were dead. You’re a drain on society. Just do it already. Kill yourself and be done.*

Chapter 29

WOMEN'S TRAUMA RECOVERY PROGRAM (WTRP)

I sat at the kitchen table, trying to choke down my Cream of Wheat, feeling helpless and fed up with my life. My weight had reached an all-time high at 298 pounds. Mine was an eating problem that had gone beyond dietary remedies and physical exercise.

My mind and body were out of sync. Ever-increasing anxiety ratcheted up my gastrointestinal issues, which frustrated and disappointed me. I'd thought once I left nursing and the hospital, my nervous stomach would get back to normal, though I no longer knew what "normal" meant.

I can't do this anymore. It'd be easy to go upstairs, get my gun, and end it. I leaned my elbows on the table and put my head in my hands. *Stop! This isn't me. God, I need help. Please guide me through this darkness. I can't keep hiding behind a mask of false happiness, mimicking positive emotions. If anyone knew how close I am to the edge, they'd lock me up because I'm crazy.* I sat up and slouched in my chair. *Maybe I should be locked up. At least I couldn't kill myself. I'd be safe.*

When I was alone in Montana, I'd thought about ending my life, but this was different. The idea felt more vivid, like a potential reality. The nursing side of me wanted to understand this gradual mental shift that kept marching ahead. I needed to find out how to reverse it.

I looked up PTSD and suicidal ideation on the internet. Not only was the information generic, but the material also mostly talked about men's experience with PTSD. I started to panic. My appointment to see Amy wasn't for another week, but I couldn't wait. I needed help. I called the Vet Center and arranged to see her the following day.

Sitting in the leather chair on the other side of Amy's desk, I blurted, "Everything to deal with PTSD seems to be geared for male veterans. I'm so frustrated and at the end of my rope. Do you know of any facilities for women?"

Amy folded her hands on her desk. "First of all. You seem kind of wound up, so take a deep breath."

I did what she said. My shoulders relaxed, and I sunk further into the chair.

Amy nodded. "Okay, there are a couple of trauma facilities the VA uses, but I think your psychiatrist has to give a referral. I suggest you call her and schedule an appointment. Do you have a plan to commit suicide?"

"I've been thinking about my guns, but I don't have a plan."

"Do you feel like you're a threat to yourself?"

"That's why I'm here. I realize this isn't me, and I need help."

"Dani, take my card." Amy handed it to me across her desk. "My email and phone number are on it. If you feel like you are going to harm yourself, call me anytime, okay?"

"Okay, thanks. I'm going to make an appointment with my psychiatrist as soon as I get to my car."

As promised, I called the Bend VA Clinic and scheduled an appointment. It was only two days away, but the idea of waiting felt nearly impossible. *I can do it,* I told myself, gripping the steering wheel. *I'll focus on getting more information, so I know what to say to the doctor and the advocate. Hopefully, they'll be able to help me.*

At home, I sat on the couch with a Diet Pepsi, my furry babies, and my laptop. First, I searched "women veteran treatment facilities" then "PTSD programs." A VA facility in Palo Alto, California came up that offered prolonged exposure therapy, something I hadn't tried. I jotted some information on a yellow pad to ask my psychiatrist about it.

My psychiatrist wore a sweater, which I thought was weird because I started sweating the moment I sat in the plush leather chair across from her clutter free, walnut desk. Her warm smile did nothing to calm my inner turmoil.

"Do you know how hard it is to find women-only trauma facilities in the VA?" I asked.

"No, I guess I don't."

"Well, they don't make it easy. That's for sure."

"Why are you looking for a trauma facility?"

I swallowed past the golf ball in my throat. "Well, I haven't been honest with you. I'm struggling. I know at our last appointment I said I was depressed, so we increased my medication, but I'm having thoughts of suicide. I've tried every form of therapy Bend has to offer. I've been in counseling for four years, and I should be better than I am. I found a place in California that has prolonged exposure therapy, and I haven't tried that yet. Do you know anything about the VA's program in Palo Alto?"

"Before we get into that, I need to know what kind of symptoms you're having."

"I'm not sleeping, I don't care about anything, and I feel numb and disconnected. I feel like it'd be better for everyone if I just wasn't here anymore. My life has no meaning. I'm miserable, and I'm afraid I'll kill myself. But I won't let anyone at home see how messed up I am because I feel like a failure. I think I need to go somewhere and get help where no one knows me."

The concern in her eyes revealed that I was probably even worse off than I thought. "I'm sorry you're struggling right now." she said. "I have heard of the facility you're talking about. It's actually in Menlo Park. I can reach out to them and see what I need to do to get you referred to their women-only program."

"Please. I can't do this anymore, and I don't want to hurt my family any more than I already have."

"Okay. I will call today and get back to you tomorrow. But I have to ask; do you have a plan to kill yourself?"

"No, just thoughts."

"This might take some time to get this set up. While we wait, you can email or call me anytime. Please make sure you continue with your group every week and set up one-on-ones with Amy when you need to. Will you be able to do this?"

"Yes, thanks for your help." The words were an automatic response. I didn't know how long I could wait.

That evening, I asked Terry, "Can you come here and sit with me for a minute?" I patted the couch next to me.

"Where's Ash?" he asked, walking toward me from the kitchen.

"She's upstairs. I had an appointment with my psychiatrist today. I haven't been completely honest with you. I'm struggling to keep my sanity. I feel like I'm losing it, and the therapies I've tried aren't cutting it. I asked her if there was a facility where I could go to get help."

"What kind of facility?"

"A women's trauma facility in California that specializes in PTSD."

His eyes softened, and he held my hand. "Well, I guess only you can make that decision, but I have noticed you've been more on edge lately. I feel like you might blow up at me for anything, and I see your patience with Ashten isn't that great either. I want you to feel better, so do whatever that takes."

I wanted to jump down his throat for mentioning I'd been on edge, but instead I said, "I'll find out more tomorrow from my psychiatrist."

"Okay, then let's just wait and see."

"Yeah, I don't want to tell Ashten until we know what's going to happen."

The next day, my psychiatrist told me she'd sent a referral to the

Women's Trauma Recovery Program in California. Two days after that, I received a call from the program coordinator. "This is a 12-week, intensive inpatient program," she explained. "There are men on the same campus but in a different building, and the classes are separate."

I collapsed onto a bar stool at the island in the kitchen, dizzy with relief. "That sounds like exactly what I need. I'm hoping this intensive program will help me break through my crushing depression.'

"Right now, we are maxed out at eight women," she said. "One of them will graduate in early January, and when she does, you can take her spot. Do you have any questions?"

"Well, I'm not really sure. Do I drive there or what?"

"One of our travel specialists will call you. Since your PTSD disability rating is 70 percent, we will pay for your transportation to get here. You can stay at Defenders' Lodge, a hotel for veterans that's located on the Palo Alto VA campus. There's a bus that takes people from the hotel to Menlo Park. When you arrive, someone will meet you and walk you over to our facility. Don't worry. We'll go over all of this again. I know it's a lot to take in."

My stomach did that fluttering thing it always does when I'm anxious. "Yeah, I'm feeling quite overwhelmed with it all."

"I bet. Just be kind and patient with yourself, and we'll see you in about a month."

"Okay, sounds good. Thanks for everything."

When Terry walked into the kitchen from work, I told him about the conversation with the program coordinator. "Hey, I'm on board for whatever you want to do," he said. By then, Ashten was 15 and more independent, so I felt more comfortable in taking time away, to maybe get a handle on this anxiety that had consumed my life.

Ashten and I had just finished cleaning up after dinner when Terry came back into the kitchen. "Can you come sit with Dad and me at the table for a minute?" I asked.

Ashten stiffened and looked from me to Terry. "Uh . . . sure."

"Don't worry. You're not in trouble. We want to talk to you about something."

We took our regular seats at the round table, facing Ashten.

"You know that I've been in counseling for PTSD for the last four years."

"Uh-huh." Her shoulders slumped, and she avoided eye contact.

"Well, I'm still struggling, and Dad and I think it would be a good idea for me to go to a treatment facility in California that specializes in PTSD."

Her brows scrunched with concern. "When would you go?"

"There might be an opening next month." I clasped my hands on the table, unsure of how much I should tell her.

"For how long?"

"The program lasts about three months."

"And you think it'll help?"

I looked at Terry and then back to Ashten. "I sure hope so, Peanut. I'm kind of at my wits end here. I'm hoping by doing this, I'll be able to be less angry and sad, so I can be a better mom and more present for you and Dad."

Her eyes got teary. "I don't think you're a bad mom."

"Thanks, Ash, but I know I can be a better mom." I got up and she stood too. I wrapped my arms around her. "It's going to be okay. Your dad will take good care of you, and we can call and FaceTime as much as we want."

Terry looked at Ashten. "We'll be okay. We can do this."

Ashten nodded. "Yeah, we can. For sure, Dad."

Getting through the holidays, trying to appear festive, and mostly failing, was painful. At the end of December, I received the call—the program would have an opening in two weeks; did I still want it? Hell yes. The travel coordinator arranged a flight and a night's stay at the

Defender's Lodge in Palo Alto.

My family gave me a bon voyage dinner. Terry, Ashten, and I went over to my parents' house for Mom's pork noodles, my favorite. The next day, Ashten came with Terry and me to Redmond airport, and we had a tearful goodbye.

The plane lifted off the runway. I watched the juniper trees on the ground get smaller and realized I was counting on this adventure to change my entire life. The next few months would dredge up memories I hadn't known were there, much less triggering my subconscious mind to react, keeping me from healing.

Chapter 30

MENLO PARK

One night at the Defender's Lodge in Palo Alto was enough. The woman who had been assigned to share the room with me seemed full of barely controlled rage. Images of her stabbing me, or trying to choke me, flashed behind my eyelids whenever I closed them to try to sleep. I got up early, showered, and called an Uber from the lobby.

I arrived in front of the main building in Menlo Park 15 minutes later and called the number I'd been given. Almost immediately, a friendly dark-haired woman, wearing sweats and a t-shirt, came out of the front entrance to escort me wherever I was supposed to go. I followed her, watching my feet hit the pavement. My heart pounded in my ears. I tried to breathe through the stress, but it didn't help. Soon we stood outside a two-story red brick building. It reminded me of the old buildings in downtown Bend, and my shoulders began to relax. My escort pushed a button on the intercom.

"Yo!" said a voice through the speaker.

"It's me. The new girl is here already."

I jumped at the loud buzz to indicate that she could open the door. She held it open for me to walk in ahead of her. Gooseflesh prickled up my arms, but I moved past her, into a gray hallway. *Okay . . . We're locked down. Keep breathing. Don't panic.*

We trudged up two flights of stairs, side by side, and we started down a narrow hallway. My tennis shoes squeaked on the shiny beige tile. She opened the door I'd just passed, toward the end of the hallway, and said,

"This is it."

I turned around and entered a tiny room with a functional desk and two metal chairs. "Have a seat," said my escort. "A nurse will be with you shortly." Then she turned and left me alone.

An older nurse came in with a clipboard. "Hi, I'm Nancy. And your name is Danielle Shine?" I confirmed my name and date of birth. "We need you to provide a clean catch urine sample."

Whoa. They don't waste any time.

"Tomorrow morning you'll also get labs drawn. This is a standard procedure for new residents. We need a baseline and to make sure you don't have any drugs in your system. To participate in our program, you must be drug and alcohol free."

"I don't drink or use drugs, so I should be good to go."

Her eyebrows rose like she didn't believe me, or maybe she was surprised. She handed me a plastic container. "We still need the sample."

Nurse Nancy came into the bathroom with me and watched as I peed into the cup. I was proud of myself for performing under such scrutiny. Back in the cramped office, she handed me several papers to read and told me to follow her.

She led me down the right side of a V-shaped hallway, past the nurses' station. Four glass windows let in natural light. Across from the windows were four closed doors on the opposite wall. She opened the second door.

"Please place your bags on the bed." Nancy waved at a bare mattress. The bed closest to the bathroom had a comforter on it, and the desk under the window was strewn with books and papers.

My roommate seems messy.

"I'm going to inspect everything you brought to make sure there's no contraband," Nancy said. "Once your bags are cleared, you can put your things inside this closet." She nodded at the narrow door to the right of my bed. "This nightstand and desk are yours too. Your roommate is in class." She opened my bag and pulled everything out, diligently running her fingers over all my clothes, checking the pockets, then left them in a heap. I felt violated but reminded myself this wasn't a vacation. I was in a trauma facility. "Okay, you're clean. The linens are down the hall on the cart. Go ahead and make your bed and put your stuff away."

She opened the door. "Come see me at the desk when you're done. If you finish early enough, you can catch the last part of class. Your assigned big sister is your roommate, Tammy. You'll meet her later."

What does that mean—class? Don't ask, just do.

I waded through the pile on my bed, putting my things away quickly so I could make it to the class, already in progress. My hands shook, and my stomach felt jittery. I glanced at my watch. It was already one o'clock. Breakfast had been six hours before, and I was prone to low blood sugar. *Oh well, I probably couldn't eat anything right now anyway.*

I went to the nurse's station. Nancy smiled and put her pen on the clipboard on her desk. "You're ready. Great." She led me down the left side of the "V" to the first door. She peered inside, then gently pushed me into the room.

Ten chairs formed a circle next to the chalkboard on the wall. Nine unfamiliar faces turned to look at me. A slender woman with short dark hair and glasses smiled and said, "Hi, welcome. Have a seat."

"Thanks." I walked over and sat in the only empty chair, directly across from the woman. Nancy disappeared from the doorway.

"We were just talking about the five-column worksheet," the dark-haired lady said. "I know you probably don't know what that is, but I assure you, you will."

Everyone laughed. I felt left out of an inside joke, but the paper they were looking at seemed similar to the ABC worksheet we used in my group at home. "My name is Carrie. I am one of the psychologists here at Menlo Park. Sitting to my right is Hannah. She's also a psychologist." The Caucasian woman next to Carrie had shoulder length, curly blond hair.

She smiled and gave a quick wave.

Seven other women of all ages, all races, sat in the circle and had one thing in common: trauma. And these women were all ahead of me in the program. I looked forward to learning more about them.

"Why don't you introduce yourself to all of us and tell us a little bit about yourself?" Carrie said.

"Okay, my name is Dani. I'm an Army veteran from Bend, Oregon. I'm married and have a 15-year-old daughter and two step-kids. The oldest is married and has two girls, so I have grandbabies."

"We're so glad you're here. Thank you." The psychologist's eyes surveyed the circle. "Let's finish up early, and we'll see all of you tomorrow."

I felt disappointed that the meeting ended early, so I didn't get to know any of them, but I assured myself that I'd learn their stories in time. Everyone got up and my heart beat faster. *Where am I supposed to go? Back to my room?*

A slender fair woman with blonde hair looked at me and said, "At 4:30 we have dinner. Do you want to come to the mess hall with us? We're all supposed to eat together. It's part of the program."

"Well, it's only 3:00. Should I meet you somewhere?"

"Yeah, meet me downstairs by the doors."

"What do I do for an hour and a half?"

"I usually do homework or take a walk . . . but you can't go anywhere by yourself yet. Maybe read a book or just relax?"

"Okay, thanks." I walked back to my room and sat on my bed. My roommate still hadn't appeared. I supposed she was one of the women in the meeting, but she hadn't introduced herself. To pass the time, I decided to organize my closet and desk.

At 4:25, my stomach growled as if on cue, and I headed down the stairs. The fair-haired woman stood by the doors with her arms folded staring into space. Apparently, she heard my feet on the stairs because she turned to look at me and smiled.

“I feel weird not knowing your name,” I said. “My name’s Dani, in case you didn’t hear me in class.”

“I’m Jackie. Nice to meet you.”

As we pushed open the doors I said, “I haven’t gotten around to eating much today, so I’m glad we’re eating early.”

“They assign times for the women that will keep us separate from the men.”

“Oh, gotcha. That makes sense.”

Five of the women had congregated outside the double doors. Jackie said, “I’ll introduce you to the others.” She pointed to a dark brown-haired woman, dressed in jeans and a flannel shirt, and said, “This is Tina.” Pointed to an Asian woman, “this is Karen, and next to her is Sandra.” Sandra was a tall redhead with a warm smile and legs for miles. “This is Maria.” She pointed to a young Latina with shiny black hair and dark brown eyes. “I think you met Patty; she escorted you when you arrived.” I remembered Patty. “And that’s it, the gang.”

Where’s Tammy? She’s not coming to dinner? Is my roommate even a real person?

In unison the women greeted me, and then we strolled across the campus together to the mess hall. I was able to stay in the moment and notice the naked winter trees and dormant shrubs. On one side of the road was an abandoned four-story building. The chipped white paint, broken windows, and boards nailed across the door made the hair on my neck stand up. Past the grass on the other side of the road was a big open space. “Hey, Jackie, the dirt looks fresh in that lot. Was there a building there?”

“Yeah, about a week ago they tore down the old mental health building. Funny thing is, the guy who wrote *One Flew Over the Cuckoo’s Nest,* Ken Kesey, used to work there as an orderly. Nurse Ratchet was based on a real person he worked with. At least that’s what they say.”

Goosebumps spread up my arms, whether from the chilly air or the

Nurse Ratchet story, I wasn't sure. "Wow. A little piece of history for Menlo Park."

None of the other women seemed interested in commenting, so we continued our walk to the mess hall in silence. Though the air was cold, sweat ran down my back. *Must be the humidity*, I thought. *Yeah, it couldn't be that you're morbidly obese and out of shape.*

We passed the main building where I met my escort. I smelled chlorine, which seemed out of place. We rounded a corner, and Jackie looked over her shoulder to say, "This is the mess hall. It's no five-star restaurant, but it fills the void."

All seven of us entered a large gray room with long tables in rows end-to-end. We were the first to arrive in the mess hall to have dinner. "You were in the military," Jackie said. "It's pretty self-explanatory. Grab your tray and utensils and follow the line."

I chuckled nervously. "Okay, this brings back memories."

I let the others go in front of me. When I got to the food, through the glass I saw two supposedly edible concoctions in square metal bins. I opted for the less suspicious one, spaghetti, and grabbed a milk carton. I followed Jackie to a smaller section on the other side of a partition. There were two rectangular tables, pushed together, and eight chairs. "The men won't be here for 45 minutes, so we have plenty of time to eat," Jackie said.

The pasta was rubbery, the sauce in need of oregano, but the predictably tasteless meal filled my empty stomach. The seven of us ate in silence. I wanted to ask who was supposed to fill the empty chair, but I didn't know the rules yet. *Will every meal be this quiet? I hope not.*

The mystery of the empty chair was answered when I got back to my room. I opened the door and there sat a black-haired, heavy woman hunched over her desk, writing something. *This must be my roomie.* I stepped forward and said, "Hi, I'm Dani."

"I'm Tammy." She glanced at me briefly, then continued writing.

Okay, not a big talker. "The nurse told me you were going to be my big sister, but I'm not sure what that means."

"Yep."

I waited, but she didn't elaborate. *Great talk.* I gathered up my shower stuff and soldiered on. Getting clean and putting on my pajamas calmed me. I fell into bed. Amazingly, I slept.

I woke early, got dressed, and waited in the lobby downstairs for my big sister, Tammy. I figured I'd talk to her and ask questions at breakfast, but she was a no show. I sat in the chair stewing, confused about what my next move should be.

One of the other residents, Patty, invited me to walk with her to the mess hall. When I returned, Nurse Nancy told me I had an appointment with my coordinator, Maureen, and to follow her. My stomach had that hollow, jumpy feeling walking down the hall. "This is it," Nancy said, outside of an unmarked, closed door.

I knocked and heard a muffled voice say, "Come in."

I slowly opened the door and stepped inside to see a woman at her desk, facing the wall, with her back to me. "I have an appointment at 9:00," I said.

"Yes, please have a seat." The woman put down her pen and turned to face me. She wore a baby blue sweater and eyeglasses with black frames. Her brown bob framed her face. She pointed to the two barrel chairs on the opposite side of her desk, and I sat in the closest one. "I'm Maureen. I'll be your coordinator for your treatment. So, how was your first day?"

I detected a slight German accent which put me at ease. One of my closest coworkers from the hospital had been German. "Kind of confusing. I wasn't sure where I was supposed to be or what I was supposed to do. My big sister, Tammy, hasn't been helpful. Honestly, I'm kind of floundering, but Jackie was nice enough to step up. She introduced me to everyone and took me under her wing."

"I'm sorry to hear that. I'm glad Jackie helped. Maybe I'll just assign her as your big sister. Tammy is almost done with the program, so it would make sense for Jackie to take on that role. I apologize for not talking to you sooner, but I was dealing with a crisis at home." She smiled sheepishly. "Admissions typically go smoother than that."

"Oh, okay." I wasn't sure what to say.

"Well, I'm back now, and the first point of business is your schedule." She handed me a white, three-ring binder.

Just the word "schedule" relaxed me. I opened the binder and saw a printed schedule with my name on it. There was a weekly outline of all the classes. *Wish I had this yesterday! Oh well.*

"This notebook contains everything you will need for your classes. In the back there are blank pages for notes. The three main sections are labeled: Interpersonal Effectiveness Skills, Distress Tolerance Skills, and Mindfulness Skills. After you leave here, you can look through the notebook and get a better feel for the topics. I assure you by the end of your time here, you will be an expert."

"Sure," I said curtly, feeling overwhelmed again.

"If you look at your schedule, you'll notice the rest of the week you'll be in basic orientation classes, which are held in the men's building next door. They consist of goal setting, medication education, suicide prevention, and opiate overdose prevention. Your first class is today after lunch. I'll have Jackie walk you over."

I tried to ignore my erratic heartbeat at the mention of the men's facility. *Alone with strange men. Don't freak out. You're in a safe place. Just breathe.* "Okay. It's nice to have an idea of where I'm supposed to be."

"Of course it is. Sorry for the confusion yesterday, but I'm back now. I'll talk to Jackie about being your big sister. She'll be your resource regarding schedules, classes, passes, and the basic rules of our program. She'll also escort you to and from your classes. If you have any further questions, please feel free to come and talk to me. My door is always open."

I left her office with my gut even more jumpy than before. Sure, I finally had a schedule. But soon I would be in classes with a bunch of people I didn't know. *Remember you're here to get better, and better here than dead. You have to be strong for Terry and Ashten.*

Chapter 31

IN-VIVO

My first weekend in the trauma program seemed to last much longer than two days. Three women had passes to leave the facility, and one of them was Jackie. Though my basic orientation had been completed, I still needed to get through an "in-vivo" experience, whatever that meant, and show two weeks of drug free urine samples. The other four women kept to themselves, so watching TV, reading, and praying for the time to go faster got old fast. When Monday finally came, I sat with the group in my first class, in the same room where I introduced myself the week before.

"Dani," Carrie said, standing next to the blackboard. "Today we're planning in-vivos. The term in-vivo means practicing in real life. I want you to list three things you've avoided in the past. Then we'll create a safe way for you to experience them and prove to your body that you can be safe while doing these things. Take a look at this." She walked over and gave me a piece of paper.

The handout explained that people who experience trauma often stay away from situations that bring up bad memories or distressing feelings, otherwise known as avoidance, something I knew well. Avoidance worked for me. My anxiety seemed more tolerable when I didn't engage in things that freaked me out. Except I seemed to avoid more and more situations. I was stuck in a retreating pattern that prevented me from getting better and moving forward. My world had shrunk. I told myself I didn't care, but if that were true, I probably wouldn't have thought about ending my life.

"The goal of the in vivo exercise is to safely confront stressful situations with our counselors and peers present," Carrie clarified. "We start off with small victories and work our way up to tackling higher SUDS provoking situations. SUDS stands for the subjective units of distress scale from zero, no stress, to 100, the most stressful situations. We have you list your trigger situations and rate them from zero to 100. Then we start you in a lower SUDS situation, so you learn it's okay to be anxious because you're safe. You get to show yourself that your anxiety is manageable, that you can ride it out and complete uncomfortable tasks. The first thing you need to do is set a realistic goal and rate your SUDS."

Okay, there's a method to all of this. I think I'm getting it now.

My first goal was simple: Spend 30 minutes walking around the mall with my peers. The thought of being in a crowded public space sent my anxiety soaring. I rated my SUDS at 70. Carrie wrote all our tasks and SUDS on the chalkboard. After the in-vivo, we would come back and talk about the experience to decide if our perceived SUDS score was accurate.

We walked outside to get on the bus. Two counselors, a short, balding guy named Matt, and a slender, dark-haired woman named Ellen, waited next to the bus with their clipboards. They checked off our names as we filed in and found a seat. As the bus lumbered out of the parking lot, I counted 15 guys and seven of us. My roommate didn't come because she was filling out the paperwork to exit the program.

I took several calming breaths and forced myself to look out the window. We passed the Palo Alto Public Library, and I fantasized about hiding in a corner, escaping in a good book. Too soon, the bus pulled into the parking lot of an outdoor strip mall, and I gave myself a mental pep talk.

It's not that busy. Just complete your task. Stay present. You want a pass to be able to leave the campus, don't you? You can do this.

Matt and Ellen stood in front of the bus. "After 45 minutes," Ellen said, "we want you to come back here, at this exact location."

"Any questions?" Matt asked. Some of the men chattered amongst themselves, but no one raised their hand.

Our female cluster exited the bus and window shopped, walking together down the sidewalk. I was grateful not to have to go inside the stores on my first in-vivo. Daydreaming about getting an ice cream slowed my heart rate, so my heightened senses felt more manageable.

From my women's group in Bend, I'd learned to be intentional to focus on the here and now, so I turned my attention to the glorious sunshine. It was snowing in Bend. I was thankful to be warm. Being outside uplifted my spirits.

"Ah . . ." I stopped on the sidewalk and tilted my face upward. "Can you believe the weather here?"

No one answered me. The others kept walking. All of us seemed to be stuck in our own heads. I concentrated on the act of walking, soothed by the rhythmic sound of my feet on the pavement.

Jackie looked at her watch. "It's about time to head back," she said. We all nodded and turned toward the bus without speaking. After everyone was accounted for, the bus returned to Menlo Park. Back in the classroom, Carrie sat in the circle across from me and asked, "How did you feel about your in-vivo, Dani?"

"Well, at first, I felt sick and kind of jittery. But after we walked around a while, I felt better." I glanced at the other six women. "I don't know how to say this, so I'm just going to say it. I wish there was a way we could feel safer communicating with each other. I know I'm the new girl, but I think it'd be helpful for all of us to let down our guard a little and try to share what we're experiencing while we're doing our in-vivos. Just a thought. Anyway, I rated my SUDS at 70 before we left, but it turned out they were more like 30."

"I think Dani brings up a great point," Carrie said. "Sometimes with trauma it feels like you're the only one experiencing these emotions, but if you allow yourselves to be vulnerable, you might find you're experiencing similar thoughts and emotions. Just something to think about." Carrie sent me a quick smile. "Great work and thanks for sharing your idea. Can you identify some of the emotions that came up for you?"

"Well . . ." I sat up straighter and took a breath. "I was nervous, but then I settled into walking on the sidewalk in a public place. When Jackie said time was up, and we could go back to the bus, I felt proud that I completed the task without running away or finding something to eat or somewhere to hide." The realization caught in my throat, and tears began to form. "I haven't been proud of myself in a long time. It feels weird."

"Good work, Dani."

Carrie moved on to the next person. I started to cry and wanted to leave, but I didn't want to be rude and get up when someone else was talking. When the group ended, I went straight to my room and flopped onto my bed. I heard a knock on the door and sat up.

Carrie poked her head in. "Hey, Dani, just checking to make sure everything's okay."

"Yeah, just exhausted."

"Emotions are hard. They can be very tiring."

"Yeah, I guess. I'm just used to taking a nap to block them out."

"Here we call that avoidance."

I laughed uncomfortably. "Yep, that makes sense."

"We want you to stay engaged with your emotions. Ride them out. Don't nap. Maybe you could do some homework or go downstairs. After every in-vivo, the kitchen sends boxed dinners. Then you can have a special treat—an hour at the pool in the main building. Our team of psychologists and therapists thought the pool would be a great way to unwind after tough in-vivo days. I hope you think so too."

I scooted to the edge of my bed. "I thought I smelled chlorine. I love the water, and I brought a swimsuit. That sounds amazing."

"Perfect. So, what are you going to do?"

"I'll go downstairs, eat, then go swimming."

"Good choice."

A glimmer of light seemed to pierce the darkness inside my mind. I'd made it through my first in-vivo and survived.

Chapter 32

Working It Out

Walking down the hall and down the stairs, I visualized floating weightless in the pool. At the bottom of the stairs, I passed the medication room on the left, and the therapists' and two doctors' offices. Though no one sat on the three couches or in the four armchairs in the large community room on my right, a sit-com rerun played on the TV. Off the community room, I entered the small kitchen where the mess hall delivered the boxed meals.

Patty, Karen, Tina, and Sandra all silently ate their dinners at the round, four-person table. None of them acknowledged me. Since all the chairs were taken, I grabbed my box and headed to the TV room, feeling sensitive and uncomfortable that no one ever talked. In-vivos were tough on everyone, but I opened up, hoping others would do the same. I didn't want them to feel forced into sharing, but I wasn't going to stop encouraging them to talk either.

I collapsed into one of the armchairs with a sigh, shoved down the tasteless turkey sandwich, and enjoyed the chips. I held onto the apple, to eat after I swam, and returned to the kitchen to throw away my trash. Karen pointed at the cabinet to the right of the refrigerator and said, "I don't know if anyone told you, but that's your cupboard where you can put snacks you pick up on the outside—that is, once you can leave campus. There's also a space in the refrigerator for you on the lower shelf on the right."

"Oh, thanks. Good to know." I went to the fridge and deposited my apple in my designated spot. "Are we headed to the pool then?"

"Yeah. It'll only be you, me, and Tina," Karen said. "Going to the pool isn't mandatory, and not everyone likes the water. Let's go grab our stuff and then walk to the main building."

After an awkwardly quiet trip to the pool together, I jumped in, swam to the surface, and floated on my back. The warm water caressed my skin and slowly melted some of the tension in my muscles. I turned and stretched my arms and legs into a relaxed freestyle across the pool, enjoying the weightlessness in both my mind and body, my best experience, so far, in the trauma recovery program.

Over the next couple of days, I began to relax into going to class, doing homework, and eating meals with the other women, though we still didn't say much. Experiencing emotions, rather than shoving them down or sleeping through them, started to seem doable—until my first strength and toning class. Sure, working out had been a normal thing for me, but that was before I gained 100-plus pounds. I had tried a CrossFit class in Bend and went home with a strained medial meniscus in my left knee. Given I had packed on even more weight since then, I anticipated limping back to my room with another injury.

The trek to the gym, next to the main building, passed in a blur of barely contained panic. The four other women ahead of me seemed unfazed. As soon as my feet hit the black mats that covered the floor, a buff guy standing in front of a mirrored wall, staring at his phone, barked: "Find a place on the mat so we can get started. I don't tolerate laziness or tardiness."

My eyes raced around the room to see if the other women were affected by his tone, but they obediently found a place on the mats. I wanted to ride one of the two stationary bikes next to the windows instead of working out with that meathead. Even better, there were rowing machines against the opposite wall. I hadn't been on one of those in years, and the idea of settling into a rhythm with a pair of oars seemed like a much better idea than doing a CrossFit class.

The muscle man wore a baseball cap. The bill rose when he looked up from his phone. My body stiffened. He pointed at me. "You, stand there."

My eyes followed his finger to the front row in the right corner. My stomach lurched. My chest constricted. My heart pounded in my ears. I ran out of the room and heard one of the women say, "Dani, where are you going?"

To a safe place.

Mid-flight, I realized I was headed back to the women's building. At the door, I punched the button on the intercom several times. The door buzzed. I threw it open and ran up the stairs to my room. Lightheaded, I flopped onto my bed and forced myself to count eight calming breaths. When that didn't help, I stripped off my clothes and turned on the cold water in the shower. I squealed under the spray, but the shock to my system helped my mind to reset. When my heart stopped racing, I toweled off and got dressed. By then, it was almost time for my next class, so I picked up my notebook and walked slowly down the hall.

The four other women in the CrossFit class eyed me suspiciously when I walked into the quiet classroom and sat in the circle. Carrie walked over and said, "Dani, I heard you ran out of strength and toning. What happened?"

I fiddled with the notebook in my lap because I couldn't look at her. "I'm not sure. I just had to get away."

"After class, can you come to my office? Maybe we can figure out what happened together."

"Okay."

I don't remember what she talked about in class because my head was filled with dread around having to go to her office afterwards. When the session ended, I continued to doodle in my notebook until everyone else had left. I thought about "forgetting" to stop by Carrie's office and going back to my room, but eventually, I walked across the hall and knocked on her door.

"Come in." Carrie gazed at me from her desk. Timmy, a black lab, the mascot for the women's Trauma Recovery Program, who doubled as a therapy dog, sat next to her. I settled in the chair across from her, and Timmy appeared at my side, putting his head in my lap. I stroked his soft ears and dissolved into a full-on, snot-dripping cry.

"What's going on for you right now?" Carrie asked.

"I miss my dogs and my family, I guess."

She handed me a tissue. "What happened in the gym today, Dani?"

"I think . . ." I choked, blew my nose, and tried again. "I think the instructor reminded me of my ex-husband and some of the male soldiers I knew. When he gave orders, I couldn't breathe. I had to get out of there."

"Okay, what exactly reminded you of your ex-husband?"

"The baseball cap he wore. He looked like Gary too. When we got divorced, I pretty much wrote him off. He cheated on me, so I packed up my daughter, and we moved back home."

"That must've been hard on you."

"Yeah, it really made me mad that he could do that to our daughter. How could he have done that to her?"

"I think maybe this would be a great opportunity to work on some of those feelings around your ex-husband. I also think it'd be a good idea for you to talk to the instructor and let him know what happened."

"I really don't want to go to his class. I've gotten hurt doing CrossFit before. Can't I just work out at the gym on my own?"

"Well, this is part of the program. He needs to know what triggered you. Maybe it would help him change his behavior. And he can modify the exercises for you."

"Okay," I said, though I wasn't okay with going back to that class or talking to that guy. *But I'm here to get better,* I told myself as I stroked my thighs. *They must have dealt with this before. You have to trust them. You've tried everything else. Just listen and do.*

Before starting the program, my all-or-nothing thinking pattern wouldn't have allowed me to go back to the class, or even to the gym, and I definitely wouldn't have been able to talk to the instructor. But two days after the impromptu meeting with Carrie, I strolled over to the free weights, near the instructor, and said, "I was wondering, can I talk to you?"

"Sure." He replaced a 30-pound weight back on the rack and looked at me.

His eyes, so much like Gary's, gave me a start, but I pushed on. "I'm sorry about the other day. You reminded me of my ex-husband—your hat and the tone of your voice. I got triggered and panicked." I swallowed hard and continued. "I'm not used to talking about things like this, so I don't really know what to do. Also, I was worried because the last time I did CrossFit, I injured my knee. And I'm heavier now than I was then, so I'm afraid I'll hurt myself."

His green eyes softened, unlike Gary's. "Thank you for being so honest. I'm sorry about triggering you. Is there anything I can do to make it easier?"

"Maybe talk to us instead of giving orders, and possibly lose the hat? And could you help me modify some of the movements?"

His face broke into a wide smile that reached his eyes. "You bet."

"Thanks so much." *More than you know.*

I chose a spot on the mat feeling lighter. Occasionally, he gave examples of how to modify the exercises, and I felt like I had accomplished something important when I finished the class. I had a voice, and it was heard. I wasn't made fun of or laughed out of the gym. This was a win. I was proud of myself for facing my fears, excited about my new sense of empowerment.

At the next class, our instructor was hatless and greeted us warmly. He played some great music, and everyone enjoyed the workout. He spoke to us instead of yelling orders. It was a better environment for everyone.

The following day, we had to get ready for another in-vivo experience. My next one sounded so simple: Sit alone and spend time with myself—no distractions, no avoidance, no isolation, just silence. Even the thought of being still like that flashed images of the rapes, burnt bodies, and stepping on the landmine behind my eyes. My hands started to sweat on my way to class. *Not yet. Don't open the vault. You must stay in control!*

Chapter 33

UNSETTLED SILENCE

I walked into the familiar classroom. The chairs faced the blackboard in a semi- circle. My legs felt weak and rubbery, so I sat on the closest chair at the end, and my knees bounced nervously.

"Dani, what is your goal for your in-vivo today?" Carrie asked.

I exhaled loudly, annoyed that she always seemed to pick me to share first. "I'm going to sit by myself on a bench outside the mall, without any distractions."

"What are your avoidant behaviors?"

"Eating, talking, and playing games on my phone."

"Okay, so you're going to sit on the bench alone, without your phone or any food for the entire in-vivo, correct?"

"That's correct." I swallowed around the lump in my throat and felt heat flash through my whole body. My arms had turned red, so I figured the rest of me looked flushed too.

"What are you thinking about?" Carrie asked me.

"I'm scared. I don't want to do this. When I'm alone, I don't feel safe. I feel like something bad is going to happen."

"Did something bad happen to you when it was quiet?"

"Yes." An image of my boot on the landmine filled my vision and I gasped.

"Can you tell us a little bit about what happened?"

"When I was in the Persian Gulf War, I volunteered to take food and water to citizens in Kuwait, and during the mission, I stepped on a landmine." My voice raised several pitches as I continued. "Time seemed to stop. I didn't want to breathe because I was terrified that if I moved, I'd get blown up."

"How long did you stay there?"

"I'm not sure. It seemed like forever, but it was probably only a couple of minutes. I didn't think I'd live, or if I did, it would be without my legs."

"Dani, I want you to focus on your safe place. Try to slow your breathing. Inhale for four seconds, hold, then exhale for four seconds."

I pictured Belknap Hot Springs—my family, the secret garden, the colorful flowers and smelling their perfume in the air, the burbling of the brook, the feel of the grass on my bare feet, the warmth of Terry's hand holding mine, the softness of Ashten's hair as I stroked it with my other hand. I focused on my breathing and felt the tension in my body release. My mind returned to the room.

"How're you feeling?" Carrie asked.

"Better." I plucked a tissue from the box on the table behind me and dried my tears. Several of my peers' eyes had gone wide with despair. "I'm sorry for freaking out over the landmine thing. It came up and just tumbled out of my mouth."

Everyone nodded and one woman said, "We've all been there."

"This in vivo might challenge you," Carrie said, "but the goal is to let yourself feel whatever you need to feel, without running away, pushing it down, or ignoring it. Just try to remain in the moment, no matter how uncomfortable you feel. Remember, the anxiety curve takes about 45 minutes. Ride the wave of anxiety so you can prove to yourself that you can be uncomfortable and safe at the same time, without using a 'safety behavior.'"

"This should be fun," I joked, trying to make light of the situation. After class, I went to my room to shove some chocolates into my mouth to subdue the butterflies in my gut. I opened the second drawer in my dresser where I kept my stash of goodies. *No, I just said I wouldn't do that in class.* Staring at a pack of peanut M&Ms, I thought: *Walk away. Just go to the bus.* Shame warmed my cheeks, and I left my room empty handed.

On the crowded bus, my stomach somersaulted and sweat trickled down my back. Jackie was my seat partner and tried to make small talk, but I couldn't focus. I muttered an apology and stared out the window.

When we arrived at the mall, everyone went their separate ways. I went in search of a place to sit alone with my thoughts, memories, and fears. Outside of a furniture store, under a tree, I found a concrete bench.

Sitting on the bench for less than a minute, my anxiety and sense of dread revved and sped into overdrive. My knees bounced. I shifted from butt cheek to butt cheek. I clasped and unclasped my hands wanting to bolt, to find somewhere no one could see me, but I forced myself to remain on my perch

I glanced at my watch every few seconds. *Please God, help me get through this,* I prayed. *Help me ride the anxiety curve to prove I can feel uncomfortable and remain safe.* I watched and waited for the world to come crashing around me, but it didn't.

What do you see, hear, and smell? I glanced up into the tree and noticed it was full of birds, chirping away, unaware of my agitated state. A few fluffy clouds dotted the otherwise blue sky. I watched as the white puffs drifted slowly to my left and remembered finding animal shapes in the clouds when I was younger. *How long has it been since I just looked at the sky, without being terrified I'd see a scud missile?*

My focus shifted back to the tree where I began to count the different kinds of birds. Some were bright blues and greens. Others were drab browns or grays. Some squawked or screamed. Others sang or tweeted. Many flitted from branch to branch, then stretched their wings and rested.

My heart rate began to slow. My breathing settled into a steady rhythm. My hands unclenched and relaxed in my lap. The sun warmed my legs. I noticed red, yellow, and bright pink flowers in the planters along the sidewalk.

The alarm on my watch jarred me. I had survived 45 minutes alone and proved to myself that I was safe in my unsettled silence. After giving myself a mental pat on the back, I pictured myself floating in the warm pool, my reward for a job well done. We had seven days to recover and set up for the next in-vivo, and I knew I could manage whatever scary task was assigned.

Later that evening, after we ate our boxed dinners, Patty, Karen, Tina, Sandra, and I walked toward the pool. Karen turned to me on the sidewalk and said, "Dani, I want you to know I think you're very brave for standing up to the gym instructor, and for facing your fear of being alone today too."

My eyes widened with surprise. "Thanks, Karen. I think all of us are brave for just being here and trying to get better."

"For real," Patty said. Tina and Sandra agreed.

I felt something shift among us, maybe a deeper connection. I didn't want to read too much into it, but I chalked up the short conversation as a win for the moment. Feeling encouraged, I decided I would offer as much acknowledgement and support as I could for the remainder of our time together in the program.

The next week, my in-vivo challenge was to eat by myself in a restaurant, without looking up the location or menu ahead of time. I was to get into an Uber, refrain from talking to the driver, and sit in uncomfortable silence. As a nurse, I had been trained to make others feel comfortable, but I knew nothing of how to do this for myself. Nervous talk had helped me to control the conversation so I could avoid my feelings.

When the Uber pulled up, a guy with dark hair and a mustache asked if I was Danielle, which I verified. Then I sat in silence in the back seat. My stomach churned, and I clasped my shaky hands in my lap. *He's just a man doing his job. You're fine. Just watch the traffic.*

I stared out the window without seeing. The 15-minute ride felt like an eternity. Eventually, he stopped at the curb. I had arrived unharmed and safe.

Inside the restaurant, cheerful Latin music played in the background. The host near the door led me to a booth. I sat on my hands while a young boy placed chips and salsa in front of me. I ate a couple of chips and wondered what to do with myself. A slender blond lady came over with a menu and told me her name was Wendy, and she'd be my server. I opened the menu but couldn't process the words. Wendy returned with her paper and pen. "Have you decided?"

I said the first thing that came to mind. "Uh . . . yeah. I'd like chicken enchiladas."

"Good choice." She scribbled on her pad. "Would you like something to drink besides water?"

"I'm good. Thanks."

"Okay." Wendy nodded and hustled to another table.

Now what? I noticed two couples at nearby tables, but I couldn't hear what they were saying. While I waited, I decided when my meal arrived, I would try to eat more slowly. In the Army, we ate as fast as possible, and in nursing, breaks often got cut short when one of our patients needed something, so my shoveling in food continued.

When my enchiladas came, I tried to identify the seasonings and pay attention to the textures. For the first time in 20-plus years it took me longer than five minutes to finish my meal. A half-hour later, I paid my bill, thanked Wendy for serving me, and summoned an Uber to come and get me. While I waited, I took pictures of the multi-colored pansies in the planters outside with my cell phone.

Resting my back against the seat in an SUV, I enjoyed the ride witout the stress of having to carry on a conversation—another victory to add to my list. I began to see progress in becoming comfortable in my own skin, something I hadn't felt in 33 years.

The more I practiced self-care, the more comfortable I became with silence when I was alone. I learned to enjoy periods I spent by myself, particularly when I was outside. Bird watching became both soothing and entertaining. Increasingly, I noticed the beauty in the surrounding plants and trees, rather than being hypervigilant about watching for people coming and going.

After that third in-vivo, I was able to reconnect with painting and writing poetry. My creative outlets, neglected for decades, became regular activities during my free time in the program. I had worried I wouldn't remember how to paint, but I decided it didn't matter. With a paintbrush in my hand, my mind entered a quiet place where time stood still. My body and mind worked together —no judgment or agenda, just peace.

I shared my revelations with Carrie in her office and asked, "Do you think my husband Terry and daughter Ashten could visit this weekend? And I'd like my mom and dad to come too. My family has always been a huge support for me, and I would really like to see them."

Carrie put her elbow on her desk and propped her chin on her hand. "Let's give you one more week. I'm excited for you that you are feeling so much better, but sometimes there are ups and downs. If you feel ready to see them next weekend, we can make that happen."

"Okay, thanks." I left her office with a smile on my face because I knew in my heart, I was ready.

One of my goals in the program was to become the best version of myself in mind, body, and spirit. In writing poetry and painting, all three aspects of me began to grow. I was awarded a pass for the weekend to leave campus, and I felt closer to God than I had in a long time, so I found a church in walking distance from the facility where I could attend a Sunday service. At the group meeting on Friday, I asked if any of the other women would like to join me at church, but everyone declined.

Having a companion to come with me would have been nice, but my anticipation was too great to let being alone stop me from going. When

Sunday came, I walked to the cheery white building in Menlo Park where huge rhododendron bushes grew on both sides of the entrance. The moment I stepped into the building, I felt I had come home. The smell of wooden benches and pine scented cleaner reminded me of the Lutheran church of my youth in Springfield, Oregon.

The piano began to play, and people started to sing a familiar traditional hymn. The pastor gave a sermon about grace and fellowship that filled me with light and love that I hadn't felt in years. My usual restless energy faded into the background. I embraced a sense of peace that I hadn't believed was possible.

On my walk back to the facility, I realized being immersed in that crowd of people hadn't stressed me out. In fact, I had a sense of belonging. Before the program, I would have been soaked in sweat and doing whatever I could to stave off panic. My chemistry had changed.

Listening to upbeat music from my earbuds, I walked back to the facility and kept on going for two more miles. There was a spring in my step, and I praised God for helping me to be strong and for guiding me to this amazing program. From that day on, taking a two- to four-mile stroll in the afternoon, in multiple laps around the compound, while listening to happy music, became part of my daily routine. At times, my mind wanted to return to the old negative dialogue, but I interrupted those thoughts and replaced them with positive ones.

My heart leapt when I remembered my family was coming for a visit on the weekend. It was perfect timing because I needed a big dose of family love just before I started my prolonged exposure portion of the program. I couldn't help but wonder: *Will they notice changes in me?*

Chapter 34

PROLONGED EXPOSURE (P.E.)

I waited anxiously outside of the facility, my head swiveling left and right, looking for Terry's white Dodge Ram. When it finally came around the corner and into the back parking lot, I ran over and threw my arms around him while Ashten, Mom, and Dad unloaded from the truck. My cheeks ached from grinning so big.

"I am so happy to see you guys! You have no idea." I hugged Ashten and gazed into her eyes. "I've missed you, Peanut."

"I missed you too, Mom."

"I love you so much."

Ashten looked away, but I caught her smile out of the corner of my eye.

Next to Ashten, my mom waited. "Thanks for making the long trek. I am really glad to see you." I put my arms around Mom, and she kissed my cheek.

Then I walked to the other side of the car and hugged Dad. "Hope the trip was okay."

"Yeah, no problem," Terry said, reaching for my hand. "You look good."

"Do you want a tour before we go to the hotel?"

"Sure," they all said in unison. After a quick lap to check out the downstairs, because only patients and employees were allowed upstairs, I introduced them to Jackie and Patty, sitting outside at the picnic table. Then we loaded into the truck and headed to San Francisco for the weekend.

On Saturday, the five of us strolled alongside the marina, took a boat out to Alcatraz, and had lunch at the Pier Market Seafood Restaurant. Walking back to the truck, my dad said, "I want to know what they're giving you here. You seem so calm, even with the crowds." He laughed. "I think I need to come here and get some help."

"They've taken me off all my meds except for one. I don't have the anxiety I used to around crowds. In the program, they teach us how to cope. They give us tools."

"Well, whatever they're doing, it's working," Dad said, and everyone else agreed.

"You seem lighter, not as stressed," Mom added.

"I feel lighter. I'm glad I came here. I really think it's helping."

Terry put his arm around me. "I'm proud of you, honey."

Ashten nodded. "Yeah, Mom, me too."

"Thanks." I wiped away tears of gratitude for our time together as well as for the change I felt inside.

On Sunday afternoon as I hugged each one of them goodbye, for the first time I could remember, I truly felt their love. Tears of joy ran down my cheeks, and I saw the tension on their faces. "Hey, I'm okay. Allowing myself to feel emotions is good for me, for all of us." I chuckled watching them all release a breath. "I love you all so much. I can't wait to get home. See you in a couple of months."

I watched the Ram truck leave the parking lot and turn the corner. I already missed them, which was much better than the numbness I used to feel. And spending time with them gave me more incentive to do the hard work that was coming. *Okay, now I can deal with my war trauma.*

Monday morning, my alarm went off, and I got ready for my first prolonged exposure, or P.E., experience. Walking under the heavy gray clouds to go to breakfast made me uneasy. After I forced down my oatmeal, along with my emotional turmoil, I entered the back office, south of the TV room, on time for my appointment. In the doorway, I waited to make eye contact with my counselor, Erica. She looked up from her paperwork and said, "Hi, Dani. Go ahead and have a seat."

Erica's office was smaller than Carrie's. A padded brown chair stood on the other side of her desk. I sat in the chair and reminded myself to take a couple of deep breaths.

"Good morning. How're you doing?" Erica asked as she arranged stacks of papers in small piles on her desk.

"I felt anxious and weird walking over here, with it being so dark outside, but other than that I'm okay.

Erica smirked. "Yeah, I would much rather have sunshine, myself. So, today we are going to start your prolonged exposure therapy, or P.E. Do you know what P.E. is?"

"Kinda. I've done a little research. P.E. therapy is the reason I chose to come here."

"Excellent. The first two sessions, we are going to go through this packet. Before we proceed, I want to make sure you understand the therapy and what is expected of you." She pushed a stack of stapled pages across the desk. "After this session, I want you to write at least two goals for yourself in regard to P.E. Next week, we are going to focus on your why and set up a plan. We're also going to go over some breathing techniques to aid you in times of distress. Before our next visit, I need you to download the P.E. app on your cell phone. We will use the app to document our visits, and you can use it to do your homework. This week is more about getting to know each other and feeling comfortable in this space. Does that make sense?"

"Sure, I need to be able to trust you in order to open up and work through my trauma."

"Exactly. Look over the packet, answer the questions, and set some goals before our next session."

"Okay, sounds good."

The following Wednesday, I sat in the brown padded chair, and we began the process. Erica turned her desk chair to face me and said, "We will record every session so you can use it for homework purposes. Let's open up the app and start recording."

I tried to ignore the butterflies in my stomach as I fumbled for my phone in my backpack, opened the app, and pushed the record button.

"I noticed the sky was dark outside again today," Erica said. "How're you feeling?"

"Praying for the sun to come out." I laughed. "Other than that, I'm fine."

Erika smiled and looked up from her notepad. "You were supposed to identify some goals for your P. E. therapy. Did you come up with any?"

"I did. My goals are to decrease my discomfort with my traumatic memories, get closer with my family, and be more personal with my peers and those around me. I also want to integrate my mind, body, and spirit to feel like a whole me."

Erica's eyebrows lifted. "Those are very powerful goals. To achieve them, we need you to listen to this recording after every session, to help you complete your assignments, and listen again every night until the next session. You need to do the work in a quiet place with no distractions. I know I'm asking a lot of you, but your homework is very important so we can meet these goals for you. Does that make sense?"

"Absolutely."

After the session, I went upstairs, sat at the desk in my room, and pulled out my *Anxiety Relief Coloring Book for Adults.* Immersed in the patterns and textures, and the movement of my hand filling in the shapes with colors that pleased me, my mind began to relax. When I felt ready, I pulled out my cell phone and opened "Homework 1" on my P.E. app.

My first assignment was to listen to the recording of the session, take notes on how I felt about what I heard, and write anything else that popped into my mind. I put in my ear buds, pressed play, and heard

Erica's voice: "The exposure, or 'imaginal', you will continue for 45 minutes, the period for the curve of anxiety. The goal is for you to see that, over time, your anxiety will decrease. Trauma can rob you of a lot of different areas of your life."

"I know," said my voice. "When I look in the mirror, sometimes I feel like I don't know who that person is."

"I know that's very painful, so let's talk about avoidance. It can come in many forms, besides opting out of doing things. Sometimes your body can become sick—like you might get a headache on the day you need to work on your trauma. Or you might forget to do your homework. Don't judge your avoidance; it's part of your diagnosis. When it comes up, we know it's PTSD. As a team, we can problem solve and help you get back on track."

"Can avoidance actually affect my memory?"

"Yes, when trauma occurs, there may be gaps in your memory because certain aspects of the event get coded under a different system. Your memory kind of has a filing system, and a traumatic event doesn't get filed properly. The idea is to refile the event so you can pull it out when you need to and put it back when you need to—without the event jumping out at you randomly and surprising you."

"Wow, I'm hopeful. This sounds like hard work, but I'm ready."

"Good. Now let's talk about the trauma—not all of it, just a two-minute summary."

"Okay, I volunteered to take food and water to citizens in Kuwait. We were on Highway 80 and saw war remnants—destruction, dark skies, the air thick with the smell of oil from the burning wells that Saddam Hussein had lit on fire. We went through Khafji, and I stepped on a landmine. I worked on that with cognitive processing therapy. There were burned-out cars and bodies. I was with soldiers I didn't know, and I didn't understand their lingo. They were all guys, except for my friend Sharon, who I talked into coming with us. I spoke out when one of the guys kicked a burnt human head across the street, and he threatened me. When we finally got to Kuwait, they started selling the food and water instead of giving it away. I was pissed that they were taking money from those desperate people. It was a really long, bad day. Smells are hard—diesel, burning flesh. I had to stop working as a nurse because of the cautery and the person, the body . . ." The words caught in my throat, and I could no longer speak.

Erica sat up in her chair. "Okay, I'm going to pull you out. It sounds like the mission was partly planned and some was unplanned. Did you get to Kuwait and then go back?"

"Yes, we stopped a lot on the way back to the base. I think I went to sleep. My memory is sketchy. I'm not sure what I did. I might've talked to my sergeant, but I don't really remember."

"Did you report the incident?"

"No, I didn't." I tossed up my hand. "Where would I even start? I was only a specialist. The guys were all sergeants."

"So, the men you were with were of a higher rank. I'm sure that changed the power dynamic."

"Yes, and being a woman, I didn't want to be the whistleblower."

"Did you have to see them again?"

"No, Sharon and I moved to the barge—the floating death trap. We always said it'd be an easy way to take out a lot of soldiers at once—just drop a bomb on the barge, and there you go."

"I can see by your labored breathing and flushed face, this road trip to Kuwait brings up a lot of emotions. Who do you find yourself blaming for it?"

"Me. Had I not volunteered to go, I wouldn't have suffered through those experiences, and my friend that reluctantly agreed to go with me wouldn't have seen all that death either."

"It sounds like the whole mission wasn't great, but we want to pick a start and stop point."

"The highway could be a start point."

"Where do you think we should end?"

"After I survived the land mine, and we headed to Kuwait."

"There's a concept we talk about called 'moral injury', where you feel you've been part of, or involved in, or witnessed something different from what you feel is right or wrong, or fair."

"I felt like there was moral injury when that soldier disrespected that corpse by kicking the head across the street. That whole interaction brought up a bunch of stuff. The biggest question was: Are we safe? And then I wondered: Who did this? I didn't know until later that it was us who bombed the highway. I thought the attack came from the enemy. You've said that trauma can piggy-back trauma. The Highway 80 and Kuwait incidents piggy-backed the trauma I suffered while being bombed at the port."

Erica nodded slowly. "One of our biggest tasks in this therapy is separating the now from then. Your brain has jumbled the time frames together, so the intensity feels the same now as it did back then. The way to disentangle it is to experience different outcomes and show yourself that the present is not the same as the past. You mentioned when you went to Kuwait, the sky was dark, and you've also told me dark days here make you uneasy."

I'd never consciously made that connection before. "Yes, on gray days, I feel anxious, afraid, and unsafe. I try to remind myself that we need dark clouds for rain because we need the water."

Her brows rose with approval. "So, you're already doing some of this work in your head, breaking up the then and now."

"I guess I am. I didn't even notice."

Over the next several weeks, I didn't hold anything back. I started to feel bad about not hanging out with the other women in the program, but I knew my time was coming to an end. Still, they forgave me.

On my last night before I headed back home, we had a pizza party and painted our nails. We gossiped and giggled until our hearts were full. When I went to bed that night, I reflected on the entire 12 weeks.

I had challenged my memories, beliefs, and courage. Before the program, I felt I didn't deserve compassion. By then, I knew that not only did I deserve to both give and receive compassion and love, but they were integral to my well-being.

I also finally internalized that I needed to cut myself some slack and acknowledge I did the best I could under the circumstances. Most importantly, I realized I wasn't responsible for the devastation and destruction I experienced and witnessed. Surviving the land mine created an opening for me to have greater appreciation for myself, spiritually and intellectually.

My brain felt like a switch had flipped. As a caregiver, I'd placed others' needs ahead of my own, but I discovered my needs and wants were important too. Once my needs got met, I was in a much better position to help others. I was ready to add spontaneity and flexibility back into my life. I felt rejuvenated and excited for the future, something I hadn't felt in quite some time.

After being gone for three months, I hoped my family could handle the new me. I underestimated how hard the transition would be, from the protected environment of the treatment facility back to real life. Not to mention, our lives were about to be turned inside out by an ugly truth that Ashten had been hiding for years.

Chapter 35

ASHTEN'S TRUTH

Driving Ashten to see her counselor, Natasha, my legs shook from tension. Ashten started working with Natasha when she was 12, for four years at that point. Terry and I began taking her to counseling, hoping to curb her angry outbursts between listless bouts of depression—like mother, like daughter. After the 12-week program, I felt better equipped to be a good mentor, but I sensed an underlying problem. At a stoplight, I silently prayed: *Please, God, help Natasha ease Ashten's suffering.*

When we walked into the office, Natasha, a petite brunette with long curly hair and kind green eyes said, "Hey, good to see you, Dani. How was your experience at the trauma facility?"

"Really good. I learned a lot about how to take care of myself so I can be a better mom, wife, and human being."

Natasha glanced at my daughter. "I'm so glad to hear that because Ashten wants to talk to you about something that came up in our counseling sessions, if that's okay with you."

Whoa. That doesn't sound good. "Okay." My hands trembled, so I shoved them into my jacket pockets.

"Follow me to my office."

Walking down the hallway, neither Ashten nor I looked at one another. Natasha turned her chair away from her desk and pointed to the two puffy recliners next to the window. Ashten and I heeded her direction, and I sat with my hands folded in my lap.

Natasha's brows furrowed. "Ashten and I have been working on some things that happened in her past. She told me you seemed much better and thought you could handle some information to help you understand what is going on with her."

I clasped my hands a little tighter. "Yes, I am in a much better place and would like to understand."

"Over the last couple months, Ashten and I have been using EMDR, and we've discovered that when Ashten was younger, she experienced sexual assault, not once but twice. She wanted you to know but felt more comfortable sharing these experiences with my help."

I inhaled sharply, and tears came before I could get a handle on the shock.

"Are you okay, Dani?" *People seemed to ask me that a lot over the years.*

"Yes," I said, though I could barely breathe.

"One of the assaults occurred at your home and included high school boys, and the second happened in a daycare situation outside of your home. They both occurred around the age of five. I'm not going to go into detail. This is Ashten's story, and it's up to her whether she wants to divulge more."

I wiped the tears from my face. "I agree. I won't push."

"As a licensed professional, I have to report this to the authorities. I'm sure you know that since you were a nurse."

"Yes, I do know that." I looked at Ashten to see her wiping her cheeks with her sleeve.

"An officer will get in touch with you via phone to schedule a time to come to your house. Then you'll need to make an appointment for Ashten to go to the KIDS Center for a more in-depth interview." Natasha swiveled her chair, grabbed a business card from her desk, and handed it to me.

With my free hand, I reached for Ashten, and she grabbed it. I held her hand tightly while Natasha went over some more information. I didn't hear all the words, and though I felt far away, I did my best to stay present, for both Ashten and me. At the end of the session, Ashten and I walked silently to the car. When we closed our doors, still teary, I turned to her. "Are you okay?"

She shrugged. "I guess so. Are you?"

"Not really, but we will get through this together, okay?"

"Okay." She turned her head and stared out her window.

I put the car in drive and made it home on autopilot. In the garage, I turned off the engine and asked, "Can I discuss this with your dad, with Terry? Or do you want to talk to him about it?"

She gazed at her lap. "You can tell him. I don't think I can."

"Okay, I love you. You know that, right? You are a strong person. You can get through this. But if you're not ready to work on this now, you don't have to."

She looked up at me. "Well, I saw you get better, so I think I can do it too. I want to do this."

"I'll be with you every step of the way, Peanut."

When we walked into the house, the dogs greeted us, and Ashten said, "I'm going upstairs to play a game on PlayStation."

I nodded with a fake smile, that I hoped she couldn't see through, and watched her climb the stairs. When she was out of sight, I walked straight to the pantry. I ripped open a bag of chips, snagged a candy bar, and shoved chips into my mouth on the way to the living room.

How could this happen? Not my daughter! This isn't fair! She was just a child. I should have protected her, kept her safe. I failed to do the one thing I was supposed to as her mother.

Dropping onto the couch, I tipped back my head to catch all the crumbs from the bottom of the bag. But the visceral ache throughout my body didn't subside. So I tried to bury the pain and panic under the chocolate that melted on my tongue—one bite after the other until the last one disappeared. Still, no help.

What the hell am I doing? This is the old me. I know now that whatever happened in the past, I did the best I could. I didn't even know about this until today. Focus on Ash. Make sure she's okay.

The empty bag and candy wrapper lay in my lap, accusingly. I rolled up the chip bag and crumpled the wrapper in my fist. *Ashten deserves better. Try to eat healthier. Everything will be fine.*

The next week, on a Tuesday afternoon, Ashten was interviewed by a female police officer. She took pictures of the upstairs, where one of the assaults occurred, and talked with Terry, Ashten, and me about both events. We didn't have much information, but we shared what we could. Before the officer left, she reminded us to call the KIDS Center to make an appointment.

Two days later, Ashten and I went to the KIDS Center, and the officer met us there. An interviewer escorted Ashten to a different room, and I waited in the lobby. I tried to read a book but couldn't concentrate on the words. I took out my cell phone and scrolled through Facebook but couldn't process the photos in front of me. An excruciating two hours later, Ashten appeared in the lobby, and the interviewer told me we were free to go.

In the car, Ash stared out her window again. Given I knew the horrors of sexual assault, I understood her silence. "I'm proud of you," I said. "I know that was hard, but you did it."

Her head swiveled slowly to look at me. "Yeah, I did it. Is it okay if I listen to my music?"

"Sure."

She put in her earbuds and returned to gazing out the window as we drove home.

Over the next month, Ashten turned inward. On our way home from school, when I asked about her day, her answers ranged from short to grunts. She seemed spacey, like her body was in the car, but her mind was somewhere else. As soon as we walked in the door, she went upstairs to do homework. I reminded myself that she was taking advanced placement classes, which required a lot of studying. Yet, I couldn't convince myself that irritable bowel syndrome caused Ashten's vomiting three of the five days before she left the house to go to school. I felt helpless.

Though I'd been eating lean proteins and more vegetables, I found myself sneaking chocolate and chips. Rather than making me feel less stressed about Ashten, eating junk food in secret made me feel like a loser.

Then, at a weekly group meeting at the Vet Center, we revisited the concept of triggers. My mind wandered to the noisy, crowded halls at Ashten's high school and the swarm of teenage boys, so like the perpetrators in one of her assaults. Triggers.

Ashten had PTSD. I realized I could help my daughter after all. I had tools and empathy to support her healing.

But I wasn't prepared for the dark emotions from my past that would surface. My combat trauma had provided a comfortable place to bury the memories of my own experiences with sexual assault. And the fledgling peace and sanity that I had worked so hard to achieve would start to unravel.

Chapter 36

HIDDEN WITHIN

My body jerked awake. Sweat-soaked pajamas clung to my skin. My pulse raced, and I gasped like I'd sprinted a 100-yard dash. Vague images and sensations flashed within seconds—twinkling Christmas lights, friends from Germany, dirty linoleum, searing pain in my vagina, nausea.

I threw my legs over the side of the bed and stared at the rectangle of light on the hardwood floor that reflected from the gap in the drapes. After what seemed like several minutes, I forced myself to get out of bed. It was Thursday and time to get ready to go to my women's group at the Vet Center.

Before the meeting began, I sat in the room and stared at the flags on the wall, one for every branch of service. The murmur of talking between the other five women barely caught my awareness. My gut ached, and my tongue felt like sandpaper. I just wanted to be an ass in a seat that day, so of course, Amy, our counselor, asked, "Dani, do you want to check in first?"

"Not really." I squirmed in my chair under Amy's concerned gaze. "Okay, I . . . I guess I'm feeling sad and overwhelmed."

"What's making you feel sad and overwhelmed?"

I began to cry. "I found out my daughter was sexually assaulted under my watch. I failed to protect her and . . ." My throat seemed to close. I gulped at the air.

"Take your time." Amy handed me the tissue box.

I wiped my tears and took a deep breath. "We had to report it to the police. I wanted to kill the bastards who'd done this to my little girl. And now flashes of my own past are haunting me—from when I was assaulted. I never said anything about this in the group because it was my fault. I didn't want to be judged. I'd been drinking and . . ." I began to hyperventilate, but I thought of Ashten's bravery and forced three more breaths into my lungs, to gather my resolve. "I was sexually assaulted by a fellow soldier in Germany and again by my sergeant in Fort Lewis."

Dizziness bobbed my head. My entire body burned like I was on fire. I couldn't get enough air.

"Dani, go to your happy place," Amy said. "Describe what you're seeing, smelling, and hearing there."

"I'm in Belknap with my family." I sucked some air. "We're standing in the grass, near the water, under blue skies. Terry's hand is warm in mine. Ashten's hair glistens in the sunlight." My muscles began to unclench.

"Do you want to talk more about this in the group today, or would you like to do a one-on-one with me?"

"I don't even know where or how to start, so I guess I'll schedule an appointment."

"Okay, if you change your mind, feel free to speak up."

"Thanks."

The exchange drained my energy. I felt boneless in the chair, but I stayed in the room for the entire hour. After the meeting, Amy checked her schedule and realized she didn't have an opening for a one-on-one session with me for three weeks. "Dang, would it be okay if you see Mandy?" Amy asked. "She's been here since January. She came right after you went to Palo Alto. Her specialties are family trauma and couples counseling."

My hands balled into fists. I wanted to scream, *Are you kidding me, another therapist? I don't want to start all over again!*

"She's really great." Amy looked up at me from her computer with hopeful eyes. "I think you two will hit it off."

I needed help, damnit. "Okay, I guess so."

Two days later, I sat in a comfortable leather chair in the waiting room at the Vet Center. My clenched jaw gave me a headache, but I couldn't seem to loosen it. Heels clicked on the linoleum floor. A woman's voice called, "Dani?"

"Yep." I looked up to see a tall, African American woman with a warm smile, dressed in a business suit. I walked toward her, and she extended her hand.

"My name is Mandy. Nice to meet you."

"Nice to meet you too." I felt an immediate connection, like I knew her from somewhere. We walked down the hall and entered her office. The way she spoke and acted reminded me of one of my roommates in Germany. I sat in the chair opposite her desk chair and got comfortable.

Mandy paged through a manila folder. "I see that you've worked in the past with a couple different therapists. I feel like this might be a fresh start for you. I spoke with Amy, and she told me you recently got back from an inpatient facility in Palo Alto."

"Actually, I was in Menlo Park, near Palo Alto. I was there for three months and worked on some combat trauma, but I couldn't shake the feeling like something else was bothering me, stuff more personal than combat."

"Okay, what kind of stuff?"

"Well, I think I was sexually assaulted a couple of times in the Army, but my memory is hazy, and there was alcohol involved."

"What do you mean by hazy?"

"It's weird, but I don't remember much of my second year in Germany. I don't know if it's because I was partying all the time or what."

"While you were in the military, did anyone ever touch you in a way you didn't want or ask for?"

"Yes, in basic training, some chick crawled into my bunk when I was asleep and ran her hands up and down my legs."

"Tell me more about that."

"I woke up with her hands all over me. I threw her on the floor and started punching her in the face. I beat the crap out of her. Two drill sergeants had to pull me off her."

"What happened afterwards?"

"They asked me what I wanted to do about the incident, and I said I wanted her kicked out. I feel okay about that time because I felt I controlled the situation."

"Did she get kicked out?"

"Yes, she did."

"Was there another situation you wondered about?"

"Well, actually two of them. The first one was in Germany. The guy who did it was supposedly a friend."

"Okay. What was the other time?"

"After I returned from the Persian Gulf, my squad leader told me I owed him for keeping me safe. He told me if I didn't have sex with him, he would tell the commander something that would keep me from getting out of the Army."

"How did that make you feel when he said that?"

"Pissed! I trusted and looked up to him. I couldn't believe I heard him correctly at first. He blackmailed me!" I started to shake, and tears streamed down my face. "I felt so awful afterwards, I scrubbed my skin raw in the shower."

"What did you do after that?"

I tossed up a hand and flopped back against the chair. "Nothing. I kept my head down, finished my paperwork to get out of the Army, and drove home to Bend."

She rested her hands on her lap, on top of my folder. "The three situations you just told me about were most definitely assault."

A sob escaped from my throat. I stood and grabbed a tissue from the box on her desk. "And I found out my daughter was assaulted too, when she was little, and I can't stop thinking about it. I should've been able to keep her safe."

Her brows lifted slightly. "Did you know when it happened? Did she tell you?"

"No."

"You didn't know, so you couldn't do anything about it. You're helping her now, right?"

"Yes, she's in counseling." I dabbed at my eyes.

"Good. She's right where she needs to be. Now it's time to work on yourself."

We talked about my family, my support system, and my happy place. Then we scheduled an appointment for the following week. "In the next session, we're going to focus on the assault you remember the most. Then we'll go from there."

"Okay, sounds good," I said, though I dreaded re-living any of those events.

Waiting for the next appointment, I distracted myself from overwhelming emotions by ignoring my new food plan. That week, I ate pizza and bought more chips and candy to chill out the swirling butterflies inside me. While indulging in my favorite salty and sweet snacks, I surfed the internet to learn more about sexual trauma in the military.

On the couch, with my laptop on my thighs, I stumbled upon the annual reports the Department of Defense published on sexual assault. The number of reported cases increased from year to year. In 2019, there were 7,825. I wondered how many victims hadn't filed reports, like me.

So, what are you going to do about it? I prayed: *Lord, give me the words to help others know they're not alone, they're important, and there's help.*

That prayer gave me a clear purpose and helped me to stay focused. If I were to show others who have experienced sexual trauma, and other forms of trauma, that there is a way out of the abyss of blame, shame, and guilt, I had to open the vault and confront the experiences I'd locked away for so long. *No more hiding or denying. I'm going to dive in and own it! Ashten did it, and so can I.*

I walked to Ashten's room and knocked. "Yeah," I heard through the door.

"Hey, it's me. Can I come in?"

"Sure."

I sat next to her on her bed, took a deep breath, and said, "I want to share something with you. When I was in the Army, I was sexually assaulted by two fellow soldiers."

"Oh, God, Mom. I'm sorry." I saw empathy in her brown eyes.

"I'm telling you this so you know you're not alone. If you ever want to talk about anything regarding your assaults, you can talk to me. I love you, and I want you to know you've inspired me to dig into my own assaults. I'm not gonna push you to tell me anything. I just wanted you to know." I stood and headed toward the door, then stopped and turned. "Can I have a hug?"

"Sure." Ash stood, put her arms around me, and held me close.

"I love you. I'm still working on my angry outbursts, but breathing and being outside seems to help. Is there anything that helps you to calm yourself?"

She grabbed the sketch pad on the corner of her bed. "I doodle. And I write sometimes." She handed the book to me. "You can look if you want."

"Okay." I opened the cover to see bright colors and intricate geometric patterns and shapes. "Wow, Ash, this is beautiful. I'm glad you found something that helps. It's important to have an outlet."

"Yeah, that's what Natasha says." She smiled with warmth that reached her eyes. "Hey, Mom, I'm proud of you."

"Thanks. That means a lot." Our intimate connection lifted some weight from my shoulders and motivated me to delve into the darkness so I could finally move on.

Chapter 37

OWNING IT

Driving to the Vet Center to see Mandy, I ached with the desire to be in two places at once. Tani had been diagnosed with breast cancer and had to have a double mastectomy, so I'd gone to Eugene to be with her. Before I left, I bought her a special blanket to keep her warm, but I wished I could be by her side for her first day of chemotherapy. Tani's courage in the face of cancer inspired me to dig deep within myself and face my truth. Between Ashten's example and encouragement and Tani's battle with cancer, I found myself realizing I could no longer take my life for granted. With Mandy's help, I challenged my recollections and my view of what happened to me.

"Dani, how responsible do you feel in regard to your assault by Sgt. Gomez?" she asked.

"One hundred percent," I blurted.

"Okay . . . Did you ask to be assaulted?"

"No." Feeling exposed, I turned my head toward her bookcase.

"Did you ask him to stop?"

"Yes." I swallowed and wondered if it sounded as loud to her as it did to me.

"Would you have gone to his room or party if you knew what was going to happen?"

"No." My eyes burned with tears.

"Would you blame someone else, tell them they were responsible, if the same thing happened to them?"

"No way." *Oh, wait. That means . . .*

"Well, then how can you be 100 percent responsible for something that happened to you, that you didn't ask for?"

"Uh, I guess . . ." I sucked in some air. "I can't. But I should've been able to fight him off, take control of the situation. We both had the same combat training." I shook my head and started to cry. "He was bigger than me. Both of the guys were bigger than me. And stronger. I tried to get them to stop, but I couldn't." I blew my nose into my tattered tissue.

"You're right. Take a deep breath and let that settle in." Her warm dark eyes held conviction. "You aren't responsible. They were bigger than you, and you could've gotten even more hurt if you had been able to fight harder. Now exhale. How does that make you feel?"

The room seemed to tilt. "I'm kinda confused and overwhelmed right now. I don't really know for sure."

Mandy relaxed onto the back of her chair with her hands clasped in her lap. "That's okay. I want you to remind yourself that you weren't responsible for what happened to you. Change the dialogue in your mind. You did the best you could at the time. Can you work on that before our next meeting?"

Though I hadn't processed the revelation yet, I felt lighter in my seat. "Yes, I will work on that."

In the days and weeks that followed, I reprocessed my thoughts about the assaults, both as they came to mind and with intention in my journal entries. Discussing the subject in my weekly group sessions at the Vet Center became easier, and we discovered most of us had suffered through some form of similar experience. By the end of September 2019, I felt ready to schedule another appointment with Mandy.

Apparently, her reputation as a helpful therapist had spread because her next available appointment was in January 2020. When the day finally came for me to speak with her, I sat in the waiting room almost vibrating with anticipation. My heart leapt with the familiar sound of heels on concrete,

Mandy's warm smile helped me to relax and enjoy the moment. "Hello, Dani. Follow me."

I sat across from her desk in my favorite brown leather chair, and she opened my folder in front of her. "Well, how have things been going for you, Dani?"

"Pretty good actually. My friend, Tani, is doing well with her chemotherapy so far. Ashten is managing her sophomore year in high school, but being a mom, I worry about her. The amount of work in her AP classes stresses her out, so I told her not to worry about getting a job this year and to focus on school instead. She's studying for her driver's permit, which is scary as hell." I chuckled and Mandy nodded.

"Even with all that, I feel like I'm making progress in dealing with my assaults. I can finally accept that they weren't my fault." I stopped as tears welled, and my throat constricted. "I don't want to give them any more power. I'm done. I'm taking my power back.

"Ashten and I commiserate about PTSD, and that's kinda weird sometimes. I find myself asking if it's her stuff or my stuff causing the arguments and confusion between us. The good news is we're able to talk through our upsets now. It's a relief that she doesn't stomp off, pissed, and in turn, I don't scrub my house to exhaustion anymore. We are works in progress."

Mandy smiled. "Wow, Dani, you've done some great work here. You are an inspiration."

"Thanks. I am truly proud of myself and my service, and I haven't been able to say that for a while."

"You should be. You're a strong and capable woman. I'm so thankful we got to know each other better."

"Me too."

"How do you feel about ending our one-on-one sessions and just following up in the group? I'm taking over the women's group for Amy next month."

"That sounds good." I got up to leave. "Thanks, Mandy. I can't tell you how much you've helped me. I am so grateful. I'll see you next week in the group meeting."

But that next meeting didn't happen. In February 2020, the entire world shut down due to the pandemic. That year of isolation, to keep from spreading COVID-19, forced me to look at my weight. At five-feet-five-inches tall, my fits and starts with trying to lose weight couldn't seem to get smaller than 298 pounds, at least not for long. The chart at the doctor's office said a healthy weight for a woman of my height and build was between 114 and 144 pounds. With the extra rolls came shortness of breath, swollen legs, and an inability to tie my shoes because I couldn't reach my feet. There were still a lot of things I wanted to do in my lifetime, and if I didn't make some lifestyle changes soon, I feared that I wouldn't get the chance.

Chapter 38

MAJOR CHANGES

With the world quarantined in 2020, we all had to adjust to staying home, separated from most of the outside world. My introverted side loved it for a while, until it didn't. More often than I wanted to admit, the isolation sucked my hope and energy. I needed human connection to survive. Thankfully, the VA set up virtual women's group meetings every Thursday on VA Video, similar to Zoom. Though it was strange sitting at home, staring at a screen, I felt grateful and relieved to see those familiar faces. I missed being with people, hugging them and hanging out, and seeing a smile instead of a pair of eyes above a mask.

The importance of my family became clearer with every passing day. Cooking together, doing laundry, playing games, watching shows and movies, and getting creative to pass the time brought us closer than we had ever been. Their love strengthened me and made me want to be a better person.

On the other hand, my waistline kept increasing. I wanted to lose weight. Heck, I needed to for health reasons. But the idea of depriving myself of my treats, when coping with having to stay inside most of the time, seemed more than I could bear.

One afternoon, a few weeks after students were finally cleared to return to school, albeit wearing masks, I picked up Ashten in the afternoon, then grabbed my laptop from the kitchen table as she went up the stairs. On autopilot, I picked up a can of diet soda and a bag of M & Ms before settling on the couch in the living room to work on my memoir.

Click, click, click went the keys just before a handful of candies landed in my mouth.

I've done it again! I promised myself I would do better. At this rate, I'll have a heart attack before I get to buy shoes that have laces again. I barely remember taking the M & Ms from the pantry. I gotta stop buying these things!

Ashten walked into the living room, her eyes wide with worry. She plopped onto the couch next to me and asked, "Mom, can I withdraw from high school? I can't do it anymore." Her brown eyes filled with tears. "I constantly feel sick and get triggered. I just can't handle it."

"Come here." I opened up my arms and Ash scooted into them. Touch still wasn't her favorite thing, but at times, she seemed comforted, like at that moment. "I think we should talk to Natasha together and see what she says. Would that be okay?"

"I guess. I can text her and ask when she can talk."

"Will you be okay until then?"

"Sure, Mom." She pulled away from our embrace and shuffled up the stairs to her bedroom.

Two days later, we masked up, went to Natasha's office, and settled into the comfy recliners. "Natasha, Ashten is struggling with school," I said. "She's nauseated every morning and vomits almost every day. I want her to be safe and healthy. What can we do?"

Looking from me to Ashten, Natasha hooked her hair behind her ear. "Well, the priority for Ashten should be her mental health. She's very resilient, but she also forces herself to do things that exacerbate her depression. She's had thoughts of suicide, so now wouldn't be a good time for her to force herself to do something that's making her sick. Maybe, for now, she could just focus on counseling and getting better. Then we can look into her taking the general education development test, or GED, so she doesn't have to go back to high school. What do you think?"

Suicide? My beautiful daughter?

Ashten sat with her head down, wringing her hands. She looked so lost and small. "We will do whatever is needed to help her," I said.

Ashten glanced up at me and mouthed, "Thank you."

The next day, we put on our masks again, went to the high school, and asked for the withdrawal paperwork in the main office. Instead of handing us the forms, the secretary asked us to wait a moment, and she picked up the phone. Soon Ashten's counselor appeared in jeans and a sweatshirt, and she escorted us to her office.

We sat in wooden chairs in front of the woman's desk. Her brows pinched as she gazed at her computer screen. "Are you sure this is the best decision?" She looked at me as if my daughter wasn't in the room. "Ashten has earned good grades in AP classes so far this year. It would be a shame not to let her finish these classes so they can be recorded on her high school transcript."

Ashten crossed her arms and shrunk in her chair. I knew what I had to do. "While I understand your concern, Ashten, her therapist, and I agree that her mental health needs to be the priority."

The counselor's eyes moved to Ashten, who stared at her lap. "I wish you could find a way for her to get her education as well as her health needs met."

When I stared at the counselor and didn't respond, after several moments, she sighed and slid a form and a pen across her desk to me. Ashten and I filled in the requested information, signed the paper, and just like that, Ashten was no longer enrolled at the high school.

In the car I said, "Okay, the main focus for you now is counseling. I want to make sure you're getting the help you need to feel safe. I love you and will do anything for you. You know that, right?"

"Yeah, I know that, Mom."

"Please talk to me if you're feeling depressed."

She turned her head toward her window.

"Are you okay with me asking some questions?" I asked.

She settled against the passenger's seat and stared out the windshield. "Yeah."

"Do you have a plan to commit suicide?"

Her gaze dropped to her lap again. "No."

"Do you think you can tell me if this changes at any time, day or night?"

"Uh . . . I think so."

"Ash, there's nothing you could ever do or say that would make me love you less, okay? I love you and just want you to be healthy. We can get you there. You believe that, don't you?"

"Yeah, Mom. I do. You did it. So I know I can too." She looked at me with those beautiful chestnut eyes, wise beyond her years.

I reached for her hand, and she grabbed mine. "You can do this. You're one tough cookie."

"So are you, Mom."

I swallowed around the lump in my throat and smiled before I turned the key to start the engine and headed for home.

Convincing Terry and Gary, her biological father, that what we had done was in Ashten's best interest was the hardest part. They didn't agree on much, but they both worried that allowing her to drop out of high school and spend her energy on individual and group therapy might work against her. Being that I had experienced the debilitating effects of PTSD, knowing the hard work it took to recover and to find tools to live an empowered life, I stood my ground. And Natalie's support helped.

I'd love to say I didn't struggle with Ashten leaving school before she'd earned her high school diploma, but that would be a lie. Still, I'd been suicidal twice. I understood the seriousness of Ashten's condition. She wouldn't be able to get her GED and go to college if she ended up dead.

Four months into Ashten's therapy, she'd learned and practiced enough techniques that she could manage emotions and triggers within the spectrum of how her brain functioned. She began to look forward to going to events instead of stressing and cowering in her bedroom. She passed the pre-tests for the GED and signed up to take the seven-hour exam the following month.

Ashten's best friend, Madi, came to live with us when Central Oregon Community College closed their student housing due to more COVID-19 outbreaks in August of 2020. Madi's friendly presence gave all of us more positive energy. She was a warm, wonderful addition to our family.

The one drawback was that Madi loved to bake. I couldn't seem to stay away from her delicious cookies, or her zucchini and banana breads. But finding myself even farther from being able to reach over my bulk to tie a pair of shoes seemed a small price for how well Madi supported Ashten through both academic and life issues.

About four months after Madi moved in with us, I noticed the girls jumping away from one another when I entered the room. They avoided eye contact when they spoke to me. I heard increased giggling at inside jokes, and I began to see touching between them, which was unusual for Ashten.

One night in December, Terry and I took Ashten and Madi to El Rancho Grande for dinner. Ashten and Madi sat shoulder to shoulder, staring at the menu. It felt intimate, like something Terry and I would do.

Getting ready for bed that night, removing my makeup, I asked Terry's reflection in the mirror, "Did you see Ash and Madi at dinner?"

He smirked like I was crazy. "Yeah, they were right across from us."

"No, I mean how they were sitting so close to each other. Do you think they like-*like* each other?" I turned from the mirror to look at him.

"What? No, I don't think so. They're just friends, right?"

"Hmm. I'm not sure." Not knowing what else to say, I went back to washing my face.

January 2021 rolled around, along with the hope for the removal of mask-wearing requirements in public. I started off the new year by organizing my closet. Ashten peeked her head in the bedroom and asked, "Mom, can I talk to you about something?"

"Sure." I hung up the shirt I had in my hand, went to the bed, and patted the mattress. "Take a load off," I said and laughed.

She sat next to me and sighed. "Well, I don't know how to say this, so I'm just going to tell you—I'm gay. Madi and I are a couple. Also I'm nonbinary. I'm identifying as they/them now instead of she/her."

Wow. That's a lot to unpack. Whatever you do, be supportive.

"Okay . . . I kinda had a feeling about you and Madi. I pointed it out to Terry, but Dad's pretty clueless about these things." We both chuckled. "I just hope you feel loved. Nothing can or will change how I feel about you. I just want you to be happy. Treat each other with love and respect. That's all I want. Be good to each other."

"We are, Mom. Madi was afraid you'd kick her out if you knew."

"No, but there will be some rules. I still want you to sleep in your own beds and leave the door open when you're playing games or watching a movie together. I guess those are the two big ones. I admit I'm confused about the they/them pronouns. In school we were taught 'they' means more than one, plural."

"I guess it is kind of confusing. There are some YouTube videos I can send you that might explain it better than I can. Basically, I just don't feel strongly male or female. They/them is nonbinary."

"Okay," I said, but my mind reeled with questions. "Are you going to share this with Dad?" felt like the safest one to ask.

Her brow furrowed. "Well, I was hoping you would tell him. Are you okay with that?"

"I guess I can, but you know he loves you and wants the best for you, right?"

"I know he does. You're just better at speaking his language."

Unsure what to say or do, I stood and said, "Can I please have a hug?"

Ashten wrapped her arms around me. My eyes welled, and I pulled away. "I'm so proud of you. You're growing up way too fast."

"I'm proud of you too, Mom. I'm gonna go pick up Madi from work. You okay?"

"Yeah, I'm good."

Ashten left and headed for Pizza Mondo, where Madi worked. I went back to organizing my clothes to keep my mind from spiraling. I completed my task and started dinner. While I was chopping peppers for fajitas, Terry got home from work and came into the kitchen.

"I have some interesting news," I said, without looking up from the cutting board.

"What news?"

"Your daughter is gay. I mean . . . your child? I don't know how to say it correctly. Anyway, Ashten's gay. She and Madi are a couple. Wait. They're a couple. I don't know. Ash and Madi are together. There." I huffed and put down the knife.

Terry frowned. "What does all that mean?"

"Well, Ashten told me she's gay and nonbinary. Which I'm not sure what that means, except she wants to be referred to as they/them, not she/her."

"The gay part I get, but I don't know about the they/them."

"I know. Ash is going to send me some YouTube videos that explain it, but I think it means Ashten doesn't feel either masculine or feminine. I'm just trying to be supportive. It's not about us—it's about Ashten. Nothing changes as far as our love for her goes. Just try to be open to it, okay?"

"Sounds confusing. I'm a simple guy that plays in the dirt. This is way over my pay grade, honey." He shrugged. "But hey, she won't get pregnant."

"You mean *they* won't get pregnant. I know it'll be hard, but try not to make her feel self-conscious and weird, okay?"

His warm brown eyes held compassion. "'I love Ashten and Madi, but there will be rules for sleeping and stuff, right?"

"Yeah, I already went over the rules and Ashten agreed." I hugged him. "I know this seems strange. I'm confused too, but together we can do anything, right?"

"Sure. Do I have time for a shower before dinner?"

"Yes, you do. I love you, honey."

"I love you too." He sauntered off to shower, and I returned to chopping vegetables.

I'd like to say I didn't struggle to understand gender identification and the transition went smoothly for us, but I slipped up with the pronouns often. Apologies were graciously accepted, but I wondered how difficult this must have been for Ashten. When I asked how things were going, I got short answers and the sense of her, no, *them* pulling away.

This may have been the normal transition from teenager to young adulthood. Ashten needed me to give *them* space to grow and thrive on *their* own. To support *their* growing independence, I focused more energy on finishing my memoir and decided I would do my best to become less confused with the pronouns.

I needed help with my story's structure and flow, so I contacted the Central Oregon Writers' Guild. The following week, I attended a class on Zoom and instantly connected with my amazing writing coach and editor. Things seemed to be looking up for me—until the next day.

Chapter 39

UNRECOGNIZABLE

I gazed into the mirror after my shower, something I hadn't done in a long time, and saw a stranger. Gone was the fit soldier, the collegiate athlete. In her place stood a large, middle-aged woman I didn't recognize. I lumbered over to the scale and stared at the glaring red numbers—still 298 pounds.

I'm way heavier now than when I was pregnant with Ashten.

My stashed candy bars provided temporary comfort, a little calm in the chaos, something pleasurable to occupy me when bored or stressed, a way to put off dealing with uncomfortable fleeting thoughts, triggers, and circumstances. Not to mention, my family showed love through cooking and baking. How could I turn down sampling the latest batch of snickerdoodles and hurt the baker's feelings?

Eating just one cookie, when a mouthwatering pile of them waited for me from the kitchen, seemed impossible. For someone who could relate to food as merely a source of energy and nutrition, my family's display of affection may have been fine. I, however, relied on food for so much more than physical sustenance.

Determined to rediscover the real me that I knew was under all those layers I had acquired over 25 years, I tried every method I could find to lose weight—South Beach, Weight Watchers, Intermittent Fasting, Medifast, and several apps purchased on my cell phone. Each new diet worked, at first, to help me drop a few pounds. I'd start to feel better about myself, even encouraged.

Then a bag of bar-b-qued chips would call me from the pantry. A lone chocolate bar that hadn't made the purge when I started the diet would tumble from between boxes on a shelf. A slice of zucchini bread here, an extra slice of pizza at dinner there, and soon the number on the scale would be higher than when I started the diet.

My urge to indulge seemed hopeless, and I would hate myself the moment my treat was consumed. My body yo-yoed from size to size. I wore 3XL T-shirts and size 24 pants. Climbing the stairs left me winded. My joints ached. I had to use a CPAP machine to manage my sleep apnea, due to obesity, and my blood sugar levels were dangerously close to full-blown Type 2 Diabetes.

Dani, something has to change. Your life depends on it.

I wanted to get smaller the old-fashioned way—through hard work and diet. Yet my efforts kept resulting in finding myself back where I started. I needed to do something about my weight before I let it kill me.

At a group counseling session at the VA, I was reminded that my emotions weren't facts, that my perceptions weren't necessarily grounded in reality. This realization had served me well in my relationships with Terry and Ashten, and even with myself. So, I decided to apply that concept to the last visage of the traumas I unwittingly held onto through food.

When I got home from the meeting, I went to the pantry out of habit, and I put my hand on a bag of chips. "Wait. Am I truly hungry?" I asked myself. "Does my body need this, or are these chips a distraction from what's going on in my mind right now?"

That was the first of many mental corrections around food. And though that mental shift of being intentional about deciding whether to eat something was pivotal, I knew I needed help to climb over this hurdle. Six years of counseling had given me clarity around my mind-body connection. My renewed relationships with family members and friends had gelled into a solid support system. I felt emotionally stronger than ever and understood that I no longer needed my big body to shield me from the attention of others. I decided it was okay for me to feel wanted and sexy instead of frumpy and unattractive. This shift in my perspective gave me the courage to seek help.

I grabbed my laptop, clunked onto the couch in the living room, and visited a website on bariatric surgery. The page said that to qualify, one had to have a body-mass-index (BMI) of 40 or more, which is referred to as extreme obesity. My BMI was 49.6. Candidates for the surgery also had to suffer from health conditions related to obesity: obstructive sleep apnea–check, depression–check, gastric reflux–check, diabetes–damn close, low back pain–definitely, urinary incontinence–so embarrassing. I had all the qualifications and health problems except high blood pressure.

Since the VA in Oregon didn't offer bariatric surgery, I would have to travel to the VA in Palo Alto, California. The website said I would need a referral, so I scheduled an appointment to go see my VA primary care provider the following day.

Terry came home from work to find me sitting on the couch, staring into space. "Hey, honey, what's up?"

"Well, I'm going to ask my doctor about bariatric surgery."

"I don't know much about that, but I think our friend's wife had the surgery and lost a bunch of weight. Is that what you're talking about?"

"Yeah." My vision blurred with tears. "I can't stand to look at myself anymore. Nothing I wear can make this body look good."

Terry sat on the couch next to me. "You know, I think you're very pretty." When I opened my mouth to protest, he added, "But I love you and want you to be happy. That's all I've ever wanted."

"I know, but I haven't been happy with my body for years, and I feel like my mind is strong enough now to do something about this. I think I substituted alcohol with food. I ate to avoid my feelings, but I think I can face my emotions now, so I don't need food to distract me anymore. I'm ready to make a change."

"Well, you know I'll support you, whatever you decide."

I reached over and hugged him. "Thank you for putting up with all my crap. I'm so lucky to have you in my life."

The next morning, I squeezed into a narrow, blue chair in the waiting room at the VA clinic in Bend. It intrigued me to think the general location where I went to heal my brain in California may also be where I got the surgery to finally heal my body. My primary physician was supportive about submitting the bariatric surgery referral.

A month passed before I got a phone call from the Movetime Clinic in Portland, the weight management group for the VA. "Before you can have bariatric surgery," the nurse said, "you have to attend a 12-week course called MOVE! When you finish the course, you can do your lab work and schedule an endoscopic EGD procedure to examine the lining of your esophagus, stomach, and first part of your intestine. If the tests show you would be able to safely undergo the surgery, you'll get it done in Palo Alto, California. We don't have any surgeons on our Portland campus who can do it yet."

"Okay, I would like to enroll in the MOVE! course as soon as possible."

"I will send you the course training book which covers healthy eating habits, nutritional advice, and physical fitness activity logs."

"Well, I've tried all of that before, but if this is what I have to do, I'm willing."

"Great. I'll send out the materials today."

"Thank you." I hung up the phone feeling cautiously optimistic.

Two weeks later, flipping through the MOVE! manual, my old, self-destructive thinking returned: *Maybe this is how you deserve to be.* I put the book on the coffee table and stared at it for several moments. *No, I won't accept that. I know better than that now.* I snatched the book off the table and started reading again.

Most of the material I had seen before, in one foray to lose weight or another, but I was determined to finally remove this obstacle. Over the next 12 weeks, I went to every class and paid careful attention to the definition of healthy portions, daily protein requirements post-surgery, and the importance of daily exercise to make the surgery successful. The biggest thing I got out of the material was this: Bariatric surgery is a *tool* that could help someone like me return to a healthy weight. The surgery wouldn't be a cure. The keys were still a proper diet and exercise.

I was ready. I wanted to live long enough to enjoy Ashten as an adult. I wanted to travel to Europe with a sleeker, healthier body. I wanted to feel comfortable in my own skin again, to recognize my reflection in the mirror, and feel that I had finally let go of my past traumas.

When I completed the Move! program, I was cleared to schedule an esophagogastroduodenoscopy (EGD) procedure at the Portland VA to make sure the surgery would be safe for me. My mom agreed to make the three-hour drive from Bend and to accompany me at the hospital. Since I wouldn't be able to ride in the car to get home for 24 hours after the procedure, I booked a hotel room for us.

Lying on the gurney, I listened to the nurses' information about the procedure, the risks and complications, what to expect, and recovery time. In the chair next to my bed, my mom grimaced at the possible things that could go wrong, but she remained quiet. I knew that issues arising from the procedure were rare. Ironically, I'd given this same speech to hundreds of patients when I worked in the MDU at the civilian hospital. Giving that information felt so much more comfortable than receiving it.

The nurse escorted my mom to the recovery area when the doctor was ready to begin. The assessment procedure only took about 15 minutes. The doctor found polyps in my stomach, but he thought the gastric bypass could still be accomplished. My mom sat up straighter in her chair when I joined her in the recovery area.

"How'd it go?" she asked.

"Well, the doctor said everything looks good. I'm cleared for surgery."

"That's good news. Any diet restrictions for tonight?"

"Nope, and I'm really craving a burger and fries."

"How about we eat at the restaurant by the hotel?"

"Sounds perfect. Thanks for babysitting me, Mom. I always feel better knowing you're here with me."

"It's no problem. That's what we moms do."

The Movetime Clinic in Palo Alto, California called two weeks after the EGD procedure. "I'll email a surgery handbook for you to read," said the nurse. "We've ordered labs to be sure you're physically healthy enough to undergo the surgery. Let's schedule an hour phone appointment so you can talk to our VA team, which consists of a psychiatrist, physical therapist, and a nutritionist. They'll design a specific diet that you must be faithful to if the surgery is going to be effective, long term. Then they will schedule follow-up appointments for two weeks post surgery, one month, and three months out. After the third post-op appointment, they will decide how frequently they want you to check in, usually every three to four months until you reach your goal weight."

The following week, the medical team interviewed me on a conference call. Apparently, they were happy with my answers to their questions because they told me the next call would come from the surgery planner. I would be informed of the date for the procedure and given information about lodging. All three of them, the psychiatrist, physical therapist, and dietician, gave me their phone numbers and email addresses to contact them if I had any questions.

Since COVID still raged in September of 2021, the hospital would allow only one support person to accompany me. I asked Terry if he could take time off work, but he had emergency septic replacements scheduled for two families. I worried about burdening my mom again, but I didn't want to take the trip alone and recover among strangers.

"Mom?" I said sheepishly into my cell phone. "I'm sorry to have to ask you again, but can you come with me to Palo Alto for the surgery? Terry can't and—"

"Of course I'll come with you," she interrupted. "The long drives give us a chance to spend time together."

Relief flooded through me, and muscles I didn't realize were flexed began to relax. "Thanks, Mom. You being there means more than you know." Her loving acceptance comforted me, and she was always easy to talk to. Her mere presence calmed me in stressful situations.

I drove the two of us down to Palo Alto a week before the surgery, to take the required COVID test, and we stayed at the Defender's Lodge. To pass the time, and to keep me distracted from my nervous butterflies over this next step in my recovery, we met for lunch at my mom's close friend's house. We also wore masks and wandered through the Stanford Shopping Center, near the university campus. The rest of the time, we watched movies and hung out together in our room.

Tuesday finally came, and I lay on a gurney in the pre-surgery area, fidgeting as four doctors from the School of Medicine at Stanford University approached me in white coats. My need for control in stressful situations kicked in and put a knot in my stomach. But I had tools to relax and go with the flow. Inhale deep—hold—release the air—hold. Repeat. I reminded myself: *They're professionals. It'll be fine. I can do this.*

A tall gentleman with brown hair and dark brown eyes grabbed my chart and approached the gurney. I deduced he was the surgeon. He glanced up from my chart. "Hello, Danielle. I'm Dr. Risenberg. I've been looking over your recent EGD results. You originally said you wanted to do gastric bypass surgery, but I think it might be better if we did the gastric sleeve instead. Any thoughts?"

"Is it because of the polyps?"

He smiled. "That's right. I forgot you were a nurse. Yes, since you have a history of polyps, we need to have access to your stomach. With the bypass, we would go around your stomach, unlike the sleeve, where we would remove part of your stomach. I think it's the safer choice, just in case, down the road, something happens, and we need to look into your stomach again."

The sleeve also meant my small bowel would be able to absorb more nutrients, so my nutrition could potentially be better than if I had the bypass. He was right—the sleeve was the better choice. "Okay," I said, "I'd rather be safe."

After I signed the surgery consent form, the anesthesiologist entered the room and started an IV. She slipped me some Versed® to help me relax, and the next thing I remembered was opening my eyes to see the pain pump next to my bed in the recovery room. The medication seemed to be working because I felt comfortably drowsy, without nausea. The nurse wheeled me upstairs to the room that would be my home for the next three days.

Sometime in the early evening, a nurse came in and strongly encouraged me to walk. "I know it must be weird being the patient since you were a nurse," he said, "but you know the drill."

I log-rolled onto my side and pushed myself into a sitting position. "I do know the drill." My chuckle became a yelp with the intense sting that ripped through my abdomen.

He pushed the walker toward me. "Don't laugh. It'll hurt."

Jeez. No kidding. I think I figured that out.

"Coughing and sneezing won't feel very good either," he added.

I grabbed the handle on the walker, and he helped me to stand. My arms and legs felt almost too heavy to move, and my mind processed in slow motion. My abdomen felt loose, like my guts were just flopping around in there. A wide compression belt encircled my middle, to decrease inflammation and provide support during healing.

The nurse pushed my pain medication button, and we shuffled down the hall. Five minutes of forcing myself to take baby steps through the sharp, breath-catching pain felt like an hour. Still woozy from the anesthesia, the descent back onto the bed into a sitting position gave me a sense of relief as well as victory. He helped me scooch my butt back so I could gently roll onto the mattress. As soon as my eyes closed, I fell asleep.

When I woke up the second time, I saw Mom in the chair in the corner. "Hey, good morning!" She chuckled. "Or should I say good evening?"

I smiled. "I guess I've been out for a while."

"How do you feel?"

"Sore. It's not horrible, but I feel like they drove a truck through my gut."

"They kind of did."

"Yeah."

"Have you eaten anything yet?"

"Nope. I can have five milliliters of Ensure tonight and more tomorrow if it stays down."

"Yummy." She smirked. "The COVID rules are kind of weird. I can only visit once a day because when I leave, I can't come back."

"Dang. Sorry, Mom."

"You know me. I'll just go to the motel to watch TV and read and knit. No worries." She'd gotten a room at the Fisher's house, located next door to the Defender's Lodge, which had rooms available for family members of hospitalized veterans.

"Well, I am really glad you're here."

"I wouldn't be anywhere else. I love you. I think I'm going to let you rest, and I'll see you tomorrow."

"Okay, love you too, Mom." I watched her walk out the doorway and wished I'd awakened earlier.

Later that evening, two residents dressed in their crisp white jackets knocked and entered my room without waiting for me to say come in. "Hi, Danielle. We just wanted to let you know that everything went well. Do you have any questions?"

I pried open my heavy eyelids and tried to focus on them. "I don't think so," I said through my painkiller haze. The short, dark-haired doctor seemed familiar, but I didn't remember the tall blond doctor, not that recognizing them behind their masks would have been easy under any circumstances.

"Well, we want to encourage you to walk as much as you can tolerate and sit up to eat for the next two days. We will check in on you and then pull your drain before you get discharged from the hospital."

"Uh . . . Okay." *Ugh. That sounds like a lot.*

Since Mom could only visit once a day, she tried to show up at noon so I wouldn't have to dine alone. The chalky Ensure coated my tongue and felt like I was swallowing a cotton ball. Once I forced down all five milliliters, I prayed that they wouldn't come back up.

The day before my discharge, Mom walked stiffly into the room and just waved when I greeted her. "Are you okay?" I asked.

"I'm fine. It's just . . . I'm nervous about driving us home on those big four-lane highways tomorrow. I couldn't sleep last night."

"Do you think I should call Terry?"

"Oh, Dan, I don't want to bug Terry . . . but I *am* pretty scared."

"I was going to call and check in with him anyway." I went to my favorites on my phone, and he answered on the third ring.

"Hey, honey, how're you feeling?"

"Well, I feel pretty beat up still, but walking seems to be getting a little easier."

"Good. How's your mom doing with all the downtime?"

"Funny you should ask. Mom is worried about navigating the four lane highways in California. So . . . I was wondering if you could possibly fly in tomorrow and drive us back to Bend?" I held my breath waiting for him to respond.

There was silence for a few seconds before Terry said, "Well, I guess I can. I'll have to make a few calls regarding work. What airport should I fly into?"

"San Francisco, Oakland, and San Jose are all pretty close to the hospital."

"Okay. I'll get on it."

"Have I told you lately that I think you're amazing?"

"Nope."

"Well, I do. I love you, honey. Thank you. Mom already looks like she feels better." I laughed, which stabbed my abdomen, but not as badly as a few days before.

The following day, Terry arrived via Uber. The minute he walked into the room, my shoulders relaxed, and I hadn't known they were tense. His warm smile made me feel safe, and I smiled back.

"I called your mom when I got in, and she said you could only have one visitor at a time, so here I am."

"Great. Just in time to watch them pull out my drainage tube. I know you love all the gross stuff." I laughed. We'd spent hours marveling over graphic shows, about medical procedures and weird things that happened inside people's bodies and loved every minute of it.

"Cool!" His wide smile and the twinkle in his eyes was like a kid ripping open a present.

An hour later, after a nurse had removed my IV, the short, dark-haired female intern came in to give me discharge instructions. "No lifting anything heavier than a jug of milk for six to eight weeks," she said. "Increase your walks, but listen to your body. If you get sore, you've done too much. Continue to use ice on your incision sites, to help manage pain and swelling, and take your pain meds on time. You can call the number on your discharge instructions if you have any questions."

"Okay. Sounds good."

"I'm going to pull out your drain now." She walked over to the bed, cut the two sutures holding the tube in place, and put gauze over the site. "On the count of three, I'm going to pull it out. Just remember to breathe, okay?"

"Gotcha." I wasn't nervous at all. I'd pulled drains many times in my nursing career. I inhaled as instructed and glanced at Terry who was holding his breath in anticipation.

"One, two, three," she said and started to tug. The exiting tube felt like a snake crawling out of my belly. The intern's eyes widened slightly, and she stopped pulling for a moment. "Oh, I guess this is the long tube," she mumbled, then yanked so hard to free the rest of the tube that fluid flew out of my abdomen and splattered onto the bed and the wall.

I cringed. *Gross. Way to go, rookie.* I looked up at Terry, whose fingers rubbed his furrowed brow. He noticed my gaze and attempted to smile.

The intern's eyes were round above her mask. "Oh my god. I'm so sorry," she said. "I didn't realize the tube was that long."

I felt sorry for her and said, "No worries. At least it's out."

Terry glanced up at the clock. "It's kinda late. Is there any way we could stay the night and avoid the five o'clock traffic? We could leave early in the morning."

I asked the intern, "Can you put in an order for one night at the Defender's Lodge and extend my mom's stay at the Fisher House for one more night?"

"Um, yeah. I'll have to ask how to do that, but we'll get it done." Her stressed dark eyes seemed to communicate that getting us a room, after we had waited all day for the tube to be removed, and then she'd made such a mess of it, was the least she could do.

"Thanks," I said.

Though I was grateful for the room, the mattress on the bed in the Defender's Lodge was a special combination of soft and lumpy. Luckily, I had pain meds to knock me out. My last thought before drifting off to sleep was: *Poor Terry.*

Early the next morning, Mom and Terry loaded up the suitcases, bobbed and weaved to get me situated in the front seat, and we headed toward Bend. We made it as far as Redding in Northern California and stayed the night in a hotel, which was a blur thanks to the narcotics. We got up early again the next day and returned home four hours later. Even with the meds, the pain was barely tolerable. Still, hope and excitement filled my chest. My next journey, my latest step toward healing, was about to begin.

Chapter 40

METAMORPHOSIS

It took me from September 2021 to July 2023 to reach my goal weight, but I did it! One night, while I was getting into my bathing suit for Terry's and my nightly hot tub time together, I stared at my reflection in the mirror and felt a wave of happiness. The image I saw was the real me, the woman I knew was inside all along. Well, almost.

I tried not to be disappointed by the unattractive ripples and folds that cascaded down my stomach, arms, and legs. *I lost 160 pounds. Did I think my skin would snap back into place? Where else would all that extra skin go? I guess I'll just have to deal with it. Damn. What am I going to do with this? I wonder if the VA would cover skin reduction surgery on my stomach.* I made a mental note to ask the doctor during my Movetime phone appointment.

That Wednesday, my cell phone rang. "Hi, this is Dani."

"Hi, Dani. This is Dr. Troutdale. How are you doing?"

"I'm doing well."

"What's your current weight? Have you had any difficulties with your diet?"

"I currently weigh 138 pounds, and I'm still doing pretty well with the diet."

"I would say so. That's great. You're at your goal weight, correct?"

"Yes, I want to stay between 135 and 140, but I have a question about the loose skin on my stomach. I've been getting rashes under the skin flap. I've used antifungal cream and powder to help, but I can't get the rash to go away."

"How long has this been going on?"

"About two months."

"If there is a medical reason for the loose skin causing problems, this could lead to an infection. If that's the case, the VA would cover the expense for a panniculectomy. You'd have to come back to Palo Alto and meet with the plastic surgery team here. Is this something you think you might want to do?"

"Definitely."

"Okay, I will put in a plastic surgery consultation request. You should be hearing from them within a week or two to schedule an intake appointment."

"Thank you, Dr Troutdale. I appreciate all your help."

An online consultation was scheduled within a few weeks of that conversation. "Hi, my name is Laura, and I'm with the plastic surgery team in Palo Alto," said a woman who appeared in her twenties, with dark coffee eyes, matching hair, and a pleasant smile. "Can you verify your full name and the last four digits of your social security number before we get started?"

"Sure." I recited those details.

"Okay, this may seem strange, but in order for me to schedule an appointment with the doctor, I need to see the rash under your skin. Are you comfortable doing this?"

"I used to be a nurse. It's just another body part, right?" I laughed awkwardly and felt vulnerable lifting my shirt, sliding down my underwear, and pulling up the flap of skin to expose the problem. "Here's the rash. I've been using antifungal cream and powder, but it's still itchy."

"Can you turn to your right for me?" she said, all business.

"Sure."

After what seemed like several minutes, though it was probably a few seconds, she said, "Okay, I am going to talk to Dr. Rohan about having you come to Palo Alto for an intake visit. After she examines you, she will decide on the best course of action. Are you available June 10 at two o'clock?"

"Yes. Can you make flight arrangements, or do I have to drive?"

"I can put in a request for our travel department to coordinate a flight for you. Is that what you would like me to do?"

"Yes, please. I live in Bend, Oregon. It's a long drive to the San Francisco area for just an appointment."

"Okay, you should be hearing from our travel people. We will see you soon."

"Sounds good. Thank you." *Wow. That was easy.*

When June 10 arrived, I took an Uber from the San Francisco airport to the Palo Alto VA and checked in for my appointment. In the exam room, I kept fidgeting with my purse on my lap. *Calm down. Take a couple of deep breaths.* I jumped, startled at the knock on the door. "Come in."

A small woman with curly dark hair and a kind gaze entered. "Hi, I'm Dr. Rohan." She extended her hand.

"I'm Dani." I reached out and shook it.

"Nice to meet you. Laura tells me you have a rash around your groin area. Can I see it?"

"Sure." I pulled down my pants and lifted my stomach flap.

"How long have you had this?"

"A few months. I've tried several treatments, which kind of help, but not really. It's pretty itchy."

"Looks like it. I want to touch your stomach. Is that okay?"

"Yes."

She grabbed the skin, which felt numb, like a parasite on my body that didn't belong to me. "If I do surgery, I would remove this entire flap of skin, maybe do some liposuction, and then insert an internal corset to stitch your abdominal muscles back together. When a person gains a lot of weight, the muscles get stretched. With major weight loss, the muscles stay separated. This extra skin has nowhere to go, so that's why it just hangs there."

"Yeah, all the sit-ups in the world couldn't fix it." I chuckled.

She smiled. "That's true. Do you have any questions for me?"

"Only one: When can we do this?"

"We could probably get you in next month."

"That would be great."

"I will need to order some labs. You can get them drawn today. Then my team will call you and schedule a surgery date. You should have someone come with you. You'll only be in the hospital overnight, but you will have to stay at the Defender's Lodge for a week. We will schedule a follow up appointment at the end of the week, and if everything looks good, you can go home."

A tear accompanied my grin. "Sign me up. I'm ready. Thank you for helping me to get my life back."

"It's my pleasure. See you soon."

A month later, Terry and I drove almost nine hours to Palo Alto and checked into the Defender's Lodge. The room was clean. There were two twin beds, a small refrigerator, and a tiny TV. We found a burger joint close to the Stanford campus and headed back to our room to channel surf.

"I'm not going to lie. I'm a little nervous," I said, surrounded by pillows on my bed.

Terry stopped changing channels and looked at me. "Why? You've had so many surgeries. You're old hat at this."

I laughed nervously. "Wouldn't it be weird if I wasn't a little scared?"

He reached from his twin bed and grabbed my hand. "You'll be fine. I'll be there the whole time."

"Thanks, honey. I love you so much. You know that, right?"

"Yes, and I love you. Try to relax."

The next day, my gown stuck to me as I lay on a hospital gurney, freshly cleaned with antibacterial soap. Meanwhile, the butterflies in my stomach had whipped themselves into a frenzy. *Breathe. You've got this.*

The nurses were great. They put me at ease with easy banter and joking about nurses not being the best patients. We all laughed in agreement. The curtain was pulled back, and Dr Rohan appeared. We exchanged hellos, and I signed the consent form. Shortly afterwards, the anesthesiologist put something in my IV, and my eyelids got too heavy to lift. The surgery lasted five-and-a-half hours. When I opened my eyes, Terry's sweet smile filled my line of sight.

"Hello, Sleeping Beauty."

"Hi." I tried to swallow around the stickiness in my throat. "What time is it?"

"It's 5:30."

"How'd it go?"

"Dr. Rohan said it went well. You have two drains in there that will have to stay for a couple of weeks. Are you in pain?"

"Actually, yeah." I grimaced with a stab near my belly button that added to the overall ache as I searched for my call light. Minutes later, a nurse arrived with pain medication. Then I fell back to sleep.

For the next six days, I slept most of the time. In my short periods of wakefulness, I forced myself to walk up and down the hallway at the Defender's Lodge to prevent blood clots. Dr Rohan instructed me to remain hunched over so I wouldn't break open the sutures. With Terry's help, we placed bags of frozen peas on the abdominal binder as I pulled up my pajama bottoms to secure the peas in place. The system worked well and kept down the swelling.

After a week in the Defender's Lodge, Terry and I were anxious to get home. At my final checkup in Palo Alto, Dr. Rohan pulled the drain on my left side, which was placed shallower than the second one, on my right, which needed to remain for another week. I had arranged for Dr. Nelson, a plastic surgeon in Bend, to check on me the following week and remove the second drain.

The drive home was long and painful. I sprawled in the back of our

Sorento on a cushion, but I couldn't get comfortable. My back hurt. My stomach ached. Not wanting to develop blood clots, we stopped every couple of hours so I could get out of the car and move.

Terry lovingly helped me scooch out of the back of the SUV. Then he carefully helped me get back in. He also watched the clock to remind me when I needed to eat and take my pain meds.

Once we made it home, I spent the next eight weeks struggling to remember not to lift anything weighing more than five pounds and keep from doing activities that would cause me to sweat. I would find myself lifting a grocery bag into the car or carrying a basket full of laundry to the washing machine, and my sutures would remind me with a hearty stab. Menial tasks of unloading the dishwasher and folding laundry rendered me perspiring and achy. I was encouraged to walk but not too far. Netflix kept me semi-sane, but I became bored and grouchy.

Slowly, the pain receded, and I began to feel human again. Day by day, week by week I stood straighter and felt stronger. Navel gazing took on a whole new meaning when I saw the smooth skin on my stomach. One morning, I glanced down at my flat, gorgeous belly, and it hit me: I hadn't seen my vagina for more than 20 years! I could see all my body parts.

More than that, between the years of therapy, the surgeries, the diligence with my diet and regular exercise, and how my spiritual relationship with God had grown and become integral to my wellbeing, I realized my mind, body, and spirit had healed. I recognized the woman in the mirror and felt whole, truly whole. Heck, I could wear a bikini if I wanted to, something I hadn't done since I was 19. I inhaled deeply and thought: *Wow, what a ride.*

As I reflected on all of the things I had done to heal over the past few decades, I realized that Terry and Ashten had undergone their own adventures. Their experiences, although sometimes painful, had transformed them for the better as well.

Chapter 41

POST-TRAUMATIC GROWTH

Much has changed in my life since the surgeries and in the past few years. Terry and I built a new, larger home in Bend. We sold our old house, and my parents have moved in with us.

As I write this, we have three acres in the middle of a quiet, peaceful pine forest. Eight chickens, whom I adore, keep me busy and our family flush with fresh eggs. I'm outlining a children's book about my feathered friends that I'm excited about writing.

Ashten is attending Lane Community College in Eugene, Oregon, studying mushrooms and soil, and is the teacher's assistant for the Mycology professor. Ashten and Madi both work at Seize the Cafe in Eugene and continue to be happy in their relationship. Ashten, Madi, Mollie, and Jackson, their core group of friends, have helped me to become a better human. I watch them lift each other up and support one another without judgment. It's a beautiful thing.

My relationship with Ashten has grown immensely. I feel closer to Ash than ever before. Having a kid in her 20s is pretty cool. Ashten makes me stretch my once inflexible brain to embrace new ideas, strive to think outside of the box, and love others in ways that I wish I could describe with mere words.

Looking back on my journey, two things have remained constant: My love for family and friends and my unwavering faith in God. My spirituality has guided me and kept the light burning inside of me, even when I thought it had been extinguished.

Thank you for reading my story. If you take away only one thing from my experience, I hope it is the realization that no one can take away your light. The brilliance of your soul may seem dim at times, but that light is always there. It just needs to be nourished.

If you are struggling with past trauma of any kind, I hope you will open yourself up to counseling, medication if prescribed, and take one brave step at a time toward becoming a better you. I'm a firm believer that we can all be more complete, more joyful humans. We just have to be willing to look into possibilities and shift some of our perspectives. I'm still growing and transforming with every passing day.

In the last few years, the biggest change for Terry and me has been cohabiting with my parents. We all have adjusted to one another's little quirks, and we are surviving and thriving. I feel blessed every day to have this time with my parents because, like all of us, someday these two key people in Terry's and my lives won't be here anymore. Without their strength and support through all of my struggles, as well as my brother Wade's and his wife Susie's, I truly believe that I wouldn't have been here to share my journey with you.

I feel more stable and loved than ever, thanks to the amazing network of people with which I've chosen to share my life. Terry, of course, my rock and the love of my life, has my deepest gratitude for his understanding, flexibility, and superhuman support. I am also grateful for the phenomenal women veterans I've met through the Vet Center, and the ladies whom I've gotten to know at our water fitness classes, three times a week.

Tani and her family have also been key players in my healing. The tailgating parties before Oregon Ducks games and family camping trips kept me human when I felt like a space alien. They've given me strength when I've felt weak and courage when I've felt like a coward. They've helped me view life with more love and compassion than I thought possible, and I will be forever grateful.

My original mission to become one in mind, body, and spirit has come to fruition. I healed my brain, which led to feeling strong enough to heal my body. Neither could have been achieved without my faith in God.

Standing outside on our front porch with Terry, waiting for Tani and Andy to pick us up to go to an outdoor concert, I am 160 pounds lighter. I went from a size 24 to a size six, and my BMI dropped from 49.6 to 22.8, which is in the normal/healthy range. I've needed some help from surgery, but it has been worth it to look at my reflection in the mirror and think: *Wow! There you are. I knew you were in there.*

My latest mission has been to get Terry to retire so I can take this new, healthy body hiking in Germany, Norway, Italy, and Spain. But for now, Yosemite and Yellowstone National Parks will work. Terry's travel ambitions are closer to home than mine at the moment, but he'll come around. He'll retire when he's ready, and he loves to travel.

Overall, life is fulfilling but still includes challenges. I use my tools to alleviate the symptoms from my PTSD and MST (military sexual trauma). There will always be days when I feel less than optimal, but I will continue to get up and get going, which is all any of us can do.

I never thought I'd say this, but my trauma has made me a better version of myself. I've grown in ways that had never occurred to me, like how I've learned to truly love myself, which has created the means for me to fully love others. One of the ways I express that love is to continue to help veterans understand that they matter. In fact, we all do. I will also continue to speak at events and consult with various organizations that support people in healing from trauma.

I hope my story has encouraged you to surround yourself with positivity and light. I hope you have discovered there is help for managing even the most difficult things in your life. If you allow yourself to be vulnerable and ask for help, you might be amazed by what happens.

Seven years ago, I couldn't have imagined wanting to be in a crowd of strangers in an open area to watch a musical. Yet here I am, waiting on the porch with Terry in front of our house, for Tani and Andy to pick us up to go see *Mama Mia!* at Drake Park in Bend. It's been five years since Tani's cancer diagnosis, and we're celebrating her cancer-versary.

I grab Terry's warm hand. "I love you," I say and give him a kiss.

"Love you too." He kisses me back.

Their Lexus SUV stops in front of us, and Tani's window slides down. "Let's go, people!" she shouts.

Her healthy, happy face stretches my mouth into a joyful grin. At the park, the four of us manage to find our seats in the front row. We sit in the white plastic chairs with a perfect view of the entire outdoor stage. The cast of *Mama Mia!* begins to sing "Dancing Queen," and Tani and I can't help ourselves. We sing with them at the top of our lungs, like we used to back in Springfield in her dad's office. Terry and Andy laugh. My heart is full.

I've come a long way from the 19-year-old who stepped off that bus in Alabama, but there are some things that remain the same. I still value family, honesty, and loyalty 37 years later. It may sound like a cliche, but I truly believe that my journey to find myself led me back to the person I've been all along.

But I'm new and improved. I'm Dani 2.0.

Where to Find More Information About Post-Traumatic Stress Disorder (PTSD)

The Body Keeps the Score: Brain, Mind, and Body in the Healing of Trauma by Bessel van der Kolk, M.D. (2015, Penguin Books)

National Institute of Mental Health (NIMH)
https://www.nimh.nih.gov

National Alliance on Mental Illness (NAMI)
https://www.nami.org

For veterans:
https://www.ptsd.va.gov

If you are a military veteran, seek help at your local Veteran Center and speak to a Veterans Service Officer. They've been immensely helpful with my journey.

www.ingramcontent.com/pod-product-compliance
Lightning Source LLC
LaVergne TN
LVHW040514210926
848480LV00005BA/1458

9798995504825